COHABITING, MARRIED, OR SINGLE

The International Institute for Applied Systems Analysis

is an interdisciplinary, nongovernmental research institution founded in 1972 by leading scientific organizations in 12 countries. Situated near Vienna, in the center of Europe, IIASA has been for more than two decades producing valuable scientific research on economic, technological, and environmental issues.

IIASA was one of the first international institutes to systematically study global issues of environment, technology, and development. IIASA's Governing Council states that the Institute's goal is: *to conduct international and interdisciplinary scientific studies to provide timely and relevant information and options, addressing critical issues of global environmental, economic, and social change, for the benefit of the public, the scientific community, and national and international institutions.* Research is organized around three central themes:

- Global Environmental Change;
- Global Economic and Technological Change;
- Systems Methods for the Analysis of Global Issues.

The Institute now has national member organizations in the following countries:

Austria
The Austrian Academy of Sciences

Bulgaria
The National Committee for Applied Systems Analysis and Management

Canada
The Canadian Committee for IIASA

Czech Republic
The Czech Committee for IIASA

Finland
The Finnish Committee for IIASA

Germany
The Association for the Advancement of IIASA

Hungary
The Hungarian Committee for Applied Systems Analysis

Italy
The Italian National Member Organization is in the process of reorganization

Japan
The Japan Committee for IIASA

Kazakhstan
The National Academy of Sciences

Netherlands
The Netherlands Organization for Scientific Research (NWO)

Poland
The Polish Academy of Sciences

Russian Federation
The Russian Academy of Sciences

Slovak Republic
The Center for Strategic Studies

Sweden
The Swedish Council for Planning and Coordination of Research (FRN)

Ukraine
The Ukrainian Academy of Sciences

United States of America
The American Academy of Arts and Sciences

Cohabiting, Married, or Single

Portraying, Analyzing, and Modeling New Living
Arrangements in the Changing Societies of Europe

CHRISTOPHER PRINZ
European Centre for Social Welfare Policy and Research, Vienna, Austria
Formerly with the International Institute for Applied Systems Analysis,
Laxenburg, Austria

IIASA
International Institute for Applied Systems Analysis
Laxenburg, Austria

Avebury

Aldershot • Brookfield USA • Hong Kong • Singapore • Sydney

© International Institute for Applied Systems Analysis 1995

Published by
Avebury
Ashgate Publishing Limited
Gower House
Croft Road
Aldershot
Hants GU11 3HR
England

Ashgate Publishing Company
Old Post Road
Brookfield
Vermont 05036
USA

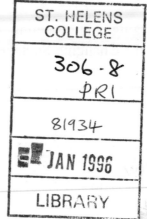
British Library Cataloguing in Publication Data

Prinz, Christopher
    Cohabiting, Married, or Single: Portraying, Analyzing
    and Modeling New Living Arrangements in the
    Changing Societies of Europe
    I. Title
    306.8094
ISBN 1 85972 187 7

Library of Congress Catalog Card Number: 95-78510

Typeset by
Publications Department
IIASA
A-2361 Laxenburg
Austria

Printed and bound by Athenaeum Press, Ltd.,
Gateshead, Tyne & Wear.

Contents

Illustrations

Tables

Figures

Foreword

A golden age of marriage, featuring youthfulness and near universality, which dominated the West European nuptiality scene during the 1960s and early 1970s, has waned. The rise of cohabitation and solo living, novel developments in living arrangements, lie behind recent declines in marriage rates. Cohabitation, whereby couples live together without the law, is not new. Prior to the 1970s, cohabiting unions were largely statistically invisible and probably socially invisible outside of the local community or milieu. There were subgroups of the population that were probably more prone to cohabitation than others – for example, the very poor, those whose marriages had broken up but were unable to obtain a divorce, and groups ideologically opposed to marriage. However, the forms of cohabitation that are the central focus of Christopher Prinz's book are new, whereby young people predominantly in their 20s and 30s live together as a prelude to, or as an alternative to marriage. Additionally, with the growth in divorce "post-marital" cohabitation has also become more prevalent either in preference to or as a prelude to remarriage. Data on cohabitation still tend to be scarce and largely emanate from surveys (a rare exception is the Swedish Census, which is an important source for this study) which can make comparative analyses problematic, as sample sizes, coverage, and definitions can vary. Notwithstanding, in the hands of a careful analyst patterns can be discerned and interpretations made. This is what is achieved in this study. A study that provides an authoritative and up-to-date review and interpretation of the development of the cohabitation phenomenon across Europe. If one is interested in changing partnership behavior, in the recent past, nowadays, and into the future across a range of European countries, this would be the place to start.

Kathleen Kiernan
London School of Economics and Political Science
May 1995

Preface

The UN declared the year 1994 to be the International Year of the Family. This declaration on the important status of the family is based on the belief that the existence and function of the family are important pillars of society. But this declaration also arises from the fear that this pillar may be crumbling. As the society changes, so does the family and all other elements of society. The number of people who prefer to live alone and the number of unions that are not legally sanctioned have rapidly increased in many European countries. Is it correct to conclude that the family and the value attached to it are in danger, and that family life is considered less important today than it was earlier?

In his 1994 New Year's address the head of the Catholic Church, Pope John Paul II, took an extreme position. He explicitly warned against legitimating all substitutes for legal marriage. Not surprisingly, his intention was to support the traditional patriarchal family. However, in a changing pluralistic society public opinion and political and legislative responses have to adapt. Legal recognition of substitutes for marriage, most importantly of consensual unions, might well serve the family better.

Demographers have been slow to reassess the value of the traditional concept of marital status. Until the beginning of the 1960s, a person's living arrangement could be predicted reasonably well by looking at the individual's legal marital status. During the 1980s, the situation altered dramatically. We know that unmarried couples have always existed; however, in the past they were so rare that little importance was attached to this living arrangement. It was also difficult to study the phenomenon because cohabitation was not yet a generally accepted lifestyle. That is no longer the case. Today, in many European countries many married couples live together before marriage, and a significant portion of the adult population chooses cohabitation instead of marriage. It is therefore no longer possible not to consider consensual unions when studying marital-status or living arrangement structures.

This study on cohabitation and marriage in Europe relies heavily on two major projects. The first is an international comparative project, entitled

"Social Security, Family, and Households in Aging Societies," undertaken at the International Institute for Applied Systems Analysis. The objective of this project was to estimate effects of changing family and household structures on social security expenditures in different countries that are characterized by rapid aging. As the study was international in scope, living arrangements had to be operationalized through the concept of traditional legal marital status to make comparative analysis possible. Most of the conclusions are conditional on the assumption that marital status is still a reasonable proxy for one's living arrangement, which is simply not true in many European countries. Information on consensual unions was not incorporated into the comparative analysis.

The second project was conducted by Åke Nilsson and Håkån Sellerfors from Statistics Sweden. In this project Nilsson and Sellerfors gathered and analyzed information on the existence, formation, and dissolution of consensual unions in Sweden and produced the most complete study on consensual unions available. Without their excellent work this study would not have been possible.

While planning and preparing this study, which finally became a discussion of the causes and consequences of cohabitation, many people contributed comments and ideas. I especially want to thank Jean-Pierre Gonnot, Nico Keilman, Kathleen Kiernan, Wolfgang Lutz, and Åke Nilsson. In addition, thanks are extended to IIASA's Publications Department.

Christopher Prinz
Vienna
April 1995

Chapter 1

Introduction, Terminology, and Concepts

1.1 Motives for the Study

Demographers have a relatively small number of basic variables on which to base scientific analysis; one of them is *marital status*. As stated by Morgan (1980, p. 633): "Marital status, like age, sex and social class, forms another pervasive personal and social characteristic." Morgan was referring to traditional marital status, a socially and legally defined condition that distinguishes between currently married, never-married, and formerly married people. In principle, marital status is determined by the presence or absence of a marital partner. However, it involves more than a personal relationship, for each marital condition is associated with socially sanctioned rights and obligations; these include children, sexuality, property, and domestic and government services. Placement in a particular marital category has wide-ranging implications for the individual and, together with age and gender, forms the most salient aspect of a person's social identity (Morgan, 1980).

The importance of marital status in determining an individual's role, social position, and expectations has led to studies on the factors affecting the marital-status distribution of a population and the nature of respective marital roles, on the one hand, and on the ways in which marital status affects other phenomena, such as fertility, economic activity, migration, mortality, and health, on the other hand. But given recent developments, is marital status still an important indicator of demographic trends?

In recent decades major social and economic changes have occurred in European societies. The changing role of women has been observed as one of the most important of these developments. Marriage has increasingly been delayed, while the age at first union formation has declined. In addition, marriage and remarriage rates have fallen markedly. In most countries, cohabitation has become common, particularly among young adults; it is considered either a transition to and from marriage or an alternative to marriage. Divorce and dissolution of unions, in general, have risen sharply. Fertility has dropped to unprecedented low levels, partly as a consequence of an increase in age of mother at first birth. The proportion of children borne by unmarried mothers has risen significantly. Also, one-person households and one-parent families have increased remarkably.

Lesthaege and van de Kaa (1986, 1987) have proposed that the mid-1960s marked the beginning of a *second demographic transition* in Europe because of the large-scale changes that subsequently occurred.[1] This second demographic transition comprises several elements:

- The transition from the "golden age of marriage" to the "dawn of cohabitation."
- The transition from the child as main element of a family to the couple as main element.
- The transition from "preventive contraception" (to avoid third and fourth children) to "self-fulfilling conception" (whenever conception is desirable).
- The transition from uniform systems of families and households to multi-form systems.

Cliquet (1991) has thoroughly examined all the available evidence and has concluded that, although there was a striking acceleration in trends in the mid-1960s, these trends were already present before this period.

The question of whether this is a second demographic transition remains unanswered. Nevertheless, remarkable changes have occurred, and these changes must be taken into account in today's scientific studies. As expressed by Linke (1991, p. 119):

> The relatively marked increase in consensual unions observed so far not only in the Scandinavian, but also in the other European countries and the further rise of this form of partnership presumably to be expected in future, gradually reduces the informational value in demographic analyses of the variable marital status.

Keilman and Prinz (1995a) write: "Still today, a breakdown by marital status of such demographic behavior as childbearing and death displays large differentials – however, given one's marital status, much of an individual's demographic behavior remains unexplained."

On the other hand, the nuclear family, a cornerstone of society, is flourishing and is indeed probably more widespread than ever before. Nevertheless, the present situation is often referred to as a cultural crisis, as well as a legal crisis. Thus, one should expect these societal changes to be reflected in legislation, but this is not the case. Interestingly, Eekelaar (1980, p. 450) points out that the "removal of the potentially oppressive aspect of traditional marriage [namely, legal obstacles toward divorce] has not resulted in an increase in marriage, for paradoxically, the liberalization of divorce has been accompanied by a progressive fall in the marriage rate." This is not a paradox since legislative changes essentially are a response to changes taking place in society.

While there is agreement that remarkable changes have occurred, no uniform method has been developed to observe these changes. One part of the scientific community appears to have overlooked the changes. For example, at a recent seminar, entitled "Demographic Implications of Marital Status," not less than 80% of the papers presented dealt exclusively with traditional marital status; alternative, new statuses and their implications on analyses were not considered.[2] Traditional analyses are interesting and important; but they will remain incomplete, sometimes even misleading, and they will often fail to discover real trends and patterns.

Another part of the scientific community has adopted a different approach. In this approach, marital status – traditionally a useful concept and variable – is no longer a measure of a person's living arrangements (with respective implications), and is therefore no longer relevant. This approach replaces the traditional marital-status concept with a more up-to-date household concept.[3] There are reasonable arguments for the latter approach, but it should be used to complement, rather than replace, the marital-status concept. A third approach that takes an intermediate position should be developed. The traditional marital-status concept should be updated so that it reflects past and current changes. This approach is taken in this study.

What should be the most important characteristic of this updated concept? The decline in marriage rates, the delay in marriage, and the increase in divorce do not necessarily make the traditional concept obsolete, but the *emergence of cohabitation* does. Men and women living together outside marriage is not new, but prior to 1970 it was largely statistically and socially invisible outside the local community or milieu (Kiernan, 1993). The emergence of cohabitation in the 1970s developed under specific circumstances. Instead of being an imperative, it was characterized by free choice; instead of being predominantly a lower-class phenomenon, it was a lifestyle chosen by the middle and upper classes (Wiersma, 1983). Today, in several countries the large majority of formal marriages are entered into only after a period of cohabitation. For some couples cohabitation is a temporary trial phase, but for other couples marriage is never considered.

Already in 1983 Wiersma stressed that "if cohabitation becomes more and more an accepted social institution, then governments and experts on family will do well to consider at length the subsequent socio-economic, legal, and de-mographic implications" (Wiersma, 1983, p. 6). Still, more than a decade later, only limited knowledge exists on this topic. As Kiernan and Estaugh (1993, p. 70) point out: "In the future, many institutions, both public and private, will need to address implications of rising levels of cohabitation, particularly if these unions become more longstanding and children are increasingly born and reared within them." It is obvious that we must learn more about the reasons for the emergence of cohabitation to deal with it socially, legally, and polit-ically. Most studies consider cohabitation a relatively isolated phenomenon and do not accept it as a type of marital status. Integrated research in the area of cohabitation is timely and necessary.

Comparing marriages and cohabitations may help us to understand the role cohabitation plays in today's societies, and make it possible to identify reasons for differences between countries in the emergence of and the speed of increase in cohabitation. Several research questions must be answered: Has cohabitation become a substitute for marriage? Is the institution of marriage threatened by the increasing popularity and social acceptability of cohabitation without marriage? How will this development affect family formation and dissolution processes? How will it affect future fertility? How will legislation and policy be affected? Are cohabitation and marriage simply two (similar or different) forms of the modern nuclear family? Is cohabitation an alternative to the ideal type of nuclear family, which is a monogamous, patriarchal family consisting of a married couple living with children, the man working outside the home and the woman being a mother and full-time housewife?

Several of these questions can only be answered sufficiently through an analysis of the future structure of the family. Surprisingly few attempts have been made to carry out *projections of cohabitation*; a major reason for this is the lack of adequate data. We should make considerable efforts to generate these projections. Such efforts include the construction of a model sophisticated enough to account for the complexity of the issue, but simple and flexible enough to adapt to the data available. Perhaps several models are needed to identify the one best suited for the problem under study. In some situations, such a model might even be a surrogate for more complex household models, depending on the research questions to be answered. These efforts should also make use of data estimates taken either directly from local sources or indirectly from calculations.

Another issue, not yet addressed explicitly, is the remarkably different development of the incidence of and increase in cohabitation in Europe. Today, fertility and mortality trends are clearly more similar between countries than are trends in nuptiality and cohabitation. With respect to these new family trends Sweden is the leading country, followed closely by Denmark. One report claims that other countries will eventually follow Sweden's lead (Lesthaege, 1992), while others find that real cultural differences will prevail (Castiglioni and Zuanna, 1992). This study tries to approach these questions by looking at 10 European countries, including not only forerunners such as Sweden but also more traditional countries such as Italy. Other countries included are Austria, Finland, France, Germany, Hungary, the Netherlands, Norway, and Great Britain.[4] Thus, some 60% of the European population (as of 1985 and excluding the former Soviet Union) is considered.

1.2 Aims of the Study

In essence this book is a discussion of the phenomenon *cohabitation* from the substantive, sociological, and statistical methodological dimensions. It combines detailed statistical analyses with speculative sociological hypotheses.

On the theoretical side, the main objective is to explain why cohabitation has become so popular and what the consequences of its popularity could be. Answers are given to the question whether marriage, as an institution, or even the family altogether, is threatened. In particular, the consequences for policy and legislation are investigated.

On the methodological side, a major purpose of the study is to analyze different concepts of living arrangements. The legal marital-status concept is no longer suitable when the number and proportion of consensual unions reach a certain level. It is, therefore, important to determine whether, and under which circumstances, the traditional concept remains a meaningful tool for analysis. New concepts that take recent family trends into account are developed, and their usefulness is compared with that of traditional concepts. In this context, important elements of the study are the projections of consensual unions, for which a suitable model is needed.

In many areas, substantive and statistical issues overlap. This is particularly true of the analyses of family-status-specific demographic developments, such as the trends in fertility, mortality, and couple formation and dissolution. Similar to the projection issue, the systematic analysis of demographic trends is undertaken in two steps: by looking at traditional family statuses only and by including new statuses, particularly consensual unions.

A major focus of the framework for cohabitation is on changing gender roles and on family and marriage laws. The study is designed as an international comparative project, hence a major goal is to compare the developments in different European countries. In particular, a cohabitation typology is developed, into which countries can easily be classified.

In summary, this book is a plea for a more serious discussion of the cohabitation phenomenon. It is addressed, first and foremost, to demographers, but family policy makers and legislators will also find the analysis of special interest.

1.3   Structure of the Study

The study consists of five chapters. This chapter introduces the terms and concepts used in the study. The main concepts of *marital status* and *union status* are clearly defined. A section on status-specific modeling from a general perspective, in particular drawing on multistate demography and the multistate projection methodology, follows. The chapter concludes with a section on the measurement of demographic differentials.

Chapter 2 is devoted to the analysis and projection of legal *marital status*. It is structured in a strict, almost itemized, manner. It first looks at data issues and then gives an analysis of population structures by marital status in the 10 countries. Next, demographic differentials by marital status are discussed, looking at fertility, mortality, migration, marriage, divorce, and widowhood/widowerhood. This comprehensive analysis of differentials is followed by a theoretical section on marital-status modeling and a section in which a projection model is applied to all 10 countries. The second chapter concludes with a discussion on socioeconomic differentials by marital status and possible implications derived from the projection results.

Chapter 3 is the core of the study. It provides a comprehensive description and explanation of the cohabitation phenomenon. The first section deals with conceptual issues, focusing on possible options and their implications. The second section discusses data issues, and the third section addresses the role of cohabitation as it has been presented in the respective literature. Next, the reasons underlying the emergence and increase of cohabitation are discussed, identifying changing gender roles as a major driving force. Subsequently, legal and political questions are dealt with in an effort to find theoretical and practical reasons for the phenomenon by looking at selected countries and at Sweden in particular. The main section tries to set up a *cohabitation typology*, assigning each country to a specific stage of development. Finally, the last section deals with expected future developments concerning consensual unions.

Chapter 4 is concerned with the analysis and projection of *union status*, mainly concentrating on Sweden (the term union status is defined at length in Section 1.5). It is structured in much the same way as Chapter 3, looking first at data issues, followed by an analysis of population structures and demographic differentials by union status – in this case dealing with fertility, mortality, couple formation, and couple dissolution. Sections on union-status modeling and on applications of the respective projection model for Sweden follow.

Chapter 5 provides a comprehensive conclusion. The first section compares the results obtained from the analyses and projections in Chapters 2 and 4. Based mainly on Swedish data, it explains to what extent marital-status analyses (and projections) lead to biased or even wrong conclusions, and why union-status analyses (and projections) are more appropriate. The second section is concerned with challenges for future research. Possibilities are discussed that would make union-status analysis feasible. An example is given of how to perform union-status projections with incomplete or missing data, using Norway for illustration. The future status of the couple is discussed, and a new and flexible registration system is introduced.

1.4   Terminology and Definitions

When analyzing marriage and cohabitation it is important to use an unambiguous nomenclature to avoid misunderstandings.[5] It is common to introduce terminology for new social or natural phenomena. In the case of cohabitation this is particularly difficult since cohabitation has not yet been fully accepted as a social institution; this fact has hindered the development of an unambiguous set of definitions. The first step is to define cohabitation terminology that provides as much information as existing marriage terminology. *Table 1.1* summarizes the terms that are used in this study, together with terms that are explicitly avoided.

Calling marriage a legal or formal union is somewhat misleading; cohabitation is neither illegal nor necessarily more informal than marriage. (The question of commitment within a partnership is discussed in detail in Chapter 3.) The term *cohabitation* does not refer to attributes such as unmarried or nonmarital, nor is trial or consensual marriage a well-chosen expression. Terms used to express nonmarital unions can easily be mixed up with the terms used to define extramarital unions; the latter unions are, in fact, relationships

Table 1.1. Marriage and cohabitation terminology.

Descriptive terms	Marriage	Cohabitation	Marriage or cohabitation
Synonyms	Marital union	Consensual union	Union
Misleading or discriminating synonyms	Formal union Legal union Conventional union Institutional union	Consensual marriage Trial marriage Unmarried cohabitation Nonmarital cohabitation	–
People involved	Married couple	Cohabiting couple	Couple
Union formation	Marriage	Cohabitation	Couple formation
Union dissolution	Divorce Separation	Dehabitation	Couple dissolution
Starting event	Wedding	Moving in together	–
Certificate	Marriage certificate	Certificate of registration	

in addition to a marital union. I therefore restrict the discussion to the terms marriages, marital unions, cohabitations, and consensual unions; other expressions are not used in this study. Both types of unions are simply called unions; two people involved in either type are called a couple, a married couple or a cohabiting couple.

A dissolution of a consensual union is called a *dehabitation* (Nelissen, 1992); this term is equivalent to the term divorce in the case of a marriage. Separation denotes a dissolution of a marital union without legal divorce. Another way to terminate a cohabitation is to marry the cohabiting partner. This type of marriage must be distinguished explicitly from other (direct) marriages, and is called *transformation* (Thornton, 1988). In this case, an existing union is transformed into another type of union without a change in actual living arrangements.

The event wedding marks the beginning of a marriage, while the beginning of a cohabitation is defined by the event moving in together. Cohabitation is usually defined as the status of couples who are unmarried, sexual partners sharing the same household. This straightforward definition is problematic because it is subjective and may have different meanings. The idea behind the subjective (sometimes referred to as phenomenological; see Trost, 1988) definition of cohabitation is that individuals themselves define cohabitation. If there were a consensus in society about the meaning of the term cohabitation there would be no problem; usually both partners define the situation in the same way. After a dehabitation, however, one partner may still look upon the past relationship as a cohabitation, while the other may not.[6] As long as the legal treatment of cohabitation remains ambiguous there will be no way of removing this subjective aspect of the definition. No valid objective criteria can be used to determine whether a cohabiting unmarried couple lives *close* enough to be considered *husband and wife*.

In this sense, the definition of cohabitation appears to be less rigid than the definition of marriage. A wedding is a legal event. Moving in together is not registered in vital statistics, although – theoretically – one is obliged to fill out certificates of registration. At the same time, however, the definition of cohabitation is more rigid. Moving in together is regarded as a prerequisite for such a union while it is not in the case of marriage. For the latter receiving a marriage certificate is sufficient for a couple to be considered married.

Any type of formation or dissolution event can easily be transferred from a marital to consensual union; however, as long as there is no registration procedure for cohabitation events, the data will remain incomplete. Current marriage law clearly defines the starting event; future cohabitation law may eventually establish an equally strict definition.

In addition, we must treat people living alone in a consistent manner. Throughout the study the term *single* refers to all people living alone, reflecting their actual living arrangement irrespective of legal marital status. Looking only at one's legal marital status, unmarried people can be divorced or widowed, if they have been married, or never married.

Creating consistent and unbiased terminology is important, but, unfortunately, must be translated into every language. Consistency in one language does not imply consistency in other languages. A list of misleading and discriminating terms used in English, German, and French to label consensual unions is given in *Table 1.2*. Based on a current essay by Fresel-Lozey (1992) on new types of "living together" I find that French is perhaps more imaginative than English in creating new terms for consensual unions. The French terms *union consensuelle* and *cohabitation* and the German terms *Lebensgemeinschaft* and *Kohabitation* may be used to correspond with the English terms *consensual union* and *cohabitation*. In all languages, particularly in French, cohabitation generally refers to two people sharing a household, but the term has increasingly been used in the literature to label consensual unions. The German term *Kohabitation* has recently been used more frequently (see, for example, Meyer and Schulze, 1983).

Table 1.2. English, French, and German terms for consensual unions.

English	French	German
Consensual union	Union consensuelle	Lebensgemeinschaft
Cohabitation	Cohabitation	Kohabitation
Concubinage	Concubinage	Wilde Ehe
Trial marriage	Mariage à l'essai	Ehe auf Probe
Clandestine marriage	Mariage clandestin	Heimliche Ehe
Consensual marriage	Mariage non institutionnel	
	Mariage privé	
Alliance without marriage	Alliance sans mariage	Gemeinschaft ohne Ehe
Unmarried cohabitation	Cohabitation de célibataires	Unverheiratetes Zusammenleben
	Cohabitation effective	
Nonmarital cohabitation	Cohabitation hors mariage	Nichteheliches Zusammenleben
Juvenile cohabitation	Cohabitation juvénile	Voreheliches Zusammenleben
Trial union	Union à l'essai	Lebensgemeinschaft auf Probe
De facto union	Union de fait	De-facto Lebensgemeinschaft
Illegitimate union	Union illégitimé	Nichteheliche Lebensgemeinschaft
	Union libre	Freie Lebensgemeinschaft
Non-ratified union	Union non ratifiée	Ehe ohne Trauschein
Living together without marriage	Vie commune sans mariage	Zusammenleben ohne Ehe

1.5   Concepts of Marital Status and Union Status

Marital status is a variable composed of several different dimensions. The traditional *marital-status concept* has been based on the legal dimension, distinguishing between never-married, married, widowed, and divorced individuals. All other dimensions are closely correlated with the respective legal status. In the past, marriage was regarded as necessary to maintain most long-lasting relationships; other marital statuses indicated a life without a permanent partner (partnership dimension). The state of not being married reflected certain types of living arrangements: living with parents, living alone, or living as a nonfamily member in an extended household. The state of being married reflected life in a nuclear family (residential dimension). The large majority of births occurred within marriage (offspring dimension).

In recent decades the different dimensions of marital status have been loosened. Changes in the legal marital-status concept are inevitable, although one can still find justifications for using the traditional concept (see Chapter 2). Once again the marital-status concept must be adjusted to reflect current living arrangements. The new concept can be derived from the application of different dimensions of marital status in a hierarchical manner.

The first criterion to be considered is the residential dimension; singles must be distinguished from couples. In this study a couple is defined as living under the same roof. The second criterion is the legal dimension. Among singles, we can distinguish the traditional four legal statuses. Legally married but separated individuals are part of the group *married singles*. Among couples, we first distinguish legally married couples from cohabiting couples. Among the latter we can also distinguish between four traditional legal statuses. People who are legally married but cohabiting with someone else are part of the group *married cohabitants*. The third criterion is the partnership dimension (only for the single population). Living as a single one can still have a permanent partner. Finally, the offspring dimension is the fourth criterion. Living as a couple does not necessarily coincide with having children. On the other hand, living as a single does not exclude living with a child, independent of the third criterion. This new concept, which considers all four dimensions of marital status, is referred to as the *extended union-status concept*. A simplified concept, called the *union-status concept*, considers only the residential and the legal dimensions.

Identifying all four dimensions in the extended union-status concept results in 26 different states, compared with 9 states in the union-status concept and only 4 states in the marital-status concept (see *Table 1.3*). In the legal marital-status concept, being married has been interpreted as living with a partner as a couple with children; classification in one of the other legal statuses has been interpreted as having no permanent partner and living as a single without children, but this is certainly an oversimplification. Considering the enormous changes in society in recent decades, an adjustment of the marital-status concept is inevitable. In the extended union-status concept all four dimensions of marital status – residential, legal, partnership, and offspring – are considered, that is, each possible combination of the four dimensions forms a separate state (for example, single, never married, without children, with partner).

Maintaining a detailed account of the extended union-status concept is useful (or even necessary) provided that demographic and behavioral differentials between individuals in different groups are significant; for example, one may want to know if never-married singles without a permanent partner living

Table 1.3. Three alternative living arrangement concepts: the dimensions of marital status, union status, and extended union status.

Marital-status concept: 4 possible statuses
1. never married
2. married
3. divorced
4. widowed

Union-status concept: 9 possible statuses

1. single	never married	
2. single	married	
3. single	divorced	
4. single	widowed	
5. married couple		
6. cohabiting couple	never married	
7. cohabiting couple	married	
8. cohabiting couple	divorced	
9. cohabiting couple	widowed	

Extended union-status concept: 26 possible statuses

1. single	never married	with child	partner
2. single	never married	with child	no partner
3. single	never married	without child	partner
4. single	never married	without child	no partner
5. single	married	with child	partner
6. single	married	with child	no partner
7. single	married	without child	partner
8. single	married	without child	no partner
9. single	divorced	with child	partner
10. single	divorced	with child	no partner
11. single	divorced	without child	partner
12. single	divorced	without child	no partner
13. single	widowed	with child	partner
14. single	widowed	with child	no partner
15. single	widowed	without child	partner
16. single	widowed	without child	no partner
17. married couple		with child	
18. married couple		without child	
19. cohabiting couple	never married	with child	
20. cohabiting couple	never married	without child	
21. cohabiting couple	married	with child	
22. cohabiting couple	married	without child	
23. cohabiting couple	divorced	with child	
24. cohabiting couple	divorced	without child	
25. cohabiting couple	widowed	with child	
26. cohabiting couple	widowed	without child	

without children have higher mortality rates than never-married singles with a permanent partner.

Two reasons are given for the creation of the simplified union-status concept. First, most of the behavioral differences between individuals can be explained by the two dimensions considered: the residential and the legal dimensions. Second, data, already difficult to obtain for the simplified union-status concept, are nonexistent for the extended union-status level, especially because several groups are very small. In the union-status concept no distinction is made between those having a child and those remaining childless (offspring dimension) or between those singles having a permanent partner and those singles without a permanent partner (partnership dimension).

1.6 Modeling Marital Status and Union Status

The concepts of marital status, union status, and extended union status describe model structures that increase in complexity. The concept chosen in a particular study depends on various theoretical and practical factors, most prominently data availability and problem complexity.

A model that is able to forecast different statuses should be independent of the concepts chosen and it should be independent of the level of aggregation chosen. Keilman and Prinz (1995b) argue that a dynamic simulation model should be the preferred model. A dynamic model recognizes transitions between statuses and hence is capable of simulating status changes in addition to changes in age structures. In contrast static models are based solely on current proportions, similar to the widely used headship rates. A static approach is not satisfactory from either a substantive or a methodological point of view. A dynamic model can answer questions such as "How would a 50% increase in cohabitation rates affect marriage?" Traditional static models do not address such interdependencies. For methodological reasons, the description of dynamics in marital and union statuses at the level of individuals is preferred over that at the level of groups, such as couples. The class of multidimensional, or multistate, models generally fulfills these model requirements.[7] Several authors have stressed the potential of this type of model (see Keilman and Prinz, 1995b, for a list of references).

The multidimensional approach has several advantages. First, the concept is very general; different categories of the state space permit entirely different applications of the model. In addition to marital-status models, the approach has been used in household models, in fertility models including parity, in multiregional models to study migration, and in labor-force models. Second, its methodology is well understood, and the model, once written in matrix form, is relatively simple. Third, the approach has been studied and applied in various disciplines – for instance, in systems engineering (linear dynamic models) and in mathematical statistics and stochastic processes (first-order Markov processes). Fourth, data of a widely different nature (for instance, population registration data, panel survey data, retrospective survey data, or repeated cross-sectional snapshots) can be used to estimate the parameters of the model.

The multidimensional approach also has limitations. First, because it relies on the concept of a state space and on categories, it can only include a small number of explanatory variables. For instance, the marital-, the union-, and the extended union-status concepts given in *Table 1.3* have three demographic dimensions (or independent variables): age, sex, and status (the last is decomposed into several dimensions). With 18 age classes (when using five-year age groups) and 2 gender classes, the corresponding models would require the estimation of 144, 324, and 936 parameters, respectively. Including additional explanatory variables is not realistically possible, particularly in the extended union-status concept.

A second, closely related drawback is that multidimensional models require large data sets to estimate these parameters. Demographers traditionally use the *method of moments* – that is, they equate model moment parameters to corresponding observed variables. Hence, a set of 144 (or 324 or 936) occurrence/exposure rates would be required to estimate the parameters of these status-specific models. Such models may demand more data than are available; the extended union-status concept is again a good example.

Third, multidimensional models are based on the Markov assumption. The model supposes that future behavior depends only on current status, and does not take into account the path by which this status is reached. In many cases this is obviously too crude an approximation of reality, and extensions of these so-called first-order Markov models have been proposed – for example, semi-Markov or higher-order Markov models. However, the problem can be reduced through a reasonable choice of the state space; hence, it is more pronounced in the marital-status model than in the union-status model, which simply includes more of the relevant dimensions.

In this study, two different dynamic multistate projection models are used to obtain future marital- and union-status structures, both run on a PC: *DIALOG*, developed by Scherbov and Grechucha (1988) at the International Institute for Applied Systems Analysis (IIASA), and *LIPRO*, developed by van Imhoff and Keilman (1991) at the Netherlands Interdisciplinary Demographic Institute (NIDI).

Marital- and union-status models must deal with the so-called two-sex problem. By definition, each marriage requires one bride and one bridegroom; hence, the projected number of married women must equal the number of married men. As a result, nuptiality rates are influenced by the composition of the population. Similar constraints apply to other status transitions, such as divorce, cohabitation, or dehabitation, and to the transition to widowhood/widowerhood in combination with mortality of married persons. In short, the two-sex problem is the inability of conventional population models to capture the changes in nuptiality rates that are produced by changes in population composition.

The most promising approach to solving the two-sex problem, the so-called *harmonic mean solution*, has been proposed by Schoen (1981). In his study he introduces the concept of the magnitude of marriage attraction. This magnitude of marriage attraction differs from the force of decrement to marriage because the force relates only to the behavior of one sex, while the magnitude relates to the behavior of both sexes. Schoen (1981) finds that the magnitude of marriage attraction equals the sum of the one-sex male and female forces of nuptiality. Even though both forces are affected by population composition, their sum is not because compositional effects on one force are offset by compositional effects on the other. In the case of discrete age intervals, those forces can be approximated by male and female occurrence/exposure rates of marriage:

$$H(x, u; y, v) = u^* w_m(x, u; y, v) + v^* w_f(x, u; y, v) \ ,$$

where $H(x, u; y, v)$ represents the magnitude of marriage attraction between men aged x to $x + u$ and women aged y to $y + v$; and $w_m(x, u; y, v)$ and $w_f(x, u; y, v)$ are, respectively, the model's male and female occurrence/exposure rates of marriage between men aged x to $x + u$ and women aged y to $y+v$. Rewriting this relationship with one-year age intervals, Schoen finds that this is a harmonic mean relationship:

$$w_m(x, u; y, v) + w_f(x, u; y, v) = \frac{c(x; y)}{\left[L_m(x) * L_f(y) \right] / \left[L_m(x) + L_f(y) \right]} \ ,$$

where $c(x; y)$ represents the number of model marriages between men aged x to $x+1$ and women aged y to $y+1$; and $L_m(x)$ and $L_f(y)$ are the corresponding person-years of exposure. The denominator on the right-hand side of the equal sign is essentially the harmonic mean of the number of men and women in the relevant age groups in the populations under observation. It can be interpreted as the total number of $(x; y)$ pairs divided by the total number of men aged x and women aged y. Since the pairs include all possible $(x; y)$ combinations, the denominators yield the number of men aged x or women aged y that are potential marriage partners to the average person in the two age-sex groups. The behavioral expectation underlying the harmonic mean solution is that the number of marriages is proportional to the average number of available partners, an expectation consistent with the usual definition of a rate (Schoen, 1988).

A major difference between *DIALOG* and *LIPRO* is the way they treat the two-sex problem. *DIALOG* is more static in that it only provides a solution to the traditional legal marital-status concept. For each unit projection interval, initial age-specific marriage rates for men and women separately result in the initial number of marriages for each sex, totaled over all relevant ages and previous marital statuses (never married, divorced, and widowed). If the number of married men does not equal the number of married women, then an adjustment algorithm corrects the numbers and translates the adjusted total marriages into adjusted age- and sex-specific marriages; this finally leads to the adjusted marriage rates. Initial, inconsistent numbers of marriages are reconciled by taking the harmonic mean. Divorce is treated in the same way, but the calculation of widowhood/widowerhood is dependent on mortality rates. The algorithm starts from death rates and widowhood/widowerhood rates for married persons of both sexes, and it adjusts the latter rates such that the numbers of new widows and widowers are equal to the numbers of married men and women who die. Death rates are left unchanged.

In *LIPRO* the two-sex problem has been reformulated in a much more general manner as a so-called consistency problem. Consistency can be defined as a situation in which the endogenous variables satisfy certain constraints. Solving the consistency problem amounts to adjusting the initially calculated number of events in such a way that these constraints are satisfied. The solution proposed in *LIPRO* can handle any relation between the statuses (that is, individuals belonging to those statuses). There are almost no restrictions. In addition to these internal consistency requirements, resulting from the state space chosen, one can also specify external consistency requirements that result from interrelationships between different models. For instance, the number of events computed from regional sub-models may be required to arrive at the corresponding number in the national population forecast. The user can specify the consistency relationships from a wide range of model parameters:

up to 60 states may be chosen, and for each consistency requirement one may select the arithmetic-, harmonic-, or dominant- (most often mortality-dominant) averaging procedure.

The advantages of *LIPRO* make it the favored candidate when we go beyond legal marital-status modeling. The exact formulation of the marital-status and union-status models and of the respective consistency requirements is given in Chapters 2 and 4.

1.7 Measuring Demographic Differentials

One of the main objectives of this study is to compare various demographic variables across statuses. For comparisons of both between countries in a given period and within countries over time, we need indicators that measure status differentials. The comparison of differentials helps to improve our understanding of underlying causes and implications of past and current marital- and union-status developments.

The type of indicators used for these comparisons is important because different indicators often result in different conclusions. Because it is not always obvious which indicators should be used for specific comparisons, in this study various alternative indicators are used. The measurement of fertility differentials may require indicators that are different from those needed for the measurement of differentials in mortality, couple formation, or couple dissolution. A common denominator of these indicators is that they are derived from age- and gender-specific occurrence/exposure rates.

Occurrence/exposure rates are useful instruments in describing human behavior, but a single summary index for a population is more easily compared with other indices than with entire schedules of specific rates.[8] The comparison of crude rates, which are single summary indices, fails to give reasonable interpretations of differences. Differences in population age distributions mask the differences between the schedules of age-specific rates. Even if the death rates of one group of the population are at each age equal to the death rates of another group of the population, the crude death rates would be different if one population is older than the other. The procedure to eliminate age differences (and possibly other variables) in the composition of the population is called standardization. In other words, to compare levels of demographic indicators (such as fertility and mortality) of different populations or different subgroups of a population, structures of the populations must be controlled.

Age-adjusted or age-standardized rates have no direct meaning in themselves (Shryock *et al.*, 1976). Because they are meaningful only in comparison with other similarly computed rates, the most useful measure is the ratio between these standardized rates. Standardization cannot substitute for a comparison of the specific rates themselves. Only through the analysis of specific rates can an accurate and detailed study be made of the variation of the phenomenon under study among populations or groups of populations. A major criticism of the standardization of rates is that "if the specific rates vary in different ways across the various strata, then no single method of standardization will indicate that these differences exist. Standardization will, on the contrary, tend to mask these differences" (Fleiss, 1981, p. 239).

There are two ways of overcoming these shortcomings of single-indicator comparisons: (1) the computation of several different indices and their validation by inspecting their consistency and (2) the computation of one index over several sub-strata, for example, separately for ages below 30 and ages 30 and above. The latter approach is particularly useful when the specific rates in the groups to be compared do not yield consistent relations across the strata. Both solutions are used in this study because they offer a sound basis for assessment and for interpretation of differences.

In the following chapters the method of direct age standardization is used; this is the preferred method if a reliable schedule of specific rates for the population under study is available. The term *direct* refers to the actual rates of the study population.[9] The data necessary for implementation of this method are the schedule of specific rates (r_i) for the study population and the age distribution (p_{si}) for a selected standard population. The equation takes the form

$$C_{\text{direct}} = \sum_{i=1}^{n} r_i p_{si} \quad \text{and} \quad CF = \frac{C_{\text{direct}}}{C_{\text{crude}}}.$$

The directly standardized rate (C_{direct}) is simply the sum (over all age groups) of the product of the specific rate of the study population and the composition of the standard population. Or, by direct standardization, we can calculate the number of events that would occur in a population if it had the age distribution of the standard population with which it is being compared. A simple summary index is obtained by dividing the respective standardized rate (C_{direct}) by the crude rate for the standard population (C_{crude}). This index or ratio is called the age-standardized comparative figure (CF), and in this study it is applied in the analyses of mortality, fertility, couple formation, and couple dissolution.

The weak point in standardization is the arbitrary choice of the standard population. There are a number of possibilities, and, theoretically, it is irrelevant which structure is chosen. The standard selected may be the age distribution of one of the groups or the total or average of the age distributions of these groups or an *external* real or theoretical distribution of some sort. Different results for the relative differences between adjusted rates are obtained depending on the age distribution selected as the standard. In fact, the choice of standard may even affect the direction of the difference between the rates for the populations being compared. Hence, it is advisable to select the standard population carefully. The general rule is to select an age distribution that is similar to the age distributions of the various populations under study. In particular, if the specific rates do not produce consistent relations across strata, or in this case across age groups, the best solution is to choose the composite or the unweighted average of two or more populations as the standard.

In Chapters 2 and 4 several demographic variables are compared across marital status and union status, respectively. Age standardization is applied in almost all cases. In addition, several alternative indicators are used for comparisons; in the context of fertility differentials, for example, these indicators include total fertility rates and life-table indicators derived from parity-specific period fertility tables.

Notes

[1] Even if these changes are all elements of a general transition, the term "second demographic transition" is probably not appropriate. It implies that this transition is the second of two related transitions. Thus far demographers speak of only one demographic transition. By this term they mean the process whereby a country moves from high birth and death rates to low birth and death rates. More specifically, the first demographic transition refers to the period of rapid population growth.

[2] This seminar was held in Germany in 1992. The most interesting of those papers are to be published in *Schriftenreihe des Bundesinstituts für Bevölkerungsforschung*, edited by Charlotte Hohn.

[3] This view is frequently taken in books that deal exclusively with household demography; see, for example, the book by Keilman *et al.* (1988).

[4] The choice of countries appears somewhat arbitrary; however, it essentially results from a study entitled "Social Security, Family, and Household in Aging Societies," carried out at IIASA. The results of this study are published in Gonnot *et al.* (1995). Only Great Britain was added to the set of countries in this study; other countries for which no information on cohabitation was available were not included.

[5] Cohabitation is increasingly used as the term to describe the status of couples that are unmarried, sexual partners and share the same household (United Nations, 1990).

[6] Using a subjective definition introduces various biases, including differences in perception between the partners. In addition, tax and social security regulations have been identified as reasons for either avoiding payments or receiving benefits.

[7] For a detailed mathematical description of the multistate population projection model see Willekens and Drewe (1984) and van Imhoff (1990). The main feature of the model is that it projects the population of all groups (or regions) simultaneously. The fundamental parameters of the model are occurrence/exposure rates, which are ratios of the number of events of a given type in a particular interval to the person-years lived in that interval by the persons at risk of experiencing that event.

[8] Occurrence/exposure rates, alternatively called rates of the first kind or intensities if the time interval (age) approaches zero, are characterized by two elements: (1) all persons in the denominator are exposed to the risk of the event given in the numerator and (2) the event in the numerator itself reduces the number of persons in the denominator. Mortality rates, marriage rates, divorce rates, and widowhood/widowerhood rates belong to this group. For any kind of life-table application (see Chapter 2) only rates of the first kind can be used. If condition (2) is not met, we apply rates of the second kind, an example being age-specific fertility rates that are also used in this study. An advantage of rates of the second kind is that they are additive; however, they are useless in a life-table approach.

[9] If specific rates are only given for a standard population, indirect standardization is required.

Chapter 2

Marital Status: Never Married, Married, Divorced, Widowed

This chapter deals with the analysis and projection of traditional marital status. As stated in the introduction, the concept of legal marital status is outdated; nevertheless, there are a number of reasons for having a separate chapter on this topic. Among other things, the study aims at comparing marital-status and union-status analyses. Such comparisons require a comprehensive analysis of the legal concept. This allows us to distinguish issues that can be dealt with by using the legal concept from questions that cannot be answered on the basis of the traditional approach.

Another aim of the study is to compare differences between the 10 European countries. For such comparative studies the traditional concept is justified simply by the lack of comparable data for other approaches. Also, a number of political issues (pension entitlements or maternity benefits) and most legal issues are discussed on the basis of traditional marital status, at least in the majority of countries. For these reasons it is worth improving traditional analysis.

The first section of this chapter is concerned with data issues, followed by an analysis of population structures by marital status for the 10 countries. In the main section, demographic differentials by marital status are discussed and interpreted, looking at trends in fertility, mortality, migration, marriage, divorce, and death of spouse. This comprehensive analysis of differentials is followed by a section on marital-status modeling and a section on the application of marital-status projection models. The chapter concludes with a discussion of socioeconomic differentials by marital status and possible implications derived from the projection results.

2.1   Data on Marital Status

Population data on marital status are easily available for all European countries. Information on current distributions is usually collected by census offices. In most countries censuses are carried out every 10 years. Information is also available for non-census years: all countries have continuous population registration systems that are regularly updated by statistical agencies on the basis of the latest census information.[1] However, it is the *perception* of marital status that is given in census statistics and not necessarily official marital status. For example, a significant proportion of those widowed and divorced regard themselves as married; or, to give a more up-to-date example, in a recent survey conducted in Great Britain, many cohabiting women regarded themselves as married (see Chapter 3).

Data on marriage, divorce, or widowhood are available from vital statistics offices and are entirely consistent with official marital status. As a consequence, marriage and divorce rates, calculated on the basis of events taken from vital statistics and person-years taken from the census or from registration systems, are generally biased. In most cases, given the overrepresentation of married persons in the census, marriage rates are overestimated, and divorce rates are underestimated.

Data on births and deaths by marital status are available from official registers; they are consistent with official marital status. Hence, fertility and mortality rates by marital status are also biased.

2.2   Population Distribution by Marital Status

In this section the marital-status distribution of the populations in the 10 countries is discussed. The distribution in 1985 is compared with the distribution in 1960 to give an estimate of the magnitude of changes over the past two and a half decades. The following changes were observed in the marital composition of the population aged 15 years and over during this period:

- There was a marked decrease in the married proportion and a remarkable increase in the divorced proportion for both sexes.
- The proportion of widowers decreased while that of widows increased.
- The proportion never-married men rose, while changes in both the level and trend in the proportion of never-married women were less pronounced.

Table 2.1 gives the marital composition of the population aged 15 years and over for men and women in 1960 and 1985. Hungary shows the lowest

Table 2.1. Distribution of the population aged 15 years and over by marital status and gender in 1960 and 1985, in percent.

Country	Women				Men			
	Never married	Married	Divorced	Widowed	Never married	Married	Divorced	Widowed
Austria								
1960	24.9	53.5	3.5	18.1	29.1	64.4	2.4	4.0
1985	24.6	53.2	4.7	17.5	32.3	61.1	3.3	3.3
Finland								
1960	29.2	55.2	2.4	13.2	33.6	62.0	1.4	3.1
1985	28.1	51.5	6.6	13.7	35.8	56.2	5.3	2.7
France								
1960	20.7	60.3	2.5	16.6	27.3	66.4	1.9	4.3
1985	24.5	56.6	4.6	14.3	31.5	61.9	3.6	3.1
Germany[a]								
1960	22.7	57.7	2.6	17.0	26.8	67.9	1.5	3.9
1985	24.4	54.3	4.4	16.9	33.5	59.8	3.5	3.2
Great Britain								
1960	21.9	63.6	0.9	13.6	25.6	70.0	0.6	3.9
1985	24.0	56.4	5.7	13.9	31.4	60.2	4.8	3.5
Hungary								
1960	17.3	64.4	2.6	15.7	23.7	71.5	1.4	3.4
1985	14.2	61.5	6.9	17.4	23.1	68.0	5.0	3.8
Italy								
1960	29.1	58.0	0.0	12.9	34.4	62.1	0.0	3.5
1985	24.5	61.1	0.4	14.0	30.8	65.8	0.3	3.1
Netherlands								
1960	26.9	63.0	1.3	8.8	30.7	64.9	0.8	3.6
1985	26.4	57.6	4.8	11.2	33.5	60.0	3.9	2.6
Norway								
1960	26.0	62.2	1.7	10.1	31.0	63.9	1.1	4.0
1985	26.2	56.1	4.7	13.0	34.3	58.5	3.9	3.3
Sweden								
1960	26.2	60.7	3.0	10.1	31.6	61.9	2.3	4.3
1985	30.0	48.4	8.7	12.9	38.7	50.4	7.3	3.5

[a]Data for Germany refer to the former Federal Republic of Germany only.

percentage of never-married men and women: between 14 and 17 percent among women and between 22 and 25 percent among men. The highest proportion of never married in 1960 is observed in Italy (34.4 percent among men and 29.1 percent among women), followed by the Scandinavian countries and the Netherlands. Italy's position is attributable to the traditional nuptiality pattern that prevailed in the 1960s.

After the 1960s, the never-married proportions clearly decreased in Italy; in other countries they increased among men, but there was no uniformity in the direction of changes among women. The highest never-married proportions observed in Europe were in Sweden: 38.7 percent of men and 30.0 percent of women in 1985.

The proportion of married men decreased from between 62 and 72 percent in 1960 to between 50 and 68 percent in 1985. The level and range for women have remained relatively stable – between 50 and 60 percent. The only exception to this general trend is Italy, which experienced an increase in the proportions of married men and women.

In most of the countries, the proportions of divorced men and women grew substantially over the 1960–1985 period, with a general acceleration after 1980. In 1960, they ranged from about 0 percent in Italy where divorce was extremely difficult to obtain to 3.5 percent for women in Austria. In 1985, the lowest proportion was still observed in Italy, and the highest proportion was found in Sweden, where 7.3 percent of men and 8.7 percent of women were divorced. No regional pattern is evident, but two countries depart from the general trend: Italy, where the divorced population remained very small, and Austria, which stabilized after 1980. In all countries the proportions of divorcées is higher than the proportions of divorcés. However, the changes in the proportions of divorced women and men are difficult to interpret, as at any given age the rate of divorce is also influenced by remarriage patterns.

With respect to those widowed, the most striking feature is obviously the difference between men and women, which is mostly due to the combined effect of sex differentials in mortality and the traditional male seniority in couples. In 1960, some 4 percent of men were widowers, while the proportions among women were between 8.8 and 18.1 percent. The highest proportions of widows are in Austria and Germany, and the lowest percentages are in the Netherlands. The proportion of widowers decreased in all countries (except Hungary), while the proportion of widows increased.[2]

The analysis of marital-status distributions indicates that substantial changes have recently occurred in the marital trends of the populations: a decline in nuptiality (stronger for men), an increase in divorce, and, although of a different order, a decrease in widowerhood and an increase in widowhood. The following section analyzes these indicators in more detail.

2.3   Demographic Differentials by Marital Status

Why should we examine differentials in fertility, mortality, and migration by marital status? To a large extent marital status also reflects (or at least has reflected) a person's living arrangement, and hence his or her lifestyle. A number of theories on marital-status differentials exist:

- Children are (were) largely born within marriage, the frequency of marriage being a proximate determinant of fertility.
- Mortality is lowest among married people.
- Migration is highest among divorcées.

Because marital status has become increasingly difficult to define, should the same demographic differentials exist? Are they still relevant? Indeed, it might be instructive to look at changes in differentials over time, changes that may have been similar or perhaps quite different in the countries under investigation. Changes in marital-status differentials over time may also indicate strong union-status differentials; however, information on the latter is usually not available. In the following, we look at trends in fertility, mortality, and migration. In the last section results derived from marital-status life-table calculations are compared.

2.3.1 Fertility

Fertility rates are higher among married women than among unmarried women; hence, marriage trends (which are discussed at length in Section 2.3.4) are often taken as a proximate determinant of overall fertility levels. This relationship is, however, less pronounced when there is a high incidence of births outside marriage. There is a weak connection between the extent of out-of-marital-union births and overall levels of fertility (Kiernan, 1993). Indeed, the discussion of fertility differentials by marital status becomes a discussion of the acceptance of childbearing outside marriage rather than a discussion of fertility levels. Nonmarital fertility also seems to be the best available proxy for the frequency of consensual unions.

A number of methodological questions arise in the analysis of fertility differentials. First, marriage must be defined. Marriage is a legal concept; today, in most European countries, only a small number of nonmarital births are actually born to women who live alone. This problem is explicitly addressed in this study: the following section deals with differentials by marital status, and a section in Chapter 4 deals with differentials by union status. Even if we have an exact definition of marriage, we must ask the question, Should the legal status of a mother be determined at the time of birth or at the time of conception? For instance, if a mother is unmarried at the moment of conception but married at the birth of her child, it has been argued that the birth is outside marriage (be it to a single or a cohabiting woman), but has a strong influence on marital behavior (Katus, 1992).[3] Another weakness of the criterion to define nonmarital births is that events following the birth are not taken into account. This shortcoming is characteristic of any criterion that is based on the status of the mother at a fixed date. If we look at the reproductive decision-making process and at social acceptance of out-of-marital-union births, a fixed date at some important moment in the process of bearing a child is the best solution. Indeed, because of data restrictions this date can only be the day of birth.

A further question in any fertility analysis is whether to use period or cohort measures of fertility. During periods of rapid change in fertility due to changes in timing or quantum or both, the difference between cohort and period fertility may be considerable.[4] However, analyses of the fertility experiences of cohorts show trends similar to those observed in recent periods (Kiernan, 1993). This study relies on period measures for two reasons: first, only period measures are available for all countries and for comparative points in time; second, the period perspective is more up-to-date, providing a glimpse at present and recent changes without having to wait 20 years.

We now compare various summary measures of fertility, all of them calculated on the basis of age- and status-specific fertility rates: total fertility rates (TFRs) with the total population in the denominator (nonspecific); total fertility rates with the population at risk in the denominator (specific); and age-standardized comparative fertility figures obtained from direct standardization. All of the indicators are computed for 1985; others are also computed for one year between 1960 and 1964. The method of direct standardization is described in Section 1.7, and the two types of total fertility rates are briefly described below.

Since the birth of a child is a repeatable event, no fertility rates of the first kind, or so-called occurrence/exposure rates, can be calculated; the denominator is not reduced by the event itself. Fertility rates are rates of the second kind. Consequently, simple summary indices are obtained by taking the sum of the age-specific rates. Fertility rates can be calculated in two ways, so we can obtain two summary indices; both are called total fertility rate, but have different interpretations:

1. *Everyone in the denominator is exposed to the risk of bearing a child.* In this case, fertility rates are calculated by dividing the number of births in a given status and age group by the person-years lived by women in this status and age group. We obtain the average number of births a

Table 2.2. Selected summary fertility indicators in 1985.

Country	Age-standardized CFFs of unmarried women[a]			Specific TFRs (all ages)		Nonspecific TFRs (all ages)	
	All ages	Below age 30	Ages 30 +	Unmarried women	Married women	Unmarried women	Married women
Austria	30	24	50	0.71	3.79	0.33	1.21
Finland	21	14	32	0.55	5.13	0.25	1.44
France	34	23	61	0.84	3.81	0.27	1.62
Germany	15	9	27	0.30	3.74	0.12	1.17
Great Britain	37	28	56	0.99	3.87	0.46	1.39
Hungary	20	14	54	0.47	3.92	0.15	1.70
Italy	9	4	21	0.19	3.98	0.05	1.51
Netherlands	13	7	24	0.27	3.61	0.09	1.42
Norway	28	21	43	0.72	4.66	0.34	1.32
Sweden	56	39	75	1.29	4.61	0.78	0.91

[a]Direct standardization; married women equal 100.

woman would have if the prevailing age- and status-specific fertility rates were to continue throughout her reproductive life from the total of these status-specific fertility rates. Hence, this indicator provides an estimate of the completed fertility of a woman on a period basis. When used for comparison, this total fertility rate – in the following referred to as TFR_{sp} (for specific) – turns out to be an extreme measure of differential fertility, since it does not take into account real marital-status distribution of the population over age groups. The equation takes the form:

$$TFR_{sp(j)} = \sum_{i=15}^{45} \frac{B_{ij}}{P_{ij}} \ .$$

2. *Not everyone in the denominator is exposed to the risk of bearing a child.* In this case, fertility rates are calculated by dividing the number of births in a given status and age group by the person-years lived by all women in this age group. Totaling this kind of status-specific fertility rate we obtain the number of children borne by a woman in the respective status on average (again, on a synthetic cohort basis). These status-specific total fertility rates – TFR_n (for nonspecific) – are additive; hence, they also represent the share of children born in the respective status. This equation is written as:

$$TFR_{n(j)} = \sum_{i=15}^{45} \frac{B_{ij}}{P_i} \ .$$

For the total population, TFR_{sp} and TFR_n are identical. Columns 1 to 3 in *Table 2.2* give age-standardized *comparative fertility figures* (CFFs) of the unmarried population – all never-married, divorced, and widowed women – resulting from direct standardization. The age distribution of the married population is taken as standard because we are interested in comparing the level of fertility of unmarried women with the level of marital fertility. This indicator is calculated over all age groups and over two sub-strata: the population below age 30 and the population aged 30 and above.

In 1985 Sweden certainly had the highest fertility level among unmarried women when compared with the respective level of marital fertility: the CFF equals 56, which means that the fertility level of unmarried women is roughly 56 percent of the level of married women. The levels of Great Britain (37 percent), France (34 percent), Austria (30 percent), and Norway (28 percent) are somewhat close to Sweden's levels. Finland (21 percent) and Hungary (20 percent) follow. Germany (15 percent), the Netherlands (13 percent), and in particular Italy (9 percent) show very low levels of fertility outside marriage.

In Chapter 1 it was concluded that single summary indicators tend to be biased because of an uneven distribution of differentials over age. One solution to this problem is the computation of the same indicator over various subgroups. Analysis of age-standardized comparative fertility figures for two subgroups of the population, women below age 30 and women aged 30 and above, shows that large age differences exist – differences that are, however, very similar in all countries – and that fertility among unmarried women aged 30 and over is two to three times higher than among unmarried women below age 30 (but only relative to marital fertility). Apart from the three countries with very low fertility levels among unmarried women, France and, in particular, Hungary show disproportionately high fertility levels at ages 30 and above.

Age-standardized comparative fertility figures were also calculated for never-married, divorced, and widowed women separately. Those results are not given in detail for two reasons: first, for Great Britain, the Netherlands, and Sweden the data are not available; second, some of the data do not seem to be plausible. For example, the fertility rates of widows in Finland are found to be twice as high as those of their married counterparts. To the extent that the figures are reliable, differences between countries are substantial. Austria and Norway show very small differences between never-married, divorced, and widowed women. In Hungary and Italy, never-married women have notably the lowest fertility rates, but this is not true for France. On the other hand, divorced women in Germany have, by far, the lowest fertility rates among all groups. No obvious reason for the differences between countries can be given; therefore, the subsequent discussion concentrates on comparing fertility of all unmarried women with fertility of married women.

Specific total fertility rates, given in columns 4 and 5 in *Table 2.2*, are an extreme summary measure of differential fertility. Most interesting is the similarity of marital fertility rates across countries. For seven countries this rate is approximately 3.8, while it is significantly larger (around 4.8) for the three Nordic countries. Specific total fertility rates among unmarried women are much lower relative to total marital fertility rates when compared with the age-standardized comparative fertility figures. The age-standardized rates are certainly a more credible measure of differential fertility.

A completely different interpretation can be derived from the nonspecific total fertility rates given in columns 6 and 7 in *Table 2.2*. These rates essentially mirror the proportion of children borne by a woman in each status, on average, and are therefore a weaker measure of differential fertility. For example, unmarried Swedish women gave birth to 0.78 children and married Swedish women bore 0.91 children – that is, 46 percent of all children were born outside marriage in 1985. Italy is the other extreme with only 3 percent of all children born outside marriage (0.05 children born to unmarried women and 1.51 children born to married women). Some comparisons between countries are interesting: for example, Finnish and Dutch married women bore nearly the same number of children (about 1.43), while the figures are quite different for unmarried women (0.25 and 0.09 children, respectively).

Fertility differentials are also an indicator of the current spread of cohabitation. Likewise, changes in fertility differentials over the past two decades are indicators of the respective increase in cohabitation. As expected, age-standardized comparative fertility figures for unmarried women in 1963, given in *Table 2.3*, are lower than the figures for 1985 in all countries. Most European countries experienced a baby boom and, in particular, a marriage boom between 1960 and 1965. During this period we observe relatively low fertility among unmarried women. Since then, social acceptance of cohabitation and childbearing outside marriage has increased remarkably. Indeed, age-standardized comparative fertility figures (column 2) have increased substantially: 137 percent on average, with small increases in Hungary and Germany and large increases in Norway, Sweden, and the Netherlands. The small increases in Austria and Great Britain are largely explained by the fact that unmarried fertility was already high in 1960. Age-standardized comparative fertility figures of unmarried women in 1963 and 1985 are given in *Figure 2.1*.

Columns 3 to 5 in the *Table 2.3* provide additional data on the substantial increase in fertility of unmarried women. These columns give information based on trends in specific total fertility rates. The decline in the period total fertility rate (33 percent, on average; Hungary clearly being an outlier) is

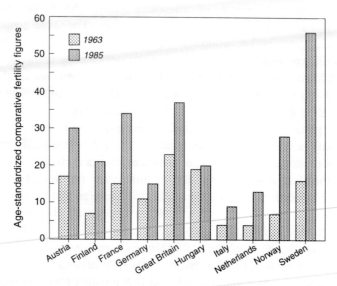

Figure 2.1. Age-standardized comparative fertility of unmarried women, in 1963 and 1985, married women equal 100.

Table 2.3. Changes in summary fertility indicators between 1963 and 1985.

Country	Age-standardized CFFs for unmarried women[a]		Changes in specific TFRs from 1963 to 1985 (in %)		
	1963	Change from 1963 to 1985 (in %)	All women	Married women	Unmarried women
Austria	17	71	−42	−43	−9
Finland	7	182	−34	−18	82
France	15	121	−32	−38	52
Germany	11	38	−48	−39	−23
Great Britain	23	62	−34	−34	19
Hungary	19	8	8	10	14
Italy	4	117	−34	−32	31
Netherlands	4	246	−52	−49	60
Norway	7	285	−41	−23	135
Sweden	16	243	−24	−18	107
Unweighted average	12	137	−33	−28	47

[a]Direct standardization; married women equal 100.

parallel to the decline in the marital fertility rate. The specific total fertility rates of unmarried women, however, have increased remarkably: 47 percent, on average. Even in a country such as Italy, where only a small number of children are born outside marriage, this rate has increased by some 31 percent. Austria and Germany are interesting exceptions with small decreases in the fertility rate among unmarried women during the past two decades.

From *Table 2.3* it appears that the overall fertility decline is largely explained by the decline in marital fertility rates. Indeed, in a majority of countries the decline in overall fertility was even stronger than the decline in marital fertility, which is a consequence of remarkable changes in the marital composition of most populations, namely, the strong decline in the married proportion. When the proportion of the unmarried population – with its lower fertility – increases, overall fertility declines even with constant status-specific fertility levels. This effect was very strong in Germany and in the Nordic countries (compare columns 3 and 4 in *Table 2.3*).

The relevance of changes in the marital-status composition of the population for the analysis of fertility, in general, and the explanation of the fertility decline since the 1960s, in particular, have been addressed in several recent publications. Most of the results show the increasing importance of marital-status changes and the respective compositional changes. Castiglioni and Zuanna (1992), for example, analyzing fertility trends in Italy between 1970 and 1990, find that, during the 1970s, the overall fertility decline in Italy was entirely caused by a decline in marital fertility, whereas during the 1980s this decline was caused by changes in the marital-status structure.[5] Prinz (1991a), analyzing the impact of changes in the marital-status structure on overall fertility trends in Austria, Norway, and Canada between 1960 and 1985, arrives at similar conclusions. Fertility declines during the 1960s were entirely due to declining marital fertility, whereas during the 1980s a large part of the decline was caused by changes in the marital-status composition.

As a consequence of stabilizing marital fertility levels in recent years, marital status seems to have gained in importance in the analysis of fertility. The substantial increases in fertility among unmarried women are largely explained by the respective increases in cohabitation – that is, larger proportions of the unmarried population are living in unions and those women presumably have substantially higher birth rates than single women. Because very little is known about fertility rates of cohabiting women, it is difficult to forecast if childbearing in consensual unions will increase and, if so, to what extent. In Chapter 4, however, fertility of single and cohabiting women is analyzed in detail using Swedish data.

2.3.2 Mortality

Mortality differentials by marital status are surprisingly controversial. Research has unequivocally shown that the mortality level of unmarried
individuals is considerably higher than that of their married counterparts. Livi-
Bacci (1985, p. 99) writes:

> This fact is well established in all countries with a sufficiently developed statistical
> system, has recurrently attracted some attention since the end of the last century
> when it was first observed, but it has not been satisfactorily explained up to the
> present time.

It is not the phenomenon itself that is controversial and partly unknown, but
the explanation of this phenomenon.

Marital status is an important factor in mortality levels. Mortality rates
are higher for unmarried individuals than for married individuals. These differences are comparable to the excess mortality of men over that of women
or to that of smokers over that of nonsmokers (STG, 1988). The apparently
consistent advantage of being married for men and women across space (that
is, for different countries) and time might suggest an almost iron law (Murphy,
1992), whose biological and social basis is worth exploring. The continuing
and consistent differences in the mortality rates of marital groups are particularly remarkable given the substantial decline in the death rates and the change
in the patterns of disease,[6] the notable decline in marriage together with the
increase in divorce, and the variety of socioeconomic structures and health-care
systems in different countries. These indicators necessarily raise the question
of whether the observed variations in mortality rates can be attributed to errors
and artifacts in the data. Misstatements of marital status on death certificates which lead to the well-known numerator–denominator bias present in all
cross-sectional data, are most problematic. Some earlier studies compared the
marital state recorded in censuses with that recorded on death certificates. One
study revealed that there is 95 percent agreement for those never married, married, and widowed but only 80 percent agreement for those divorced (Morgan,
1980). However, the evidence strongly indicates that mortality differences
remain sizable even after correction for possible misreporting.

Another statistical artifact may be adding to the confusion on mortality
differentials; certain attributes of people in the respective marital-status groups
may account for the marital-status pattern of health and mortality. For instance,
lung cancer is strongly related to smoking habits. Murphy (1992) finds that
marital-status differentials of lung cancer in Britain during the 1970s and 1980s
fit exactly with the marital-status distribution of the prevalence of cigarette

smoking some years earlier. Hu and Goldman (1990), however, conclude that mortality differences persist even when the effects of socioeconomic status and other observable factors are controlled.

If observed marital-status mortality differentials are not, and certainly not only, a statistical artifact we can instead assume causation. If we assume causation, we should expect that, across time and space, similar factors are responsible for the excess mortality of unmarried individuals. Livi-Bacci (1985, p. 102) states: "The interpretations of the excess mortality of the unmarried population are still the same as those advanced since this pattern was observed in the second half of the nineteenth century." Several hypotheses have been put forth to explain the more favorable mortality experiences of married individuals, but two main factors have been held responsible for the differences: the *protective* and the *selective* role of marriage.

Hypotheses testing the first factor posit that a beneficial, protective effect of marriage, stemming from a variety of environmental, social, and psychological factors, makes the married state healthier than the unmarried state. One way that marital status is thought to affect health is by acting as either a protective factor or a risk factor in relation to stress. Morgan (1980, p. 638) writes:

> The precise links between stress and health are unclear. However there is evidence to suggest that certain forms of stress predispose towards specific diseases, as for example in the relationship between occupational stress and coronary heart disease.

The married state has been viewed as protecting against stress by providing the individual with a well-defined and socially accepted role. Not having a family, never-married individuals lack one of the most salient identities within society.[7] Occupying a particular marital status not only exposes an individual to specific amounts of stress but also tends to be associated with differences in the availability of social support in the form of a kin network. The latter might play an important role in relation to the onset, the course, and the outcome of an illness.

Another way in which marital state has been related to health and illness is through the lifestyles and physical environment that may serve to expose or shield people from particular diseases. Unmarried people may expose themselves to more dangerous environments and lifestyles; for example, motor vehicle accidents and cirrhosis of the liver among never-married men are important factors in accounting for this group's mortality rates (Morgan, 1980). Certain features of the marital relationship itself, most notably the sexual relationship and the bearing of children, may also be factors conferring either risk or safety.

The second factor given to explain the higher mortality rates of unmarried people is based on the premise that marriage is selective: it selects healthier persons and leaves among the never married a higher proportion of persons with serious health problems. Similarly, remarriage selects the healthiest individuals from among widowed and divorced persons. The selective effects of health on marital state are likely to be influenced by the extent to which a particular illness or disability is stigmatized in the society. Some authors called this effect *permanent selection* and distinguish it from the so-called *temporary selection*. The latter situations occur when persons who are gravely ill, who are undergoing a serious operation, or who are engaged in a dangerous temporary activity postpone marriage to a less hazardous period of their life (Livi-Bacci, 1985).

A third selection is also worth mentioning: *post-marital selection*. This implies that marriage can only be sustained by healthy people and that physically or emotionally handicapped persons are more likely to get divorced (Weingarten, 1985).

For those divorced and widowed a number of additional reasons for excess mortality have been identified. First, marital disruptions – through divorce or through the death of a spouse – have been posited to be severe life stressors (Weingarten, 1985) or life events (Vallin and Nizard, 1977). In particular, during the period immediately following a life event there is a high probability of accidents, disease, or death. Since members in the young age categories are more likely to experience a divorce or an early death of a spouse in the recent past than those in the old age groups, this factor would partly explain the extremely high mortality rates among those divorced and widowed at young ages. In the case of the loss of a spouse, a severe source of stress arises from bereavement. In the case of divorce, the severest period of stress and its adverse effects on health has been shown to occur prior to the divorce action itself; this indicates that marital breakdown is likely to contribute to the morbidity and mortality of those classified as still married and of those who are legally divorced (Morgan, 1980). An interesting explanation for the higher mortality among those widowed has been given by Hu and Goldman (1990). Their results suggest that the cause of death of a spouse places the surviving partner at a higher risk of dying. For example, an accident may injure both persons but may result in one dying before the other. In other circumstances, an infectious disease may debilitate the surviving spouse. In these cases the high mortality rates of widowed individuals could be considered a statistical artifact.

Some interesting conclusions arise from an analysis of marital-status differentials by cause of death. Morgan (1980) reports that the 1965–1967 morbidity data for England and Wales gave no cause of death, among either women or men, for which mortality rates of married persons were greater than that of unmarried persons. However, there are significant differences in the size of those differentials. According to STG (1988), mortality differentials are largest for deaths from external causes and respiratory diseases and smaller for cardiovascular diseases and cancer. This would explain the age pattern of observed mortality differentials: death from external causes dominate in early adulthood, whereas at older ages diseases with a small differential dominate mortality.

The most probable explanation of mortality differentials is a combination of all the factors mentioned so far: the protective role of marriage, in particular in relation to stress; temporary and permanent selection of marriage; effects from life events; the age pattern of different diseases; and statistical artifacts. Indeed, most researchers would agree that a combination of various factors have, in fact, produced the observed differences. Nevertheless, the similarity of death rates of never-married, divorced, and widowed persons, albeit with quite different explanations for their respective sizes, is somewhat surprising. It is clearly difficult to estimate the contribution of various factors to the observed excess mortality of the unmarried population. A number of attempts have been made to explain the phenomenon, but little quantitative evidence has been derived from empirical studies. Both Livi-Bacci (1985) and Hu and Goldman (1990) have tried to assess the possible impact of selection in determining the higher mortality of the unmarried population. Their hypothesis was straightforward: the lower the proportion remaining never married (or divorced), the higher the frequency of the less healthy and the impaired, and the higher the respective excess mortality. Indeed, Livi-Bacci finds that a significant portion of the excess mortality of never-married women can be attributed to the permanent selective role of marriage. Among men, lifestyle seems to change significantly when one's status changes from never married to married, obscuring the relationship between the never-married proportion and its excess mortality. In general, the results obtained by Hu and Goldman support the selection theory, particularly for never-married persons. In their study of 16 developed countries, they find that, on average, a 10 percent increase in the percentage of persons who are never married is associated with a 3.4 percent decline in the death rate for those persons. However, their study shows that significant regional patterns exist, and that there is only little support for the selection argument for divorced persons.

Goldman (1993) has published a paper criticizing the possibility of estimating the role of marriage selection with aggregate cross-sectional data. Using a mathematical simulation model she demonstrates that many inferences derived from observed patterns are simply not justified. Essentially she proves that a particular correlation between the proportion single in a population and its excess mortality relative to the married population can arise from very different combinations of relative marriage risks, relative mortality risks of the healthy and the frail, and initial proportions of the healthy population. She concludes that it is highly unlikely that the analyst will be able to use aggregate patterns to distinguish between selection and causal explanations and that longitudinal data may offer the only promising approach.

Two main questions arise in the study of mortality differentials by marital status in the 10 countries under study: Are the results consistent with previous findings? How do the results relate to the different theories reviewed above? In the study of mortality differentials the analyst may select either mortality or survivorship as a base for comparisons. Hansluwka (1986) points out that this is not a semantic problem but one with far-reaching implications for measurement and interpretation. Due to the complicated relationship between mortality and life expectancy, opposite conclusions may be drawn. Pollard (1982) explains that changes in life expectancy may be expressed as a weighted function of mortality changes of individual ages plus the interaction effects of those mortality changes, interaction effects which may influence trends in differentials in life expectancy. Pollard concludes that "it is dangerous to use the expectation of life for this purpose (i.e., the measurement of mortality differentials) but, in case the main interest is on survivorship rather than mortality, the use of the expectation of life is clearly appropriate."

The obvious conclusion from this discussion is that we should, in principle, concentrate on mortality and for comparative purposes that we should also look at life-expectancy differentials. Therefore, most of the discussion focuses on age-standardized comparative mortality figures (CMFs) obtained through direct standardization. The age distributions of the total population are taken as standard; CMFs are calculated for both 1965 and 1985.

Table 2.4 summarizes some indicators derived from direct standardization for the year 1985. There is an amazing similarity in age-standardized comparative mortality figures over the 10 countries. For never-married and widowed women and for married men almost identical CMFs are obtained for all countries. Given the significant sociodemographic differences between the countries, including the size of the respective marital groups, the proportion living in consensual unions, the mortality level, the health and social security systems, and the income levels, the extent of these similarities is surprising,

Table 2.4. Selected gender-specific summary mortality indicators in 1985.

Gender	Age-standardized CMFs (ages 20 +)[a]				Ratio of CMFs Unmarried/Married	
	Never married	Married	Divorced	Widowed	Ages 20 +	Ages 60 +
Austria						
Women	111	76	127	110	1.43	1.40
Men	127	88	144	154	1.56	1.36
Finland						
Women	111	85	111	107	1.27	1.22
Men	135	86	146	134	1.58	1.35
France						
Women	111	84	104	114	1.30	1.25
Men	134	88	129	167	1.58	1.35
Germany						
Women	111	81	138	110	1.34	1.31
Men	118	89	167	169	1.52	1.36
Great Britain						
Women	108	80	98	113	1.37	1.36
Men	112	89	110	140	1.42	1.36
Hungary						
Women	119	99	130	104	1.07	0.99
Men	127	91	156	141	1.51	1.27
Italy						
Women	113	82	145	109	1.35	1.31
Men	131	90	135	146	1.51	1.37
Netherlands						
Women	109	87	107	112	1.25	1.20
Men	121	91	125	153	1.39	1.29
Norway						
Women	115	79	118	108	1.38	1.35
Men	121	89	145	148	1.45	1.34
Sweden						
Women	115	89	111	107	1.22	1.17
Men	129	87	134	119	1.46	1.35

[a] Direct standardization; CMF for total population equals 100.

even though these similarities are in line with findings from other studies that have used different indicators.

For all marital statuses the age-standardized mortality figures (columns 1 to 4) are notably smaller for women than for men. As was found in most other studies, marriage seems to be more beneficial for men than for women – at least measured in terms of mortality. On average, and for most of the 10 countries, there is a clear *benefit sequence* among both sexes. Among men, excess mortality over the marital group is highest for widowers and lowest for never married, while among women it is highest for divorcées and lowest

Table 2.5. Life-expectancy differences by marital status in 1985, in years.

| Country | Life-expectancy differences: Married minus Never married | | | | Life-expectancy differences at birth: Married minus Divorced or Widowed | | | |
| | At birth | | At age 60 | | Divorced | | Widowed | |
	Women	Men	Women	Men	Women	Men	Women	Men
Austria	2.6	5.7	1.3	1.7	3.4	7.7	3.8	10.4
Finland	2.5	6.0	1.0	2.2	2.7	7.5	2.0	6.3
France	2.5	6.5	0.9	2.1	1.6	6.3	3.8	12.6
Germany	2.1	4.4	1.0	1.7	3.2	7.1	3.7	13.4
Great Britain	2.2	4.0	1.0	1.7	1.5	3.1	3.1	5.9
Hungary	4.0	6.3	1.0	1.6	2.5	7.9	2.1	8.3
Italy	2.6	4.8	1.2	1.8	2.8	3.9	2.1	7.2
Netherlands	1.9	3.5	0.6	1.4	1.9	4.0	2.3	8.9
Norway	2.6	4.3	1.1	1.7	2.6	6.2	2.2	10.2
Sweden	2.8	4.6	1.3	2.1	2.4	6.1	2.4	4.1
Unweighted average	2.6	5.0	1.0	1.8	2.5	6.0	2.8	8.7

for widows. An exception to this general trend are those divorced in France and Great Britain; these groups have the lowest CMFs among all unmarried groups. Except for divorcées in Germany, Hungary, and Italy, none of the female groups have CMFs as large as any of the male unmarried groups.

These marital-status-specific results are partly a consequence of the age range considered for the calculations of CMFs given in columns 1 to 4. In columns 5 and 6, CMFs of all unmarried groups are compared with respective CMFs for married groups. Calculated for age groups 20 and over, the gender-specific results are confirmed: for all countries excess mortality is significantly larger for men than for women, with ratios of 1.5 compared with 1.3 on average. If we only look at the population aged 60 and over, the age when most deaths occur, differences between men and women become much smaller. While excess mortality of unmarried women is largely independent of age, excess mortality of unmarried men is roughly two times higher at age 20 and above than at ages 60 and over. For Austria, Great Britain, and Norway no gender differences are observed beyond age 60. Differences between countries in the CMF ratios are particularly small for elderly men: excess mortality of about 35 percent was calculated for 8 out of 10 countries; lower excess mortality was obtained only for Hungary and the Netherlands.

An alternative measure of differential mortality is given in *Table 2.5*: life expectancies calculated on the basis of age- and marital-status-specific mortality rates, both at birth and at age 60. Essentially the data confirm the results given in *Table 2.4*. Among men in the unmarried population, widowers show the lowest life expectancy and never-married men the highest life expectancy. Life-expectancy differences are again much smaller among women than among men. A major difference from the results obtained from the analysis of CMFs is that among women this measure gives no consistent difference or sequence in the three unmarried states. In a majority of countries widows seem to have slightly higher mortality than divorcées or never-married women. Divorcées seem less disadvantaged in France, Great Britain, and the Netherlands.

In contrast to the findings obtained from the analysis of age-standardized comparative mortality figures, insignificant differences are found when comparing life expectancies at birth with those at age 60. In both cases men's excess mortality exceeds that of women by between 80 and 100 percent. However, the variations over age found through the use of direct standardization seem to reflect age-specific differentials more appropriately than the comparison of life expectancies.

Whether selection effects could be a major cause of marital-status differentials in mortality can best be examined through time trends of appropriate mortality indicators. Intuitively, the striking similarity of age-standardized comparative mortality figures between countries, notwithstanding significant differences in the proportion of people living in various marital statuses, does not strongly support the selection theory.

Table 2.6 gives percentage increases during the period from 1965 to 1985 in the ratio of age-standardized comparative mortality figures between unmarried and married individuals. The table distinguishes between ages 20 and over and ages 60 and over and considers those never married and divorced separately. Unfortunately, information for 1965 is not available for Italy. Four major conclusions can be drawn from the table. First, age differences are insignificant with regard to changes over time. In all countries and for all marital-status groups percentage changes for ages 20 and over and ages 60 and over are almost identical (except for divorced men in Germany and Hungary). Second, excess mortality of never-married and divorced men and women increased in 78 percent of all cases. This increase is somewhat surprising as the 1960s marked a marriage-boom period. Third, increases in excess mortality of unmarried women were significantly larger than those of unmarried men. Fourth, no consistent differences between the never-married and divorced groups were detected. In the majority of countries, the two groups experienced changes in the same order of magnitude among women, while among men increases were small or zero for the never-married group. Notable exceptions to this general trend are divorced women in France and Hungary and divorced men in Germany (both groups have disproportionately large increases) and divorced

Table 2.6. Changes in summary mortality indicators between 1965 and 1985.

| Country | Percentage increase in the ratio of age-standardized CMFs: Never married/Married | | | | Percentage increase in the ratio of age-standardized CMFs: Divorced/Married | | | |
| | Women | | Men | | Women | | Men | |
	Ages 20+	Ages 60+	Ages 20+	Ages 60+	Ages 20+	Ages 60+	Ages 20+	Ages 60+
Austria	16	19	9	3	21	21	14	13
Finland	10	8	11	6	–6	–8	–5	–10
France	5	3	–3	–11	20	21	46	48
Germany	6	7	–6	–11	1	0	2	15
Great Britain	14	15	9	7	15	16	9	10
Hungary	–3	–7	–10	–18	7	8	6	–5
Netherlands	9	10	1	–1	2	7	–25	–28
Norway	34	37	15	12	29	30	14	18
Sweden	5	6	15	13	11	14	4	7
Unweighted average	11	11	3	0	11	12	7	8

An increase of, for example, 16 percent means that the ratio of CMF was 16 percent higher in 1985 than it was in 1965; e.g., for never-married Austrian women, aged 20 years and over, the CMF ratio increased from 1.26 in 1965 to 1.46 in 1985.

women in Finland and divorced men in the Netherlands (both with dispro-portionately small increases, or indeed decreases, when compared with the respective changes among the never-married groups).

The pattern of change in excess mortality of widows and widowers, which is not shown in *Table 2.6*, is less uniform. In most countries, CMFs increased slightly between 1965 and 1985; however, substantial increases were observed among women in Austria and Norway, while decreases were observed among both sexes in Germany and Sweden.

Hu and Goldman (1990) find almost identical time trends in excess mortal-ity among the three unmarried statuses. They use a more complex measure of differential mortality, "relative mortality ratios," which are essentially expo-nential parameter estimates obtained from a log-linear model that adjusts for specified covariates, including age. In their explanation of time trends, Hu and Goldman identify three possible factors: increased protection effects, a greater degree of selection, and the inappropriateness of the chosen measure of differ-ential mortality. As to the third factor, the agreement of two different measures on time trends suggests real changes rather than measurement artifacts.

Both Livi-Bacci (1985) and Hu and Goldman (1990) find evidence of se-lection effects among the never-married population. The results in the present study indicate only a slight relation between the excess mortality of the unmar-ried and the relative size of the unmarried group. Excess mortality of those divorced increased substantially almost everywhere and at all ages, while the divorced proportion increased significantly in all age groups. At an aggregate level this conclusion also holds for the never-married population, which did not decrease in relative size. Hungary, for example, is the only country where excess mortality among never-married women did not increase, and it is also the only country where the proportion of never-married women declined significantly. In 1985, there was no relation between higher age-standardized comparative mortality figures and lower proportions of the population in the respective group in any of the 10 countries. However, the analysis of age-specific trends shows decreases in the never-married proportion between 1965 and 1985 for most age groups beyond age 35 for women and at older ages for men. This is only a weak confirmation of the existence of selection effects since excess mortality of the never-married population increased at all ages irrespective of the trend in the never-married proportion. At least, some of the gender difference in time trends, namely, the significantly large increase in excess mortality among never-married women, seems to be attributable to selection effects.

If misreporting of marital state on the death certificate were an important source of bias in mortality rates, then part of the increase in the CMFs among the divorced population could be explained by the drop in misreporting over time. Since being divorced is likely to be less stigmatized today, the reported number of deaths among those divorced and, hence, excess mortality of this group are likely to increase.

A major residual factor in the explanation of excess mortality, in general, and of respective increases over time, in particular, must be protection. Increased protection through marriage is difficult to prove, but it is suggested by the results in this study. Whether this would be increased protection from stress due to a stable family life, from a more dangerous environment, from a lifestyle chosen by unmarried individuals, or from other types of protection cannot be derived from aggregate mortality data.

It seems that the conclusion can be drawn that increased protection through family life is a major reason for excess mortality increases in the unmarried population; however, another observation is the emergence and rapid increase in the proportion living in consensual unions. If a larger proportion of the unmarried population is living in a family, excess mortality of the unmarried should be declining. The question then becomes, Are only legally married couples protected through family life or are couples in general protected? Has the excess mortality of singles over couples changed? Obviously, very little can be concluded from the analysis of marital-status differentials in mortality.

The increasing divergence between legal and actual family status increasingly invalidates the relationship between marital status and mortality. On the basis of marital-status data, certainly nothing can be determined about the mortality and lifestyle of cohabiting couples.

In conclusion it seems that neither increased protection of marriage nor a greater degree of selection into marriage can explain the increase in excess mortality of the unmarried. Heterogeneity within marital-status groups has certainly increased, making marital-status mortality analysis increasingly irrelevant. If within-group variance becomes larger than or as large as between-group variance the categories chosen must be changed. Weingarten (1985), for example, has argued that remarriage should be treated as a distinct status, since remarriage is uniquely stressful in itself because of problems with former spouses, potential stepchildren, or absentee children. To achieve the required within-group homogeneity one certainly has to distinguish never-married or divorced singles from never-married or divorced cohabitants and possibly first marriages from remarriages. These distinctions are made in Chapter 4, which analyzes mortality differentials by union status using Swedish data. Reasons for the increase in excess mortality are also identified.

2.3.3 Migration

Marital-status differentials in migration trends have not been as thoroughly analyzed as those in fertility and mortality trends. A major reason for this is the lack of adequate data. In most cases marital status is not reported in migration statistics. Hence, a comparative analysis across the 10 countries is not possible. Instead, in this section a number of issues and problems are raised, and data for Great Britain are used for illustration.[8]

An internationally comparable measure of spatial mobility is the proportion of the population that changes residence during a fixed period of time. Migration information by age and sex is collected in France, Great Britain, the Netherlands, and Sweden, but only the British data include marital status as well. Based on age-specific proportions of changes in residence, which is sometimes referred to as the residential mobility rate (Long, 1992), a number of summary indicators can be calculated, but only two are used in this discussion. First, age-standardized comparative migration figures are computed, based on direct standardization and using the total population of each sex as standard. These age-standardized migration figures are calculated for two subgroups of the population: those aged 15 to 29 and those aged 30 and above. Second, so-called mobility expectancies are calculated. This is the expected number

Table 2.7. Summary migration indicators for Great Britain in 1981.

Marital status	Age-standardized comparative migration figures[a]				Relative mobility expectancies[b]			
	Women		Men		Women		Men	
	Age 15–29	Age 30 +	Age 15–29	Age 30 +	Age 20	Age 40	Age 20	Age 40
Never married	94	112	89	103	1.05	1.08	0.97	1.10
Married	194	85	233	89	1.00	0.84	1.15	0.88
Divorced	160	159	181	200	1.48	1.68	1.82	2.10
Widowed	107	112	108	108	1.07	1.19	1.08	1.14

[a]Direct standardization; total population equals 100.
[b]Relative mobility expectancies equal the ratio of the mobility expectancy (number of years with moves) of group x to that of the total population.

of years with moves during the remaining lifetime for a hypothetical cohort, assuming that rates of moving and mortality remain unchanged (Long, 1992). The mobility expectancy is the equivalent of the e_x column in an ordinary life table and is calculated analogously.[9] In *Table 2.7* ratios of resulting mobility expectancies (relative to the total population) are given. Two age ranges have been selected: ages 20 and above and ages 40 and above.

Available data reveal that migration is most frequent among the divorced population and least frequent among the married population. This pattern is supported by the British data. Among both sexes and independent of age, mobility expectancy is highest by far among the divorced population, with ratios ranging from 1.48 for women at age 20 to 2.10 for men at age 40. A strong age dependency is evident for the married population. Beyond age 30, married men and women move significantly less often than their unmarried counterparts, independent of the indicator chosen to measure mobility. Up to age 30, however, rates of residential mobility are highest for married persons. Age-standardized comparative migration figures for the 15–29 age group are even higher for married than for divorced persons. The high mobility of these age groups among the married population is due to the large proportion of recently married couples and the fact that marriage is highly likely to lead, in the short term, to a change of residence. Interestingly, differences in mobility between never married and widowed are minor.

The relationship between marital status and mobility is quite complex. Events in the life cycle, such as marriage, divorce, or the death of a spouse, can certainly be the reason for a change in place of residence. However, the relationship between various life-cycle events, or the connection between the marital career and the migration career, cannot be studied with aggregate data. Such analyses require longitudinal data, which, with the aid of the chronological sequence of events, provide an opportunity for reconstructing the connection between family biography and migration biography (Haug and Priester, 1992). Indeed, in the study of migration a major advance in the 1980s has been the adoption of a life-course perspective and the use of longitudinal data (see Mulder and Wagner, 1992, for references).

Using event–history data we can also distinguish two different aspects in the relationship between marital status and migration: pure status dependence and event dependence. In studies of the first type a question arises: Does occupying a certain marital status influence the probability of the occurrence of a change of residence? Analyses of the second type must address the question, Does the occurrence of an event in the marital career influence this probability? If the related events occur simultaneously they are referred to as synchronized events (Mulder and Wagner, 1992).

In the study of the influences of the marital career on the migration career the analysis of synchronized events permits a distinction between the short-term effect of getting married and the long-term effect of being married. An interesting example of such an analysis is given by Mulder and Wagner (1992). They use data from the German Life History Survey, carried out in 1981–1983, to estimate the parameters of a log-linear model of occurrence/exposure rates. Two of their findings are most relevant. First, if only status dependence is considered, unmarried individuals seem to move two to three times more often than married persons.[10] When event dependence is included in the model, unmarried individuals move less often than married individuals with regard to short-distance moves (short-distance moves make up the large majority of all changes of residence). Second, newlyweds move 20 to 30 times more often than all others (married and unmarried) over short distances. Over long distances, they move two to five times more often than unmarried individuals and six to twelve times more often than married persons. A similar life-course analysis could be carried out on other life-cycle events, such as divorce or death of a spouse.

Such detailed conclusions cannot be derived from the analysis of aggregate data such as those presented in *Table 2.7*. If information on mobility by marital status were available for several countries, however, it could help to explain the roles, statuses, and behaviors associated with marital status in different national settings. In a comparison of the United States, Great Britain, Ireland, and Japan, Long (1992) speculates that mobility may be lower for single men than for single women if men have prior claim to the parental residence or have greater economic resources to purchase housing. He points out that marital-status differentials in residential mobility could arise from employment or housing policies that favor married couples over singles. Such policies could influence not only the mobility of individuals but even marital status itself.

As the study of migration has recently gained in prominence we can expect better-quality data, which allow more detailed analyses and comparisons to be made between various European countries. Mobility differences between marital and consensual unions are also highly interesting; however, apart from a general knowledge of higher flexibility among the latter, no information is currently available.

2.3.4 Marriage, divorce, and death of spouse

The population composition by marital status, which is discussed in Section 2.2, and its development over time are to a large extent determined by marital-status dynamics. In this section we examine marriage, divorce, widowhood/widowerhood, and remarriage rates in 1985 and their changes between 1960 and 1985.

Increment–decrement marital-status life tables conveniently describe and compactly summarize the marital life-course patterns experienced by a given (real or synthetic) cohort. Such multistate life tables represent the most advanced stage in a development process that began with the construction of single-decrement life tables. A limitation of these single-decrement life tables is their reliance on only one avenue for exiting a state. Multiple-decrement life tables were proposed to remedy this limitation; these tables allow for multiple paths for departing a state. Typical illustrations are cause-of-death life tables or conventional nuptiality tables showing attrition from a cohort due to death and marriage. Subsequent experiences of individuals once they exit the life-table population are not followed up. Thus, entrants and particularly re-entrants into the life table are not permitted (Espenshade and Braun, 1982).

Generalization of the life-table methodology is needed to keep track of individuals in various states. Except for the state of death, most states are transient and may be left and re-entered. The multistate, also called increment–decrement, life table is the ideal solution; it permits simultaneous entries into (increments) and exits from (decrements) the alternative states in the life table. The key feature of all increment–decrement life tables lies in their formulation as simple Markov-chain models (Espenshade and Braun, 1982). We assume that each individual at a given age, present at a specific time in a given state, has the same propensity for moving out of the state as all others at that age and in that given state (the population–homogeneity assumption) and that this propensity is independent of the individual's past (the Markovian assumption).

Multistate life tables can be applied when analyzing marital status (or union status). In short, increment–decrement marital-status life tables permit us to describe and summarize compactly the marital-status life-course patterns experienced by a given cohort as they age and as they move from one marital-status category to another. Analyses of marital-status life tables allow us to calculate several life-course indicators and to answer a number of important questions: What proportion of a cohort marries? What is the probability that a marriage will end in divorce? What proportion of marriages ends in the death of a spouse?

Country-specific results of selected marital-status life-table indicators have been calculated based on average occurrence/exposure rates for the period 1981 to 1985. The results are given in *Table 2.8* for women and *Table 2.9* for men. The following tabulation shows how they were calculated from standard life-table functions.

Proportion of persons ever marrying:	$\Sigma\, d_{nm}\, /\, l(0)$.
Average duration of a marriage:	$T_m(0)\, /\, \Sigma\, (d_{nm} + d_{dm} + d_{wm})$.
Proportion ending in divorce:	$\Sigma\, d_{md}\, /\, \Sigma\, (d_{nm} + d_{dm} + d_{wm})$.
Proportion ending in widowhood/ widowerhood:	$\Sigma\, d_{mw}\, /\, \Sigma\, (d_{nm} + d_{dm} + d_{wm})$.
Average duration of a divorce:	$T_d(0)\, /\, \Sigma\, (d_{md})$.
Proportion of divorced remarrying:	$\Sigma\, d_{dm}\, /\, \Sigma\, (d_{md})$.
Average duration of a widowhood/ widowerhood:	$T_w(0)\, /\, \Sigma\, (d_{mw})$.
Proportion of widowed remarrying:	$\Sigma\, d_{wm}\, /\, \Sigma\, (d_{mw})$.

The sums run over all age groups (age-interval identifiers have been omitted to simplify the notation); d_{ij} represents the number of transitions from state i to state j; $T_i(0)$ is the total number of person-years lived in state i at and above age 0; and $l(0)$ is the radix. The indices indicate marital status (never married, married, divorced, and widowed).

Column 1 in *Tables 2.8* and *2.9* gives the proportion of the population ever marrying by age 50, a useful marriage indicator. It ranges from very low levels in Scandinavian countries and in Germany (with a minimum of 62 percent among men in Sweden) to very high levels in Hungary and Italy (with a maximum of 96 percent among Hungarian women).[11] On average, 83 percent of all women but only 77 percent of all men marry at least once. Among men, significantly larger proportions marry a second time, a fact that is also evident from the large proportions of widowed and divorced men remarrying

Table 2.8. Selected marital-status life-table statistics for women between 1981 and 1985.

Country	Marriage statistics				Divorce, widowhood, and remarriage			
	Proportion ever marrying	Average duration of marriage in years	Proportion ending in divorce	Proportion ending in widowhood	Average duration of divorce in years	Proportion of divorced remarrying	Average duration of widowhood in years	Proportion of widows remarrying
Austria	82.7	30.7	23.8	52.3	22.1	57.1	16.8	1.7
Finland	79.7	31.3	25.4	51.2	26.2	41.3	17.4	2.0
France	85.2	32.7	21.2	53.7	24.2	52.8	17.4	2.4
Germany	79.0	30.6	24.6	51.6	18.0	63.9	15.9	1.5
Great Britain	85.6	30.8	25.6	46.4	17.7	63.2	16.4	3.9
Hungary	96.1	26.7	27.5	48.0	17.9	63.5	16.8	5.5
Italy	90.1	32.7	3.0	91.4	20.3	58.3	19.9	2.5
Netherlands	84.0	32.5	24.7	51.5	24.6	48.5	17.4	1.8
Norway	78.8	32.1	25.2	50.6	26.3	42.6	16.6	1.3
Sweden	68.7	28.0	33.8	43.5	26.3	43.5	16.5	1.0
Unweighted average	83.3	30.8	23.5	54.0	22.4	53.5	17.6	2.4

Table 2.9. Selected marital-status life-table statistics for men between 1981 and 1985.

Country	Marriage statistics				Divorce, widowerhood, and remarriage			
	Proportion ever marrying	Average duration of marriage in years	Proportion ending in divorce	Proportion ending in widowerhood	Average duration of divorce in years	Proportion of divorced remarrying	Average duration of widowerhood in years	Proportion widowers remarrying
Austria	80.1	30.4	23.3	18.2	14.1	72.4	10.2	9.3
Finland	71.5	30.7	25.0	17.4	18.4	50.1	10.4	7.4
France	80.2	32.5	20.8	19.3	15.4	66.8	10.6	8.1
Germany	72.1	29.7	24.4	19.1	13.4	72.6	9.8	10.4
Great Britain	80.3	30.5	25.4	19.0	12.1	73.3	10.9	10.7
Hungary	89.2	26.9	27.5	18.2	11.8	73.5	9.2	15.7
Italy	87.5	32.5	3.2	58.3	8.8	79.8	12.4	11.8
Netherlands	77.6	32.4	24.2	19.9	16.0	62.4	10.2	8.6
Norway	71.2	31.7	25.3	18.5	19.0	50.3	11.0	3.8
Sweden	61.7	27.7	33.6	16.9	20.2	48.7	10.9	4.7
Unweighted average	76.8	30.5	23.3	22.5	14.9	65.0	10.5	9.1

given in columns 6 and 8 in *Table 2.9*. The number of marriages per person is approximately 1.2, with very little variation between countries. No correlation is evident between the prevalence of marriage (column 1) and its average duration (column 2).

The proportion of marriages ending in divorce over the life course of a given or synthetic cohort is a very useful indicator of marital stability. In the early 1980s roughly one-fourth to one-fifth of all marriages were projected to end in divorce. The only exceptions were Sweden, with one-third of all marriages ending in divorce, and Italy, with only 3 percent.

Because of gender differences in mortality and in age at marriage, roughly half of all women's marriages end in widowhood, while less than one-fifth of all married men experience widowerhood. Due to relatively small differences in mortality, variation over countries is minor and mostly reflects differences in divorce rates. Hence, Italy is a clear exception.

Among those divorced, between 50 and 80 percent of men and between 40 and 65 percent of women remarry; the lowest proportions remarrying are observed in the three Nordic countries. Among both sexes a high correlation is evident between low proportions remarrying and long durations of a divorce. This correlation is not apparent among those widowed. Mostly due to their older age, the proportion of widows and widowers remarrying is very low, in particular for women. The smallest proportion remarrying is observed in Sweden (1 percent of Swedish widows); the largest is found in Hungary (15 percent of Hungarian widowers).

Durations of marriage, divorce, and widowhood/widowerhood differ by country and gender. The average duration of a divorce among Swedish women is almost as long as the average duration of a marriage. Except for the Nordic countries, the average duration of a divorce among men is generally less than half as long as the average duration of a marriage and even shorter than the length of widowhood for women.

Different proportions of the population are affected by marriage, divorce, and widowhood/widowerhood. An interesting measure obtained from the marital-status life table is the average proportion of lifetime spent in each marital status. *Table 2.10* gives the population-based expectation of future life in state i; hence, it gives the proportion of person-years lived in state i by all persons, or $T_i(0)/T(0)$.

In Hungary women enter their first marriage at a very young age; therefore, their married life, on average, exceeds their never-married life in length. At the other extreme are Swedish men who spend almost two-thirds of their life in the status never married. Among women, widowed life exceeds divorced life –

Table 2.10. Proportion of lifetime spent in each marital status between 1981 and 1985, in percent.

Country	Women				Men			
	Never married	Married	Divorced	Widowed	Never married	Married	Divorced	Widowed
Austria	43	39	7	11	50	43	5	3
Finland	47	36	8	10	56	36	5	2
France	42	40	6	11	49	44	4	3
Germany	48	37	5	10	56	37	4	2
Great Britain	43	41	6	10	50	43	4	3
Hungary	33	45	8	14	46	46	6	3
Italy	39	40	1	20	46	44	0	10
Netherlands	43	39	7	11	51	41	5	3
Norway	48	36	7	9	56	36	5	2
Sweden	56	28	9	7	63	28	7	2
Unweighted average	44	38	7	11	52	40	5	3

with the exception of Swedish women; however, men spend only 2 to 3 percent of their lives as widowers in most countries. Italy is again an exception with large proportions of lifetime spent in widowhood/widowerhood and negligible proportions in divorce. The data, however, only reflect legal marital status and do not indicate time spent as a single or as a couple.

Of particular interest are trends in marriage and divorce rates during the past three decades in different countries. Trends in marital-status dynamics have recently been analyzed in a number of studies (Gonnot and Vukovich, 1989; Roussel, 1989; Haskey, 1991; and Kiernan, 1993). Some of the findings from these studies are included in the following discussion. *Table 2.11* gives the number of marriages per 1,000 individuals of the total population (the crude marriage rate) and the number of divorces per 1,000 married couples between 1960 and 1985.

Although the crude marriage rate is influenced by changes in the age composition of the population, its interpretation remains straightforward, and trends over time roughly mirror trends of more sophisticated marriage indicators such as the proportion ever marrying. The prevalence of marriage rose during the 1950s and continued to rise in all countries except Austria and Germany in the early 1960s. During this period mean ages at first marriage declined. Marriage rates peaked in 1965, with more than 90 percent ever marrying in all European countries (Haskey, 1991). Interestingly, differences between countries were also lowest at that time.

Table 2.11. Crude marriage rates and divorce rates from 1960 to 1985.

Country	Marriages per 1,000 total population				Divorces per 1,000 married couples			
	1960	1965	1975	1985	1960	1970	1980	1985
Austria	8.3	7.8	6.2	5.9	5.0	5.9	7.9	8.8
Finland	7.4	7.9	7.2	5.3	4.3	6.0	9.0	8.5
France	7.0	7.1	7.3	4.9	2.8	3.4	7.1	8.3
Germany	9.4	8.3	6.3	6.0	3.6	5.1	6.4	8.6
Great Britain	7.5	7.8	7.7	6.9	2.1	5.9	12.0	13.3
Hungary	8.9	8.8	9.9	6.9	6.6	8.4	9.9	10.9
Italy	7.7	7.7	6.7	5.2	1.5	1.0	1.1	1.2
Netherlands	7.6	8.8	7.3	5.7	2.2	3.3	7.5	9.9
Norway	6.6	6.5	6.7	4.9	2.8	3.7	6.8	8.6
Sweden	6.7	7.8	5.4	4.6	5.0	6.7	11.1	11.7
Unweighted average	7.7	7.9	7.1	5.6	3.6	4.9	7.9	9.0

The period 1965 to 1970 marked a turning point. The mean age at first marriage increased, and the prevalence of marriage decreased. The decline in marriage rates started in Sweden, where it was particularly fast, and it slowly spread to the rest of Europe. Based on crude marriage rates, the decline was much more modest in Great Britain than in all other countries, while it was particularly fast in the Netherlands. Declines in marriage rates were much steeper at younger ages, while the rates were relatively stable at older ages. Today couples marry at older ages and over a wider range of ages than couples in the recent past.

The abrupt changes in the patterns of marriage in the early 1970s have been ascribed to a number of factors (Haskey, 1991): the emergence of cohabitation as a permanent feature in couple formation; the delay of marriage; fundamental changes in attitudes toward marriage and partnership; evolving aspirations concerning family size and lifestyle (individualization); and changing economic conditions. While these factors play a role, they do not satisfactorily explain the substitution of cohabitation for marriage (reasons for this replacement are discussed at length in Chapter 3).

Except in Italy (between 1960 and 1970) and Finland (between 1980 and 1985), divorce rates (divorces per 1,000 married couples) increased in all countries and at all ages between 1960 and 1985. In some countries, such as Hungary, Austria, and in particular Germany, the increases occurred gradually over the whole period, but in the other countries, most importantly France, Great Britain, the Netherlands, and Sweden, a rapid increase occurred during the 1970s. In 1960, Hungary had the highest divorce rate, followed by Austria and Sweden, but by the 1980s Great Britain had taken the lead. Interestingly, by 1985 Great Britain also had the highest crude marriage rate in the sample. Italy, again, appears as an outlier with the smallest number of divorces per 1,000 married couples and virtually no increase over time. Beginning in the mid-1980s many European countries experienced a period of stabilization in divorce rates. Differences between countries have declined over time. This decline, however, may be due to the selection of countries; only one Southern European country with a low divorce rate has been considered.

The rapid increase in the prevalence of divorce in Europe has been attributed to a number of causes. In general, since World War II, obtaining a divorce has become progressively easy and relatively inexpensive. The rise in the incidence of divorce, therefore, may partly be attributed to changes in divorce law and especially to the widening and liberalization of grounds on which divorce may be granted in European countries (Haskey, 1991). Changes in divorce laws and their impact on divorce rates have been well documented and analyzed.[12] Divorce rates began to rise first in Eastern Europe where divorce laws were liberalized earlier than in most countries in the West (Kiernan, 1993). In an analysis of West European countries Festy (1985) finds that substantial changes in divorce legislation were introduced between 1965 and 1975. Examining the timing of the revision in divorce law, he also finds that countries that introduced liberal legislation early (Great Britain and Sweden in this sample) experienced a much greater increase in the divorce rate than those that did so later.

Increases in divorce have also been attributed to other factors (Manting, 1992): the increase in labor-force participation of women leading to economic independence; individualization; changes in marriage trends such as the delay of marriage; and changes in attitudes toward marriage as a lifetime commitment. The selectivity of married couples and the emergence of cohabitation have been given as reasons for the recent stabilization in divorce rates. Unstable cohabiting couples do not marry, but rather separate before they marry (Bumpass, 1990). Trends in marriage, divorce, and cohabitation rates appear highly related and seem to have the same origin. Chapters 3 and 4 provide more information on the role of cohabitation in divorce and marriage rates.

2.4   Modeling Marital Status

In Section 1.6 multistate projection models were identified as the most suitable models for projecting the marital-status composition of a population. They are dynamic simulation models, and, provided the required data are available, they can operate in any state space. In this section the exact formulation of the

Table 2.12. Transition flows in the marital-status model, no external migration.

Status before transition	Status after transition				
	Never married	Married	Divorced	Widowed	Death
Never married	–	M	*	*	D
Married	*	–	S	W	D
Divorced	*	M	–	*	D
Widowed	*	M	*	–	D
Not yet born	B	*	*	*	*

B=birth, D=death, M=marriage, S=divorce, W=widowhood/widowerhood, – =no event, * =impossible event.

four-state marital-status model and its consistency requirements are described. The benefits of the scenario approach to population projection, in general, and the advantages and problems of scenario setting in a marital-status model, in particular, are investigated.

2.4.1 The marital-status projection model

The marital-status concept comprises four possible statuses: never married, married, divorced, and widowed. Ideally only the married state indicates life with a partner and with children. With four marital statuses and excluding external migration, there are five possible transitions (*Table 2.12*): three for marriages (first marriage, remarriage of divorced, and remarriage of widowed) and two for marriage dissolution (divorce and loss of spouse). Another four transitions result from the exit from the state space (death). All newborns (entry into the state space) are never married, but they result from the natality of women in all four categories.

For each sex we have the following component-of-growth equations over the time interval t to $t + h$, h being one projection interval which is set at five years in the case of our marital-status projections:

$$
\begin{aligned}
P_n(t + h) &= P_n(t) + B(t, t + h) - M_n(t, t + h) - D_n(t, t + h) \ , \\
P_m(t + h) &= P_m(t) + M_n(t, t + h) + M_d(t, t + h) + M_w(t, t + h) \\
&\quad - S(t, t + h) - W(t, t + h) - D_m(t, t + h) \ , \\
P_d(t + h) &= P_d(t) + S(t, t + h) - M_d(t, t + h) - D_d(t, t + h) \ , \\
P_w(t + h) &= P_w(t) + W(t, t + h) - M_w(t, t + h) - D_w(t, t + h) \ .
\end{aligned}
$$

In these equations, P is population and B, D, M, S, and W are as listed in *Table 2.12*. The index indicates marital status (never married, married, divorced, or widowed).

The number of newly married or divorced women must equal the number of newly married or divorced men, and the number of new widows or widowers must equal the number of deaths among married men or women. Thus, we have the following constraints or consistency requirements (the indices denote gender and marital status):

$$M_{s,\sigma}(t,t+h) + M_{d,\sigma}(t,t+h) + M_{w,\sigma}(t,t+h) =$$
$$M_{s,\varphi}(t,t+h) + M_{d,\varphi}(t,t+h) + M_{w,\varphi}(t,t+h) \ ,$$

$$S_\sigma(t,t+h) = S_\varphi(t,t+h) \ ,$$
$$D_{m,\sigma}(t,t+h) = W_\varphi(t,t+h) \ ,$$
$$W_\sigma(t,t+h) = D_{m,\varphi}(t,t+h) \ .$$

Within a multistate demographic framework, male events are modeled independently of female events, and conditions arising from the constraining equations are not likely to be fulfilled. To obtain consistent flow figures for men and women, a number of possibilities arise. In the *DIALOG* projection model – which was used to produce population projections by marital status – mortality dominance is assumed to obtain consistency between the number of deaths and the number of widows/widowers. In the case of marriage and divorce, differences observed in the number of events between sexes are averaged by using the harmonic mean method (see Section 1.6).

2.4.2   The scenario approach to population projection

Recently several authors (Ahlburg and Vaupel, 1990; Lutz, 1991; Lutz and Prinz, 1991; or Cliquet, 1993) and agencies (EUROSTAT, 1991; United Nations, 1992) have chosen to study population scenarios instead of the more traditional variants. A scenario approach to population projection may be defined through several characteristics. Lutz *et al.* (1993) have identified four basic elements of the scenario approach: the if–then nature of the calculation is emphasized more than the likely prediction; all assumptions are explicit and offer a sensitivity analysis over the assumptions chosen; all possible components of change are addressed separately (if one is chosen to remain invariant, it must be justified); and the connotation of a somewhat larger number of scenarios is given. A general goal of population projections is to provide a basis for reasonable policies. If the goal is to have robust policies, an important contribution of the scenario approach is to provide a sensitivity analysis that indicates which variables are less stable than others even under identical scenario assumptions. Indeed, policies must take into account the uncertainties of critical variables.

The crucial question, of course, is what alternative assumptions should be made for future fertility, mortality, and migration and in marital-status projections for marriage and divorce. A major limitation of most, if not all, population projections is the assumption of the independence of demographic variables. Fertility, mortality, and migration are treated independently, and the assumptions are made separately for each. Independence is critical in standard population projections, but it becomes especially problematic in marital-status projections. Dependencies cannot be neglected. For example, the death of a spouse is a function of gender differences in mortality and the age at marriage; the incidence of divorce is related to the prevalence of marriage; and remarriage depends on both divorce and widowhood/widowerhood. Fertility, mortality, and to some extent migration depend on the marital-status composition of the population. All variables are strongly related to one another; however, it is not obvious whether fertility and mortality differentials between marital statuses will continue, increase, or rather disappear in the future.[13]

Nevertheless, marital-status-specific fertility rates have been more stable than overall fertility rates, that is, changes in overall fertility rates are to varying degrees a consequence of changes in the marital composition of the population. Hence, if predictions of future marriage behavior were available, uncertainties arising from assumptions on future fertility could be reduced. For example, the baby boom during the 1960s has to a large extent been attributed to the boom in marriage; if the latter boom had been projected, population projections would have been more accurate. Given the increasing numbers of consensual unions, however, it seems unlikely that projecting future marriage behavior will be easier than projecting future fertility behavior.

For the purpose of marital-status projections, the future of marriage and divorce rates should be investigated in detail. In this study, however, only one assumption of constant rates is used for several reasons. First, this procedure is justified because marital status alone, disregarding consensual unions, does not provide a complete picture. Marital-status trends must be investigated in detail with cohabitation trends. These latter trends, as shown in Chapters 4 and 5, have a significant impact on the legal marital-status composition. Various scenarios are, therefore, only used in the context of union-status projections. Second, comparability between different approaches and models is only given assuming constant rates. It would be difficult to compare marital-status and union-status projections under a scenario with high divorce rates since increased divorce rates would have different consequences under different projection models.

The comparison between the two types of status-specific projections is a major intention of this study. Third, comparisons between countries are easier under constant rates than under varying rates. Trends in one component of the population might affect different countries in different ways which would complicate the analysis further. Finally, the problem of interdependencies of various demographic variables can be avoided. It would require a substantial effort to handle all kinds of dependencies in 10 different countries.

2.5   Population Projections by Marital Status

During the 1970s Denmark, Great Britain, the Netherlands, Norway, and Sweden produced official population forecasts in which individuals were classified not only by age and sex, but also by marital status. Since marital status is no longer a good indicator of one's living arrangement – and, hence, demographic behavior – in these countries (except in the Netherlands) the marital-status projection models are no longer used. It has not been employed in Norway since 1981, and in the remaining countries the marital-status models were applied only during the 1970s. There are benefits from using marital-status projection models, even with regard to the future size and age structure of the population (see Prinz, 1991a), but in this section it is the future marital-status composition that is of interest.

Even if we assume no further declines in marriage rates and no increases in divorce rates, the marital composition will change substantially. *Table 2.13* gives actual and projected proportions of married men and women for two large age groups; ages 15 to 59 and ages 60 and above. On average, the proportion married is expected to decline at all ages. Among elderly men the decline is an amazing 17 percentage points. This decline in the married proportion might largely be compensated by a corresponding increase in the cohabiting proportion; however, for elderly men, part of the decline is due to an equalization of the unfavorable sex ratio in 1985.[14] There are, however, significant differences between the 10 countries. Italy does not follow the trend evident in other countries; apart from elderly men, the marital composition does not change. Among elderly men, the decline in the married proportion is particularly strong in Finland, Germany, and Sweden. In all countries the decline is caused by a remarkable increase in the never-married proportion. Changes are more modest in Austria, Hungary, France, and Great Britain. The increase in the divorced proportion is approximately 4 to 5 percentage points, except in the three Nordic countries where it is somewhat higher.

Table 2.13. Proportion of married men and women in 1985 and 2030.

Country	Ages 15 to 59 (in %)				Ages 60 + (in %)			
	Women		Men		Women		Men	
	1985	2030	1985	2030	1985	2030	1985	2030
Austria	59	58	56	52	35	33	77	62
Finland	57	51	53	46	36	29	74	52
France	62	57	58	53	42	36	76	63
Germany	61	56	55	46	37	36	79	57
Great Britain	61	58	56	51	44	42	75	63
Hungary	70	65	66	61	37	28	77	64
Italy	67	70	62	62	42	42	79	73
Netherlands	61	58	56	51	46	36	78	60
Norway	60	50	54	45	46	35	73	54
Sweden	50	39	44	34	45	27	69	42
Unweighted average	61	56	56	50	41	34	76	59

Among elderly women, changes are most significant in the three Nordic countries, Hungary, and the Netherlands. In contrast to men, the decline in the proportion of elderly married women is caused by an increase in the divorced proportion – which in 2030 is projected to be very close to the never-married proportion. Sweden is an exception; the proportion of elderly divorced women increases from 7 to 17 percent, and the never-married proportion from 10 to 25 percent. The widowed proportion declines in the elderly population among both sexes in all countries, except Hungary and Italy.

Changes are more modest among the working-age population. The widowed proportion does not change significantly, and the divorced proportion generally increases slightly (up to 2 percentage points). In both sexes the decline in the married proportion results from an increase in the never-married proportion. Changes are again largest in the Nordic countries and Germany. Among both sexes and both age ranges, differences in the married proportion between countries increase because the marital composition changes much more rapidly in some countries than in others under constant rates assumptions.

The projected changes in the marital-status composition cannot completely explain the changes in actual living arrangements. The results suggest further, sometimes substantial, increases in cohabitation, but we do not know the extent of these increases. For Sweden, projections of consensual unions are undertaken in Chapter 4. Nevertheless, we can address a number of issues by looking at legal marital status, as is done in the following section.

2.6   Socioeconomic Differentials

Behavior in general – not only with regard to fertility, mortality, and migration – is strongly linked to living arrangements, and hence at least to some extent also to marital status. Information on union status should also be considered in studies on demographic behavior. In this section, however, the focus is on marital-status differentials in behavior, looking at various issues such as labor-force participation, income, retirement, health, illness, and household formation. If legal marital status has an effect on some of those factors, the changes expected in the marital-status composition of the population will have important consequences on the society and economy of European populations.

2.6.1   Labor-force participation and income

Women's economic activity is an important factor that shows pronounced differences by marital status in most European countries. *Table 2.14* gives so-called labor-force participation rates for married and never-married women, and the total number of years worked by women during their active life, a figure that results from these labor-force participation rates, in five countries.

In 1985 the labor-force participation rates of never-married women between ages 35 and 39 were between 40 and 100 percent higher than those of their married counterparts. Between 77 and 93 percent of all never-married women and between 42 and 60 percent of all married women belonged to the labor force. Totaling all age groups, marital-status differences range between 10 working years during active life in France and more than 16 years in the Netherlands.[15] Generally, activity rates are significantly lower among all Italian women and married Dutch women than among women in other European countries in this table. These marital-status differentials in female economic activity were significant in 1985, but, with the exception of Austria, they have declined substantially since 1970. This decline in differentials is essentially due to the more than proportional increase in participation rates among married women. This trend is expected to continue.

The economic activity pattern by marital status in Scandinavian countries is different from that in other countries. Female economic activity is very high, differentials are small, and, in some age groups, labor-force participation rates of married women exceed those of never-married women. This characterizes a situation where female behavior increasingly mirrors male behavior, that is, virtually everybody belongs to the labor force. This may be the trend toward

Table 2.14. Economic activity of never-married and married women in 1970 and 1985.

	Labor-force participation rates between ages 35 and 39 (in %)				Total number of years worked, calculated from period participation rates			
	Never married		Married		Never married		Married	
Country	1970	1985	1970	1985	1970	1985	1970	1985
Austria	82.7	92.9	48.1	55.9	32.4	35.2	21.6	22.4
France	80.3	85.5	35.6	60.0	35.8	35.1	19.7	24.9
Germany	89.0	91.6	41.1	56.5	40.1	37.3	20.8	24.2
Italy	50.2	76.8	25.5	46.9	20.1	28.4	12.0	17.8
Netherlands	80.0	87.4	23.3	42.0	33.7	34.1	10.4	17.6

which other countries will converge in the long run. If so, marital-status differentials in female economic activity will be reversed.

Married men have the longest period of economic activity, while never-married men have the shortest period. Although data on these differences among men are limited, they indicate that the total number of years worked during active life is between 35 and 38 years among never-married men and between 42 and 45 years among married men.[16]

To some extent the situation in Scandinavian countries, with high activity rates among married women, is attributed to the high proportion of part-time jobs. Women work both fewer days per month and fewer hours per week than men, but nevertheless they make up a considerable part of the labor force. Part-time work is particularly common among mothers with preschool children. Therefore, the situation in the Nordic countries can, to a considerable degree, be attributed to the definition of the term *labor force*.

Even among those who belong to the labor force, substantial differences exist by marital status. This is best demonstrated by income differentials, given in *Table 2.15* for the Netherlands for the year 1986. Several conclusions may be drawn from this table. There are notable differences between all employees taken together and full-time employees only. These differences are due to a relatively low proportion of full-time employees (65 percent) among never-married men and women.

Never-married women seem to earn only slightly more than married women. This is, however, due to fewer hours worked among those never married; the income of never-married women is some 37 percent higher if only full-time employees are considered. Fewer married women are in the labor force, and those in the labor force are likely to have significantly lower incomes than never-married women. Among men the relation is exactly the opposite:

Table 2.15. Income differentials by marital status in the Netherlands in 1986.

| Marital status | Average annual disposable income (in guilders) | | | | Proportion of full-time employees (in %) | |
| | All employees | | Full-time employees | | | |
	Men	Women	Men	Women	Men	Women
Never married	14,200	13,000	20,100	18,600	65	65
Married	32,800	12,300	33,100	13,600	98	85
Divorced	20,500	19,400	20,500	19,500	100	99
Widowed	27,800	20,200	28,300	21,400	96	89
Average	26,400	14,200	29,500	16,700	88	80

there are more married men in the labor force than never-married men, and married men have substantially higher incomes.

These gender differences are quite interesting and difficult to explain. They cannot be attributed to education, which is closely related to income, as the educational attainment of married partners tends to be very similar. Rather, and in particular in a country where economic activity of married women is as low as in the Netherlands, it is due to social selection. We find a high proportion of highly educated never-married women in the labor force, while among married women those with lower household incomes – which happen to be those with lower education – are overrepresented. The reverse relationship among men is to a large extent due to the age structure – the never-married population is, on average, much younger than the married. It is also due to selection, quite similar to mortality, and due to fewer family responsibilities of unmarried men.

What are the possible effects of these marital-status differentials in labor-force participation and income on the economy? If cohabitants were to behave like their married counterparts, which is not likely to be the case, observed marital-status differentials would remain valid. As long as marriage is replaced by cohabitation, the increase in the proportion of unmarried would be irrelevant; changes would arise from increased economic activity of women only. If marriage is not fully replaced, the increase in the never-married proportion could reduce overall participation rates, particularly among men. Alternatively, those men could be replaced by women, thus having relatively little impact on the size of the labor force. The labor force could also grow if economic activity of women, in particular married women, increases. If cohabitants behave unlike their married counterparts, effects on the labor force and hence the economy would largely remain unknown as long as their behavior is unknown.

Living arrangements have some effects on the countries' pension systems. In most European countries pension benefits depend, to some extent, on the individual's working history. Depending on work histories of cohabitants, increases in the proportion of unmarried women would raise pension expenditures, due to their higher economic activity and their higher incomes.

A recent comparative study on the effects of changes in living arrangements on the performance of pension systems arrives at interesting conclusions about retirement income differentials by legal marital status (Gonnot *et al.*, 1995). While per capita pension benefits of widows are relatively high – due to the existence of survivorship pensions – benefits are particularly low for divorced and single women.[17] On the other hand, it is this group of single and divorced women whose working life usually exceeds the retirement period, whereas married and widowed women, on average, work for a shorter time than they receive pension benefits. It is evident that the provision of survivor benefits must be reconsidered. The increasing proportion of divorcées might make an extension of such benefits to this group necessary.[18] On the other hand, if economic activity of women continues to increase, survivor benefits may become obsolete.[19]

2.6.2 Morbidity and illness

In this section, morbidity (or health) differentials are discussed; these are not necessarily the same as mortality differentials. The World Health Organization defines health as "a state of complete physical, mental and social well-being, not merely the absence of disease and infirmity." It is reasonable to expect that population groups with high mortality rates also have high morbidity rates, since death is often preceded by a period of illness or injury. Morgan (1980, p. 633) writes:

> Although it is recognized that health encompasses more than mere survival, death rates have formed the main indicator of the relative health experience of population groups, for death unlike morbidity is usually an unambiguous and easily measured event. However, the extent to which differences in mortality rates in today's advanced industrial societies reflect differences in health in terms of freedom from disease and disability is unclear.

The relationship between mortality and morbidity is not straightforward, and relatively little attention has been given to marital-status differentials in morbidity and health behavior. The questions that were asked by Verbrugge in 1979 are still largely unanswered: How do marital groups differ in rates of acute and chronic conditions, disability from them, and utilization of health services? Which marital groups are most often committed to institutions for health problems? Do the marital groups with the highest mortality rates also

Table 2.16. Mortality and hospital use by marital status in England and Wales in 1971.[a]

Indicator	Women			Men		
	Never married	Divorced	Widowed	Never married	Divorced	Widowed
a. Age-standardized comparative mortality figure	126	128	122	122	144	140
b. Age-standardized comparative hospital-use figure	185	129	125	292	197	230
c. Ratio (b/a)	1.5	1.0	1.0	2.4	1.4	1.6

[a] Direct standardization; total population equals 100.

have the highest rates of morbidity, disability, and health-services use? Due to a lack of data this study cannot answer these questions. Instead, some interesting and important issues and aspects are discussed.

Table 2.16 compares data on mortality differentials by marital status with data on hospital-use differentials. The data are taken from the 1971 census conducted in England and Wales; unfortunately, more recent data were not available.[20] To calculate age-standardized comparative summary indicators – cumulated over ages 20 and above – direct standardization is used, with the married population taken as standard. Men and women are treated separately.

Once again, we observe significant excess mortality among all three un-married states, with somewhat larger differences between never-married men and previously married men. Unmarried individuals have notably higher rates of hospital use than married people. The greater representation of unmarried people among hospital patients holds for both men and women and for all ages; the only deviation from this general pattern is among women aged 20 to 29 years, probably reflecting the larger proportion of obstetric admissions in this age group among those married. As shown in *Table 2.16*, marital-status differentials in hospital use were generally greater than the difference in mortality rates. Among both sexes, never-married individuals clearly had the highest rate of hospital use in relation to their mortality rate; for all three unmarried states the hospital use/mortality ratio was significantly higher among men than among women. While both mortality and hospital-use differentials are much more pronounced among men, an interesting conclusion can be drawn from the respective mortality and hospital-use levels. For all four marital statuses and at each age, mortality rates of men exceed those of women; however, during childbearing age (ages 20–49) and beyond age 80, hospital-use rates are significantly higher among women, irrespective of marital status.

These data are old and limited to one European country; nevertheless, the observed patterns are likely to be representative. A number of reasons are responsible for the larger differentials in hospital use by marital status. Only data on in-patient care were considered in this study; the differential rates of hospital-bed use are partly accounted for by differences in out-patient services. In contrast to the in-patient sector, it is the married population that is overrepresented among hospital out-patients (Morgan, 1980).

When trying to explain health differentials one must be aware that illness is both a physical and a social event (Verbrugge, 1979). Individuals with a particular physical symptom may or may not perceive it. If they do perceive it, they may consider it intense or mild, and opt for various health actions or no action at all. Health data from many sources reflect physical and also social and socio-psychological factors. Hence, differences in illness, disability, and health-services use occur because of two factors: different physical risks and different propensities to perceive symptoms, evaluate them, and take health actions. With certain behavior the relationship between morbidity and mortality could be reversed. If health actions are taken early in the course of a particular disease, mortality rates may eventually be significantly reduced. Preventive health care would have similar effects.

Both physical risks and illness behavior may vary with marital status. The finding that the differences in rates of hospital use between marital-status groups are generally greater than the differences in mortality rates suggests that social needs are as dissimilar as clinical needs. While differences in clinical needs might also be discovered by mortality data, the additional excess hospital use mostly reflects differences in social needs. The latter differences are obviously most pronounced among the never-married population. It may be that never-married individuals – and, to a lesser extent, previously married people – are less able to tolerate the stress from an illness due to the smaller amount of social support available to them, and are therefore more likely to employ coping responses, such as seeking medical advice (Morgan, 1980). This effect may partly be offset by the enhanced likelihood of a married person – due to the presence of a spouse – to seek professional medical care in times of illness.

Even if we do not know the reasons for the observed illness behavior differentials, we may make a number of relevant projections for the future. Hospital costs will grow substantially, not only as a consequence of aging but as a result of the expected increase in the number and proportion of elderly people living alone. Insofar as health-care policy is concerned a particularly important issue is whether the differential rates of service use by married and unmarried people, and particularly their use of hospital in-patient care, can be regarded as indicators of their relative needs or whether they reflect an inappropriate use on the part of unmarried people or nonuse by those married. Strategies should be found to balance clinical needs and service use. Data for various countries are needed to discover variations in societies in the roles attached to the different marital statuses and the effect of such differences on the stress associated with these states.

Marital-status information is useful for estimating future health-care expenditures, even if the role of cohabitation is unknown. If illness behavior is largely determined by existing social and family networks, differences between married and cohabiting couples will be relatively small. However, the extent of conformity between the need for health services and the legally defined marital status will certainly diminish in the future.

2.6.3   Headship rates and households

Several demographers have suggested that the "old-fashioned" marital-status concept should be replaced by the "up-to-date" household concept (Keilman *et al.*, 1988). Is the marital-status distribution indeed irrelevant for analyzing and projecting a country's household composition? Can we still infer household formation processes from marital-status structures and trends?

Recent attempts to model household dynamics and processes are confronted with a number of difficulties: the definition of a *household* in national family and household statistics differs across countries; little agreement exists on appropriate procedures for analyzing and building models; difficulties remain in linking household theory (sociological perspective versus economic perspective) to household modeling and forecasting; the complexity of household demography makes matching theory and data collection difficult (the specific data needed for advanced models hardly exist); the necessary longitudinal analyses are difficult and expensive compared with the straightforward registration of marriages and divorces.

To avoid these difficulties, it seems justified to use marital-status information for analyzing and projecting households. But there are other reasons, too. Marital-status analysis is useful as a first step, even if more sophisticated models and data are available. And such analysis is a necessity in comparative studies, as the definition of a household is different from country to country, and data are almost never comparable.

Marital status still covers a significant part of the demographic processes involved in household formation and dissolution, processes which should be looked at in detail. Recent increases in the number of households were undoubtedly not only due to demographic changes. Important nondemographic factors include the general economic situation of a country; the economic well-being and independence of women (which is strongly influenced by women's labor-force participation); housing availability; urbanization; and changes in norms, values, and social behavior. Reasonable future estimates of the nondemographic parameters are difficult to obtain, irrespective of the model used. The analysis and projection of marital status can only assist the analysis and the projection of demographic parameters.

A well-known way of projecting the number of households is the *headship-rate* method. This method requires only the number of heads of household in each age group and by sex as a share (in percent) of the population in each age–sex group. The results of any population projection are then applied to current headship rates of the population in each projected age–sex group to obtain the future number of households. A major shortcoming of this method is that household dynamics are not included: the headship rate describes the results of dynamic processes, but these processes themselves remain a black box. The headship rate is not a rate in the demographic, occurrence/exposure sense, since it focuses on changes in stocks and not on flows (Keilman and Prinz, 1995b). Also, the definition of *head of household* as implicitly meaning the person who bears the chief responsibility for the economic sustenance of the household is outdated in most European countries. Therefore it has been suggested that the members of the household designate one among them as a *reference person* with no implication of headship. Following UN practice, today the term *householder* is used to denote either household head or reference person. Most of the 10 countries in this study use the reference-person concept; however, the way this reference person is defined differs largely from country to country. In Austria, Italy, and the Netherlands the reference person is explicitly determined by the household members themselves; in Norway and Sweden it is the oldest person; in Germany and Great Britain it is the person entered first on the census form; in Finland it is the person with the highest income subject to taxation; and in France it is a predetermined person depending on the family composition of the household. Only Hungary still uses the concept of a family head.

Irrespective of the exact definition, the householder concept is the only one that is, to some extent, comparable between countries. Time-series analysis of past headship (or householder) rates may help to estimate future changes in these rates, thus including some kind of economic or behavioral trends.

Alternatively, a scenario approach using different settings of future headship rates could be chosen.

A number of extensions and improvements to the simple headship-rate method have been suggested (see Kono, 1987). Among them are the consideration of the marital-status dimension. This enables the estimation of not only the effect of changes in a population's age and sex structure on the future number of households, but also effects of changes in the marital composition of the population. Combining a dynamic marital-status projection model with the static age-, sex-, and marital-status-specific headship-rate approach one arrives at a semi-dynamic or hybrid household projection model (Prinz, 1991a).[21]

The concept of head of household seems increasingly inappropriate; however, notwithstanding the various definitions of a reference person, headship rates by age, sex, and marital status are surprisingly similar between countries. *Table 2.17* gives marital-status-specific headship rates for the age group 40–44 and for ages 15 and over, for censuses taken in six countries in 1981. Headship rates for married men remain at about 95 percent between ages 30 and 69, and below 5 percent for married women. Norway is an exception, with 20 percent of all married households headed by women; this possibly demonstrates a higher degree of gender equality in Norwegian society. Among those in the unmarried states, headship rates are – at all ages – clearly lowest among the never-married population. Differences between the divorced and widowed populations are minor, although headship rates are at most ages somewhat higher among the widowed group. At younger ages, those divorced and, in particular, never married tend to live in their parents' households. Differences between unmarried men and women seem to reflect the degree of women's economic independence. In Great Britain, Austria, and Norway headship rates among the unmarried are significantly higher for women, while in Italy and France the opposite is observed.

Given the relatively consistent findings over countries, the use of the householder concept for the projection of households seems less problematic. In trying to assess the usefulness of this approach – the combination of dynamic marital-status projections and static marital-status-specific headship rates – Prinz (1991a) compares the method retrospectively with other approaches. For instance, using marital-status-specific headship rates reduces the deviation from observed household numbers by more than half when compared with simple age-specific headship rates. Prinz (1991a) also gives some evidence for the increasing importance of the marital-status component in household changes over the period from 1960 to 1985. Averaged over a number of countries, decomposition of household changes reveals that during the period

Table 2.17. Headship rates by marital status in 1981, in percent.

Gender	40–44					15+				
	Never married	Married	Divorced	Widowed	Total	Never married	Married	Divorced	Widowed	Total
Austria										
Women	56	4	82	82	17	27	5	80	76	27
Men	53	96	68	87	90	19	93	66	72	68
France										
Women	59	2	74	84	12	23	2	69	70	19
Men	63	97	90	92	93	26	97	86	72	74
Great Britain[a]										
Women	40	5	83		14	21	5	82		22
Men	40	96	69		89	18	95	72		72
Hungary										
Women	31	3	71	76	13	16	4	64	53	17
Men	33	97	64	85	90	12	91	61	57	72
Italy										
Women	29	2	78	91	7	15	2	76	73	16
Men	42	97	79	92	92	13	96	80	79	70
Norway										
Women	56	19	77	83	27	31	22	79	90	35
Men	38	80	64	78	76	21	77	68	88	61

[a] In Great Britain divorced and widowed are combined.

1960–1970 some 57 percent of the increase in the number of households was due to increases in total population size, 8 percent was due to age-structure changes, only 1 percent was due to changes in the marital composition, and the remaining 34 percent was due to economic and other nondemographic factors. During the period 1980–1985, however, 22 percent of the increase in the number of households could be explained by changes in the marital composition of the populations. Age-structure changes were responsible for 33 percent of the change, the influence of total population size declined to only 24 percent, and the residual part declined to 21 percent.

The importance of marital-status changes for household formation and dissolution processes has not diminished; in fact, it has even gained in significance since the slowdown of economic development in most industrialized countries. Inclusion of consensual unions, that is, using a union-status projection model in combination with union-status-specific headship rates, will certainly improve the estimation of the number of households.

Notes

[1] Among the 10 countries in this study, Italy is an exception: population structures by marital status are available only for census years. Thus, the most recent information for Italy is from 1981.

[2] For a more detailed analysis of changes in the marital composition in 14 industrialized countries, including an analysis of the elderly populations, which have experienced pronounced changes, see Gonnot and Vukovich (1989).

[3] In principle, similar problems arise in the discussion of union-status differentials in fertility.

[4] For example, there is general agreement that total fertility rates (TFRs) of the 1950s and 1960s overstated ultimate fertility, whereas those of the 1970s and 1980s understated the prospective fertility of the generations passing through their reproductive ages (Council of Europe, 1991).

[5] Castiglioni and Zuanna (1992) use an adaptation of the formula presented by Berent and Festy (1973). This formula decomposes overall fertility into three components: age structure, marital-status structure, and marital fertility. For simplification, fertility of unmarried women was not considered.

[6] The patterns of disease have changed dramatically, for instance, with the reduction of infectious disease and the increase in lung cancer and ischemic heart disease.

[7] Presupposing that being unmarried equals living without a family, an assumption which is increasingly incorrect; see Chapters 3 and 4.

[8] The data for Great Britain are from the Office of Population Censuses and Surveys, *Census 1981: National Migration*.

[9] The only extension to the ordinary life table is that the number of years lived by the survivors, L_x, is multiplied by the respective residential mobility rate, hence giving the number of years with moves lived by the survivors. As a consequence, the e_x column gives the expected number of years with moves during the remaining lifetime.

[10] Mulder and Wagner (1992) do not distinguish between never married, divorced, and widowed, but only between unmarried and married.

[11] The figures would be much lower if calculated on a cohort basis. The figures obtained by Sardon (1986) for the 1960 birth cohort, based partly on actual cohort data and partly on the assumption that current trends were to continue, are generally some 10 percentage points lower.

[12] Increases in the level of divorce sometimes preceded changes in legislation, suggesting that the laws have only adapted to public opinion.

[13] Gonnot (1995), for example, takes an extreme position. Both fertility and mortality rates are assumed to be independent of marital status – that is, marital-status differentials are ignored.

[14] Because of World War II, sex ratios of 55 men per 100 women were observed in 1985 in some European countries. By 2030, the ratio is expected to be at about 75 men per 100 women.

[15] Totaling age-specific labor-force participation rates over all age groups gives the average number of years worked per woman during active life (synthetic cohort perspective).

[16] It should be noted that differences between never-married men and never-married women are insignificant.

[17] Benefits for married women are also low, but these women are assumed to have additional income as a consequence of being married, be it through their husband's earnings or pension benefits.

[18] Currently, only in France are survivor benefits also payable to divorced spouses. In Norway divorcées receive a transitional grant on the death of their former spouse.

[19] Prinz (1995) shows that this would be possible if the pension systems considered the number of children borne by a woman, i.e., if women were granted additional entitlements for each child born.

[20] In this particular data set, hospital-use rates refer to patients in nonpsychiatric hospitals per 1,000 of the respective population.

[21] A similar hybrid household projection model was developed at the Netherlands Central Bureau of Statistics (Latten, 1992). The static household component is incorporated in this model in a way that is different from the model suggested in Prinz (1991a). Instead of marital-status-specific headship rates, Latten applies a set of five household position proportions to each dynamically projected marital-status group.

Chapter 3

Cohabitation

During the past three decades, remarkable societal changes have increasingly led to a variety of alternative living arrangements, emerging in different countries at different speeds and intensities. By far the most prominent new way of life, almost fully accepted in many countries, is cohabitation. In several countries the majority of marriages are entered through cohabitation of varying length, and the number of couples preferring long-lasting cohabitation to marriage and particularly to remarriage has increased rapidly. Cohabitation has gained in significance to such a great extent that it can no longer be disregarded in marital-status analysis. In an increasing number of countries it is possible to analyze cohabitation since the amount of information on it has also grown, though not as fast as the phenomenon itself.

An interesting, almost contradictory, aspect of cohabitation is that in most countries people continue to live in nuclear families, but they increasingly reject marriage. A major objective of this chapter is to explain why this has happened and what we can expect in the future.

The first section deals with conceptual issues. It discusses the definition of cohabitation established in Section 1.4. Next, data issues are presented, including a rough sketch on the spread of cohabitation in the 10 European countries included in this study. The third section treats several interpretations of the phenomenon, focusing both on the role of cohabitation and on differences usually found between marriage and cohabitation. In the following section, reasons for the emergence and increase of cohabitation are presented, in particular pointing to the changing status of women, a driving force for many recent societal changes. Section 3.5, looking at cohabitation law, is particularly important to understand the discrepancy between the unpopularity of marriage and the popularity of the nuclear family. This section presents possible ways to regulate cohabitation both theoretically and practically and compares legislation in various countries. The next section sets up a *cohabitation typology*, assigning each country to a stage of development of the phenomenon on the basis of data on cohabitation and data on covariates that can be measured more easily than the phenomenon itself. The final section gives a more qualitative outlook on the future, based on this typology and on the reasons for the emergence and spread of cohabitation.

3.1 Conceptual Issues

What is a consensual union? At what stage can two individuals be called cohabitants? Who is authorized to judge whether a couple is (or was) cohabiting? The answers to these questions depend on how we define cohabitation; therefore, the definition must be unambiguous. Several situations prove that the acceptance of a cohabitation as a living arrangement matters – for example, when granting social security benefits after the death of the cohabiting spouse or when terminating alimony payments. Definitions do exist in legislation, and in most cases legal practice must establish what is meant by those definitions.

What does a term used in legislation imply? One reason why definitions differ is that some are used to deprive someone of a right, while others are used to grant a right. For the latter purpose definitions are usually more restrictive. Theoretically, it is possible for two people to be considered a cohabiting couple in one regulation and separate individuals in another. As clearly pointed out by van de Wiel (1980, p. 213), "This inevitably leads to unpredictability as to someone's legal position and should be avoided as much as possible."

Whatever the definition of legally recognized cohabitation, there would be some unions that would not fall within its compass. Deech (1980, p. 301) states: "Just as there is now a feeling that certain cohabiting partnerships ought to be treated as beneficially as marriage, so there would then be a demand for justice to those unions that did not fall within the new definition of cohabitation." This dilemma can be exemplified by the question of length of cohabitation required to qualify as a legally accepted consensual union. If, for example, cohabitation were to be legally established after living together for one year, the rejected partner of a nine-month union might feel that exclusion of this union is unfair. It may be that one can never satisfactorily and exhaustively define cohabitation.

Legal practice must decide whether a consensual union exists or has existed, but the situation is quite different with regard to data collected through censuses and surveys. As already discussed in Section 1.4, usually a subjective definition is applied: couples (or individuals) themselves define cohabitation. Of course, a definition is also suggested by the authorities. Cohabitation is defined as the status of couples who are sexual partners, not married to each other, and sharing a household. In some cases this definition includes homosexual partners; in other cases it does not.

The definition of cohabitation remains a challenging issue. Section 3.5 on cohabitation law demonstrates how this subjective approach could also be integrated into legislation to arrive at a complete definition of cohabitation.

3.2   Data on Cohabitation

Most research on cohabitation suffers from one common problem: the lack of adequate data. Because of the absence of legal registry and a fixed date of inception, data on cohabitation are much more difficult to assemble than marriage data. Vital registration and censuses – which cover the entire population – traditionally record only marriages. Only in a few countries are consensual unions reported in censuses. As provocatively stated by Sogner (1986, p. 27): "If there is no marriage, there is nothing to register until the bureaus of statistics get up enough stamina to ask the pertinent questions." Of course, there has been reluctance to record consensual unions for several reasons. The phenomenon was not considered to be of any importance. Also, one hesitated to ask questions about this type of union, since cohabitation did not have general social approval. Or, one feared false reporting.

It is evident that questions concerning cohabitation should be included in censuses taken in Europe. Censuses, however, are usually conducted at 10-year intervals, and information based on a 10-year time lag would not help much in understanding rapidly changing social processes such as cohabitation. Therefore information stemming from sample surveys must be used. There are several problems connected with survey data, in general, and survey data on cohabitation, in particular.

First, there are problems in defining the term. The definition of cohabitation (for example, concerning its length) is ambiguous and varies from study to study. Second, the formulation of relevant questions is crucial. Third, sample design and sample size are difficult to determine. Cohabitation is still a relatively rare phenomenon in some countries, and in these countries a national sample will yield relatively few cohabiting couples. Samples vary strongly with regard to structure, for example, age structure and educational composition. Fourth, cohabitation may be a sensitive topic. A number of people claim single-person residence when they actually live with someone else. Among the reasons for this practice are to pay lower taxes, to secure higher social benefits, and to hold on to an apartment just in case the relationship ends. Fifth, retrospective surveys presuppose that timing and type of events can be recalled accurately; this is difficult to do in the case of cohabitation as couples are sometimes unsure of when they started cohabiting. Sixth, surveys give information over the period covered by the questionnaire for survivors only; mortality and emigration cannot be captured. Finally, nonresponse is likely to be selective. Couples that are uncertain of their legal situation are more likely to refuse answering the questionnaire.

Some limitations have been studied in detail. Keilman (1992) has investigated the possible impact of different definitions on comparative analyses between European countries, using a simulation approach. He modeled trends in consensual unions and compared model results for various projections based on different definitions. He concluded that trends in cohabitation during the past few decades are not distorted by different definitions. Overall levels, however, may be higher or lower depending on the definition and hence a comparative cross-sectional analysis might be hazardous, unless it is combined with a time-series analysis.

Evidence of the sensitive attitude toward cohabitation comes from the General Household Survey in Great Britain where close to half of all never-married cohabiting women and more than half of all divorced and separated cohabiting women originally presented themselves to the interviewer as legally married (Brown and Kiernan, 1981). Women who were originally noted as married had been cohabiting for a longer time (28 months, on average) than women who were immediately identified as cohabitants (13 months, on average); the former group also included a large percentage of mothers (50 percent). These observations stem from information obtained in 1979. Acceptability has certainly increased since then. A similar situation may, however, be observed today in Southern Europe.

Concerning the starting date of a cohabitation, a Swedish study (Blanc, 1987) found that there is a tendency for women to report a starting date that is one year prior to marriage; presumably, these women know their marriage date and count backward one year to obtain the date of initiation of cohabitation. The data for this survey were taken in 1981 of the oldest cohort; therefore, this observation may not reflect the current situation.

The number of consensual unions recorded in surveys is usually underreported, but the downward bias is even larger in population censuses because of problems with registration of the actual dwelling place of the respondents. In the early 1980s, the underestimation of consensual unions amounted to between 30 and 50 percent in Norway, France, and England and Wales (Keilman, 1992). At that time the bias was somewhat lower in Sweden, but it has increased recently (Nilsson, 1992). On the basis of the Population Census and the Survey on Living Conditions, Nilsson estimated the number of cohabitants in 1975, 1980, 1985, and 1990. The figures in the surveys were some 12, 19, 18, and 32 percent higher than those given in censuses. He identified several reasons for the differences. In 1975, both cohabitants were interviewed in the survey; hence, the difference between the census and the survey estimates was fairly small. Today the census has a strict definition of consensual unions.[1] Since 1980, only one member of the consensual union has been interviewed, resulting in an increase in the difference between the two estimates. In the 1990 census, similar to censuses taken in other European countries, the number of nonrespondents increased from negligible levels to 3.7 percent. However, selective nonresponse only explains part of the increase in the difference between the two estimates (the difference was 18 percent in 1985 and 32 percent in 1990). Nilsson's estimates show that the problem of downward biases does not necessarily disappear with increasing acceptance of consensual unions.

Data on cohabitation are scarce and generally emanate from surveys (see Linke, 1991, for more information on European surveys). This makes comparative analyses problematic. For six of the ten countries included in this study, the most reliable data on cohabitation are from surveys: Finland, the 1985 Labor Force Survey; Norway, the 1985 Health Survey; Great Britain, the 1986–1987 General Household Survey; the Netherlands, the 1985–1986 Housing Demand Survey; Italy, the 1983 Survey on Family Structures; and France, the 1985–1986 Family History Survey. Austria, Germany, and Hungary collect cohabitation data in their micro-censuses.[2] Only the Swedish data are taken from the 1985 census.[3]

From the map in *Figure 3.1* a clear regional distribution can be derived. Cohabitation is widespread in Nordic countries, particularly in Sweden, while it is rare in Southern and Central Europe.[4] France, Germany, Austria, Great Britain, and the Netherlands show comparable levels of cohabitation. It should be emphasized that this map is based on data taken in the mid-1980s and that in some countries, particularly Norway, the prevalence of cohabitation has increased substantially in recent years.

Table 3.1 provides data on the prevalence of cohabitation of women by age. Cohabitation is very common at young ages – more than 45 percent in the 15–19 age group in eight out of ten countries, and even more than 90 percent

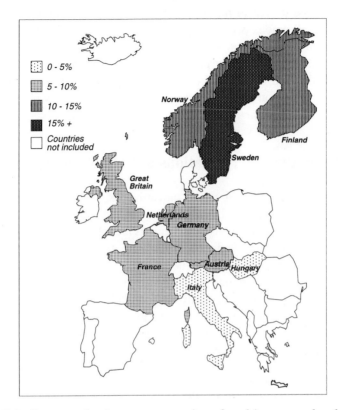

Figure 3.1. Consensual unions as a proportion of total (consensual and marital) unions in 10 European countries in 1985.

Table 3.1. Proportion of consensual unions among all unions by age of women in 1985.

Age	Swe	Fin[a]	Nor[a]	Fra	NL	GB	Ger[a]	Aus	Hun	Ita
15–19	92.7	49.7	75.0		63.0	50.4	30.0	45.4	8.2	4.2
20–24	77.1		47.0	35.8	36.3	29.0		18.7	3.3	2.1
25–29	48.1	23.9	23.0	14.0	15.9	12.8	6.2	5.9	2.4	1.8
30–34	29.6	11.6	12.0	10.1	6.7	6.8		3.9	2.7	1.6
35–39	19.2	7.1	7.0	6.0	4.0	4.3	2.0	3.2	2.9	1.1
40–44	13.0			5.5	2.2	3.7		2.9	2.9	1.1
45–49	10.2	3.7	3.0		2.1	2.8	2.0	2.1	3.1	1.0
50–54	8.7				1.8	1.5		2.0	2.7	1.0
55–59	5.9	3.7	3.0		2.3	0.9	1.9	1.5	2.7	1.1
60–64	4.7				1.8	1.2		2.2	3.0	1.4
All ages	19.9	11.4	10.8	8.8[b]	7.7	6.2	4.7	4.2	2.9	1.4

[a] The data are given in broader age groups.
[b] Estimate.

in Sweden – and decreases rapidly with age. The proportion of consensual unions among all unions is less than 5 percent beyond age 45 in all countries except Sweden.

Substantial differences in age patterns exist between the countries (compare, for example, the distribution in Great Britain and Hungary in *Table 3.1*). Age patterns of cohabitation are analyzed in detail in Section 3.6, which sets up a typology of cohabitation.

3.3   Alternative Interpretations of Cohabitation

Data on cohabitation are still scarce; nevertheless, this topic is increasingly discussed in the demographic literature. Not surprisingly, most research is undertaken in countries where consensual unions are relatively widespread, such as France, the Netherlands, and most prominently the Scandinavian countries. Cohabitation is not always treated in the same manner; its interpretation varies, and different roles and functions are assigned to the phenomenon. A large part of the differences is due to the actually observed differences between countries and over time in the prevalence of cohabitation, but the particular approach taken is also essential. In this section several interpretations of cohabitation given in the literature are reviewed.

3.3.1   Deviant phenomenon or social institution

A phenomenon can be called deviant for many reasons. For example, from a statistical point of view, it does not follow the pattern of statistical normality (Trost, 1980). In this sense, cohabitation – as a relatively new phenomenon – had to start as a deviant phenomenon in all European countries. To be deviant is to act contrary to or to oppose, in some way, the norms and expectations of society. According to Lesthaege (1992, p. 8), the emergence of cohabitation originated in the desire to behave in a deviant manner: "During the initial phase, cohabitation signaled plain protest against authority in general and against conformity and conventionalism of petty bourgeois marriage." This opinion is not really supported by Swedish data which indicate that cohabitation was pioneered by the working class; J. Hoem (1986) finds that there is no evidence that modern cohabitation started as a campus movement. Norwegian data support, at least partly, the notion that modern cohabitation originated as a practical living arrangement among the unconventional intelligentsia and subsequently spread to other segments of the population (Blom, 1992).

Today, in several European countries a statistically normal pattern is to start a union by cohabiting. If more than half of those at age 20 cohabit, and if the majority of marriages are preceded by cohabitation for some period of time, cohabitation can no longer be called a deviant phenomenon. Trost (1980, p. 19) states that in Sweden "we can now say that, far from being deviant, cohabitation has become a social institution."

Marriage and cohabitation are two social institutions that do not compete with each other but exist alongside each other (Trost, 1985). This opinion is shared by several authors. Sogner (1986), for example, stresses that these changes seem so fundamental that we can talk of a revolution in the old European marriage pattern. She calls it the "new European cohabitation pattern." Leridon and Villeneuve-Gokalp (1989, p. 222), referring to the situation in France, state that "cohabitation is no longer a mere prelude to marriage but a type of union in its own right which is increasingly replacing marriage."

Cohabitation will likely be gradually accepted as a social institution in all European countries. As cohabitation becomes more common, cohabiting couples will generally find it easier to rent an apartment or to open joint bank accounts. Conversely, the fact that cohabitation has become easier to arrange undoubtedly makes this lifestyle an option for people who otherwise might have chosen to marry (Blanc, 1984).

3.3.2 The role of cohabitation

Various interpretations of the role of cohabitation are found in the literature. These different options need not be exclusive. Due to the heterogeneity of cohabiting unions the alternative types of cohabitation listed below exist at the same time in all countries, although to largely varying degrees.

For many couples, cohabitation is and was a prelude to marriage. It is a transitional stage that either is terminated or is transformed into a legal marriage (Wiersma, 1983). Cohabitation obviously functions as a test or trial marriage. Successful unions are transformed into marriage, and others are simply dissolved. In 1975, Trost speculated that if this assumption is correct "the marriage rate will increase again in some years . . . , many marriages between two partners not fitting together will never be formed, those marriages being formed will be 'happier' and thus the divorce rate will be lower" (Trost, 1975, p. 682). Today we realize that these speculations were wrong. Marriage rates continue to decline, while divorce rates continue to increase, and the number of couples cohabiting continues to increase. Cohabitation is a complex phenomenon and cannot simply be identified as a premarital phase. The processes leading to cohabitation are far more complicated (Sections 3.4 and 3.5 take up this discussion in detail).

Couples who do not perceive their cohabitation as a trial marriage have various views on their relationship. Several types of cohabitation might be identified. Increasingly, cohabitation is seen as an alternative to marriage. It can be a rejection of marriage as an institution or a true alternative (Wiersma, 1983). Leridon (1990a) concludes that consensual unions in France seem to constitute a new type of union, often transitory, which differs from marriage. This approach postulates that the change in the form of unions (from married to unmarried) is accompanied by a corresponding change in the content of relationships, with respect to norms and expectations. A comparison of the behavior of cohabiting and married couples should demonstrate whether this is true. Section 3.3.3 offers some findings of such comparisons from the existing literature; new findings are discussed in Chapter 4. Leridon (1990b, p. 480) cites:

> Whereas marriage postulates both stability and fertility, the outcome of consensual unions is much more open: breakdown is not desired, but is increasingly accepted when it occurs; marriage is not rejected, but is not regarded as urgent; a child may act as an element of stability in the relationship, but is not considered as obligatory.

Lewin (1982) provides another interpretation. Lewin argues that, if differences between married and cohabiting couples are negligible, then cohabitation is not an alternative to marriage but rather a variety of it. The increase of cohabitation "does not pose a threat to marriage, since most who cohabit without marriage have no objections to marriage, feel the same norms applicable to both marriage and cohabitation, and even intend to marry eventually" (Lewin, 1982, p. 763). He maintains that cohabitation primarily would mean a postponement of the wedding until a time when the wedding ceremony serves as a rite of confirmation rather than a rite of transition. Under this interpretation, cohabitation is somewhat equal to marriage; the distinction between cohabitation and marriage is not important. Both marriage and cohabitation may serve as equal markers of the establishment of a joint household (Manting, 1992).

Cohabitation is sometimes interpreted as an alternative to being single. At the onset of the process, marriage is not even considered; the decision to cohabit is only a consequence of the time one shares with each other. Independence is highly valued, whereas commitment has a rather low value (Manting, 1992). In those countries where consensual unions function as precursors to marriages, we may get a better theoretical understanding of the phenomenon by considering similarities and dissimilarities between cohabitants and singles (Rindfuss and van den Heuvel, 1990).

One must stress that large variations with respect to cohabitation have been observed, both between and within countries, as motivations and behavior of individuals differ. In most countries support is found for each perspective described above. The different interpretations are equally relevant and certainly not exclusive. The consequence is that for an understanding of the cohabitation phenomenon all groups of individuals, singles as well as married and cohabiting couples, must be compared simultaneously. This is done in Chapter 4.

3.3.3 Commitment in consensual and marital unions

Cohabitation has many of the characteristics of marriage: shared dwelling, economic union, sexual intimacy, and not infrequently children. Is there any real difference between the two? In this section, an answer is given on the basis of several studies that have looked into the topic of commitment to the partner. It does not compare demographic differentials (such as fertility, mortality, and couple formation and dissolution) between the two types of unions; these are discussed in Chapter 4.

Whether one finds differences in commitment to the relationship depends on the definition of commitment. In a summary of US studies, Macklin (1978) finds cohabitants appear to be less committed to the relationship than married couples when commitment is measured in terms of dedication to the continuation of the relationship or in terms of reluctance to terminate the relationship. However, the differences are not significant when commitment is measured in terms of relationship satisfaction, exclusivity of the relationship, or division of labor within the household. Therefore, it does not come as a surprise that different studies arrive at different conclusions. Lesthaege (1992) poses the question: Is there a commitment crisis? This is an interesting question, but no conclusive answer has been given. For instance, some authors conclude that the observed postponement of marriage and parenthood signals a weakening of commitment; others find that marriage and parenthood are taken more seriously and that commitment has been strengthened.

What does the term commitment imply? In a partnership, each individual tries to achieve a balance between the need for personal separateness, on the one side, and the need for identification as a couple, on the other side. Wiersma (1983) calls the act of achieving a balance between these two needs the "degree of individuation." Since each partner must find a balance, this process also involves the difficulty of trying to match two possibly different utility functions. In the past, when asymmetric, institutionalized gender roles were readily internalized (Lesthaege, 1992), adjustment of positions to a final equilibrium was relatively easy. It seems obvious that recent changes in gender roles have made this convergence more difficult, causing "individuation" to increase or commitment to decline.

A study by Wiersma (1983), comparing 164 married and cohabiting couples in the Netherlands and the United States, finds that cohabiting couples are less committed to their partners than married couples. Cohabitants are less likely to idealize their partner as the one and only, and the thought of living without their partner causes significantly less "panic" among cohabitants than among married persons. Both types of couples are very much partner oriented, but the cohabitants tend to be less dependent on their partner. Cohabitants occupy a more autonomous position in relation to other societal institutions, such as the church or the extended family, and their attitudes show greater liberalism and progressiveness. On the other hand, Wiersma concludes that, because a legal marriage document is lacking, mutual trust is the binding principle for cohabitants. In this sense, commitment between cohabitants must be strong.

Similar findings are reported by Lesthaege (1992) in a study on Belgium. He concludes that individuals in consensual unions clearly demand more from their relationship than those in marriage. Cohabitants scored higher on "mutual respect and appreciation," "tolerance and understanding," and "happy sexual relations." On the other hand, they feel more lonely and more depressed than those who are married. Those findings might be an explanation for the high rates of dissolution of consensual unions (see Section 4.3.4).

A study on Sweden by Lewin (1982; see also Section 3.3.2), comparing 111 cohabiting and 101 newly married couples, reports on no differences in the norms the respondents found applicable to marriage or cohabitation. He does not find significant differences in attitudes toward friends, financial responsibilities, emotional and sexual fidelity, and living arrangements. Lewin therefore concludes that there is no difference in commitment between the two and, hence, in the content of the two types of unions.

An interesting finding is described in a French study by Leridon and Villeneuve-Gokalp (1989). Among other things, they looked at the average number of unions reported by the respondent at the time of the survey (including the current union). Married couples reported 1.08 unions, on average, in the 21–44 age group, confirming that ever-married persons have rarely had previous union partners other than the spouse. For cohabiting couples, the average is noticeably higher (1.40, on average), which is mostly due to the fact that marriage to another person preceded the current cohabitation. The reported number of unions was 1.20, on average, for never-married cohabiting couples, so they conclude that the choice of cohabitation does not necessarily lead to a higher degree of union instability.

Most studies seem to find some differences between cohabiting and married couples. These differences could be in behavior, in attitudes, or in the perception of their relationship. To explain these differences a first step is to find out who prefers cohabitation to marriage. Meyer and Schulze (1983) find that cohabitants are usually young, economically independent, often urban, politically liberal, and Protestant. It is mostly women, in particular economically active women, who seem to regard cohabitation as a long-term alternative to marriage. Having identified the types of people that prefer to cohabit it should be possible to find out why those people do so. The following section is exclusively concerned with that particular question.

3.4 Cohabitation and Changes in Gender Roles

Why did the phenomenon of cohabitation emerge? Why did it spread so rapidly? What are the reasons for the substitution of cohabitation for traditional marriage? The emergence and increase in cohabitation is just one element of what has frequently been referred to as the "second demographic transition" (Lesthaege, 1992; van de Kaa, 1987); other elements include the decline in marriage and fertility and the increase in divorce (see Section 1.1). Since these phenomena are closely linked to one another, it is reasonable to assume that they all have the same origin. This common root can only be the changes in gender roles brought about by the women's movement.

In her brief summary of the seminar entitled "Gender and Family Change in Industrialized Countries," Oppenheim Mason (1992) writes that "it is simplistic to attribute post-modern family change to women's emancipation."[5] I agree with the term simplistic, but the women's movement is certainly the most prominent reason for all the societal and demographic changes that have taken place during the past three decades. The women's movement is not a simple concept but rather can be decomposed into several components which are certainly interdependent and which are important to the framework of cohabitation.

The increased economic independence of women is a major component of the women's movement. Increased education and employment are radically changing women's position in the family. Having their own incomes women are no longer dependent on men. Consequently, the degree of equality in household responsibilities increases. Also, it is financially possible for women, and hence for the couple, to divorce and lead independent lives. The increased economic independence is essentially a consequence of increasing labor-force participation rates of women, caused by technological and economic changes that, in turn, have led to an increasing demand for labor, in particular a demand for women in the labor market.

A second major component can be summarized as changes in social norms and values. Women are increasingly pursuing their own career. The influence of traditional values and the prevalence of sexist ideologies, which in the past have strongly influenced marriage behavior and family life, have rapidly decreased, while women's educational achievements have increased. Equal treatment of men and women has been achieved – in theory, but certainly not in practice.

A third component is the so-called biological independence of women. The availability and use of birth control methods, the revolution in contraceptive techniques in the 1960s, and the legalization of abortion have created a new situation. Women are now able to determine the time and the number of conceptions, allowing them to have an independence that was previously unknown.

Finally, we should not forget the feminist movement. It is certainly difficult to assess its impact. In this study I rely on a report by Chafetz (1992). Chafetz concludes that "the role of feminist movements is to serve as an accelerator to change, one which acts rapidly, and in some instances strongly, where movements are intermediate-sized or larger, and with a greater lag time where they are smaller."

The women's movement has directly or indirectly been credited as the main cause of change by most authors writing on cohabitation. Some of them emphasize the economic independence of women (Chafetz, 1992; Lesthaege, 1992); others stress biological independence (von Krbek, 1980); and still others focus on changing social norms (Haskey, 1991). Most authors, however, attribute the observed changes to various elements of increased independence of women (Meyer and Schulze, 1983; Sogner, 1986; and Wingen, 1985).

Why has the women's movement affected the relationship between men and women? In what way has it led to the substitution of cohabitation for marriage? One theory is given by Chafetz (1992), who tries to put the whole issue of the relationship between gender and family change in what she calls a "process model." She identifies five phases. In the first phase, macro-structural economic conditions change through technological change and economic expansion. In the second phase, opportunities for women, especially in the labor force, but also in higher education, expand. In the third phase, labor-force participation rates among all women, including married women and mothers, rise; this results in a double workday for women and a significant change in relative spousal power resources. Eventually, in the fourth phase, the family changes, including a decline and delay in marriage and fertility and an increase in divorce and cohabitation. At the same time, the women's movement emerges and grows. In the fifth phase, public opinion regarding gender and the family changes, further accelerating the family change.

Obviously, some of the changes that are referred to as part of the second demographic transition are more affected by the women's movement than others; they are more easily explained through changes in the status of women. Pinelli (1992), for example, concludes that the increase in divorce and in births outside marriage are more closely related to the independence of women than, for example, to the decline in fertility. The relationship is also less clear in the case of cohabitation and marriage. Sogner (1986, p. 31) writes: "The passion between the sexes ... no doubt remains the same, as does the simple desire for intimate social and emotional company with other human beings." The nuclear family does not seem to be threatened, quite the contrary. Cohabitation, however, is increasingly replacing marriage. What is the reason for this replacement?

As a consequence of women's and men's changing roles, the tendency has been toward convergence of the traditional roles of the two sexes (Sogner, 1986). The roles of partners have become less differentiated and are allocated more flexibly. When gender roles become interchangeable, the traditional competitive advantages of marriage, with the husband's function as provider and the wife's role as homemaker and caregiver, are no longer self-evident. More weight is put on the emotional and qualitative aspects of married life. If demands are too high, they cannot be met or they can be met in other forms of living arrangements. Opting for cohabitation instead of marriage, people, women in particular, expect adjustments in the distribution of responsibilities and duties within the partnership, the family, or the household to overcome the well-known "double burden of women" (Meyer and Schulze, 1983). Women expect better chances for self-realization with the new gender roles.

It may be concluded that, in general, the quality, and not the intensity, of the commitment to the partner has changed and that the changing roles of men and women have increasingly led to traditional marriage being inappropriate. Kiernan and Estaugh (1993, p. 70) state:

> On a day to day basis there may be little to distinguish between the two types of unions and there may be more variation within marriage and cohabiting unions than between them. The major differences between the two types of union are less to do

with the private domain and more to do with their relationship to the institutional framework of our society.

But why should cohabitation be more appropriate? Getting married implies accepting the existing – partly restrictive and, in many areas, outdated – marriage law. Due to the lower degree of institutionalization, cohabitation improves the bargaining position of both partners. We will never be able to really understand why cohabitation suits couples better than marriage without taking a look at marriage and cohabitation laws. Demands, particularly legal demands, have changed mostly as a consequence of the women's movement. Andrup *et al.* (1980, p. 32) find:

> Legislation and the application of laws, jurisdiction, and administration have not been capable of adapting the complex of rules and regulations pertaining to family law to the very far-reaching changes which have occurred over the last century in the functions and consequences of couples living together.

A major point is that demands are more heterogeneous than ever before. Marriage is the preferred legal form of partnership for some people but is not acceptable for others. The following section discusses pros and cons of alternative options for regulating cohabitation, both at a theoretical level and in practice, by looking at existing laws on cohabitation for some of the countries in this study.

3.5   Legislation and Policy

The purpose of this section is to discuss the relationship between legislation and family change and to give examples of and explanations for the problems that may arise when the legislature tries to deal with this change. Arguments are given for the necessity for legislation on cohabitation. Several alternative proposals to deal with cohabitation are discussed and compared in detail. On the basis of this legal framework, actual cohabitation laws are reviewed.

3.5.1   Changes in legislation, gender roles, and behavior

Liberal laws and policies on consensual unions are occasionally put forward as a major reason for the rapid increase in cohabitation. While restrictive policies obviously hinder the development of new types of living arrangements, the causality between legislation and behavior is not so clear. As precisely stated by the Swedish jurist Agell (1981, p. 311):

> It is impossible to state to what extent recent legislation has actually contributed to the marked decline in the marriage rate.... Since the popular knowledge of legal rules is rather limited, it is generally speaking doubtful whether legislation on a particular matter will have any great effect on patterns and behavior.

In general, we know that changes in law are not a precondition to, but rather a consequence of, certain changes in behavior. As a rule, social behavior and norms seem to change faster than legal regulations do (Wingen, 1985). Cohabitation did not arise in answer to liberal laws on such relationships; rather, an inconsistent and often confusing legal treatment was adopted once significant numbers of consensual unions were observed. Even if no causal relationship between behavioral changes and changes in cohabitation law can be determined, the way in which legislation is formulated might play a part and influence further developments. While there does not seem to be a causality between the emergence of cohabitation and the legislation on it, there certainly is a strong causal relationship between the popularity of cohabitation and traditional marriage law. In many European countries, large parts of current marriage law date back to the nineteenth century. Society has changed and so has partnership, but marriage law has remained virtually unchanged. There is little doubt that inappropriate marriage laws are major reasons for the emergence and the rapid spread of cohabitation.

Traditional laws are increasingly in conflict with legal requirements, mostly as a consequence of the changing gender roles. Today, at least for many couples, neither the man's provider function nor the woman's caretaker function is applicable. Since the traditional family roles of the two sexes have become increasingly less differentiated, marriage law must be adjusted. Commitment to the partner has changed; therefore, the institution of marriage increasingly imposes a pattern of life or obligations that couples feel limit their freedom. Current marriage law explicitly expresses the traditional division of labor, including the woman's responsibility to care for her husband and children and her few responsibilities in financial matters. The intention of marriage and family law is the protection of women and children. Marriage law may, therefore, be held to be a large-scale attempt to create an artificial dependence of the man on the relationship and an obligation for him to maintain the relationship that corresponds roughly to the woman's dependence on him (Andrup *et al.*, 1980).

It is occasionally argued that society's expectations about the roles of spouses, and not marriage laws themselves, intrude on the life of married people (Eekelaar, 1980). Norms and values, on the one hand, and legislation, on the other hand, are strongly related. Expectations from friends, relatives, or authorities are probably equally important, but these expectations can be influenced by appropriate legislation. Women and men hope and attempt to escape from their traditional roles by preferring cohabitation to marriage, both legally, to avoid certain obligations, and socially. Due to its slow degree of institutionalization, cohabitation improves the bargaining position of both partners; partnership can be defined according to individual needs and to the commitment desired.

Divorce law, which can be interpreted as a reflection of the loss in function of marriage law, is a good example of the adaptation of family law to new legal requirements. Today, divorce is a functional necessity in view of the social changes; it is a safeguard without which living together would become a practical impossibility or at best extremely risky. Andrup *et al.* (1980) describe how the intrusion into the freedom and privacy of couples is slowly loosening. The absolute ban on divorce is abandoned and progressively replaced by a judicial decision based on the principle of guilt, by a joint agreement by the partners to end the marriage, and by unilateral termination of marriage given certain conditions of guilty behavior. Andrup *et al.* argue that all industrial and postindustrial societies are moving toward this direction and that, eventually, the principle of a right to a unilateral unconditional termination of marriage will be generally recognized.

We should also emphasize that partnership has increasingly become more heterogeneous and, as a consequence, legal demands have become more diversified. For these reasons marriage is still appropriate for a large part of the population. For an increasing portion, however, marriage and marriage law are no longer acceptable. We must determine whether there is a legal demand or even a necessity for legislative actions for this part of the population.

3.5.2 Legal requirements

The present situation, with increasing numbers of consensual unions and decreasing numbers of marital unions, is often referred to as a cultural crisis. A general fear of the consequences this development could have on family life in the future has been observed. In fact, however, the nuclear family is flourishing. Nevertheless, the change in behavior is certainly a serious threat to our existing family law, which is held to be absolute and fundamental. Andrup *et al.* (1980, p. 32) express the problem precisely: "The crisis is a legal one. It is the legal treatment of the family which is in the process of dissolution, not the family itself." There is little doubt that legislation on cohabitation is needed.

Legislation should serve the people and their demands. It is a basic concept of justice to be consistent and to protect parties that need protection. Legislation on cohabitation can only be meaningful to the extent that the rules are adapted to the changing functions and aims of present-day living situations.

A direct consequence of increased levels of cohabitation is a simultaneous growth in the number of court cases involving cohabitants. While there exists a fairly well-defined set of laws and precedents governing legal marriages, no such set exists to govern cohabitation. The ambiguity in court cases involving cohabitants has also led to a concern for a well-defined set of laws that govern this type of relationship (Eekelaar, 1980). Legal confusion on cohabitation continues in all European countries, including Sweden (see Section 3.5.4). Laws and regulations are often contradictory, usually in a way that benefits the state treasury (Wiersma, 1983). As the number of cohabitants increases, government agencies will unavoidably be called upon to respond to these changes and modify policies and laws accordingly. In the following section, alternative legislative options to deal with the observed changes in behavior are discussed.

3.5.3 Some alternative approaches to cohabitation law

Cohabitation must be dealt with legally as an additional part of family law, similar to the laws on marriage, divorce, and children. To address this issue, three fundamental questions must be answered; these questions are similar but certainly not identical. First, should a cohabiting couple have the same rights and obligations as a married couple? Second, should marriage be encouraged and cohabitation discouraged (or vice versa) or should no preference be given to either type of union? Third, should marriage law be changed or should cohabitation law supplement existing, traditional marriage law?

The answers to those questions will certainly depend on the attitude toward the changes in behavior that have occurred and will continue to occur. By cross-classifying the three questions one arrives at a kind of *legal framework* into which virtually all proposals regarding the legal treatment of cohabitation can be grouped. *Table 3.2* summarizes some alternatives. The classification in the table is a framework for discussion; the answers to the three questions are not always straightforward and depend on the interpretation of the respective proposal.

The first option, no regulation of cohabitation, is the most restrictive approach. It does not take into account individual or legal demands. It is the most extreme interpretation of the *neutrality ideology* (Agell, 1981) reflecting

Table 3.2. Nine alternative options to regulate cohabitation.

Option		General treatment	Union preference	Current marriage law
1	No legislation on cohabitation	Inequality	Marriage	Unchanged
2	Laws on engagement concerning cohabitation	Inequality	Marriage	Unchanged
3	Special rules on cohabitation	Inequality	No preference	Unchanged
4	Uniform rules on both types	Equality	Marriage	Unchanged
5	Private contracts on cohabitation	Inequality	Marriage	Unchanged
6	Private contracts on both types	Equality	No preference	Changed
7	Consideration of the individual only	Equality	All unions discouraged	Changed
8	Functional approach to cohabitation	Inequality	Cohabitation	Unchanged
9	Functional approach to both types	Equality	All unions	Changed

"freedom of choice": individuals must choose between regulation and non-regulation. This solution must be combined with public education on the suitability of marriage for long-term relationships. Legislators would not issue any rules governing cohabitation, and marriage law would not be changed. The main argument against the legal recognition of cohabitation stems from the assertion that married couples and cohabitants have different expectations and intentions. If couples choose to cohabit without marrying they may do so precisely because they do not wish to allow their relationships to be governed by the laws pertaining to marriage (Blanc, 1984). If cohabitants are dissatisfied with their legal position and believe that they are suffering an injustice, they should marry. Therefore, cohabitation would not be a legally recognized status (Deech, 1980). Such a view, however, does not take the heterogeneity of today's relationships into account. Apart from greatly unequal treatment between married and cohabiting couples, such a solution would certainly discourage new living arrangements. In most European countries this solution is obsolete, since certain steps have already been taken away from this restrictive view.

The second option in *Table 3.2* was proposed by von Krbek (1980). She recommends leaving marriage law unchanged and applying existing provisions (in this case German provisions) on engagement to cohabitation. These provisions do not grant damages for the dissolution of cohabitation, but they allow claims to be made for damages suffered and expenditures incurred by the partners as a result of having lived together.[6] This solution accounts for the fact that some legal activity is needed, since a marriage contract has been rejected and a special contract has usually not been entered into. Instead of applying parts of the marriage law to cohabitation, a separate law is applied. A major disadvantage of this solution is the unequal treatment of cohabiting and marital couples in comparable living situations. This proposal aims at encouraging marriage as the basic contract within family law. Again, this approach would be reasonable for a certain group of cohabitants but would be inadequate for others. It also does not take into account the increasing number of children born outside marriage.

The third option is to leave marriage law unchanged and to establish special rules on cohabitation wherever necessary. This is the most practical but, at the same time, most confusing and unsystematic solution. The basic principle of this solution is nondiscrimination – the legislation is based on marriage, but equal rights for cohabitants are introduced if justifiable (van de Wiel, 1980). In theory no preference to either partnership is expressed. The question of equality cannot be answered uniformly, since it depends on the specific question at stake. Undoubtedly, the frequency of cohabitation creates a need for legislation on certain questions. Cohabiting couples would not enjoy better benefits than married couples, and likewise couples that have cohabited for a long time would receive the same benefits as married couples. On the other hand, the rapid increase in cohabitation indicates the couples' wish not to be regulated as if they were married. Because of social needs in particular areas (for example, with regard to children), legislators must introduce special rules on cohabitation, following the general rule *as many regulations as necessary and as few as possible*. A policy of legislation on cohabitation is needed in those areas where practical solutions are required, without aiming at full equality with married couples. This option has the advantage of solving some problems but also has distinct disadvantages. It is difficult to balance the desire not to enact rules for couples that do not want rules for their cohabitation with the necessity to protect the weaker party in a union. For the individual about to make a choice, it would be difficult to arrive at an overall view of the legal differences between marriage and cohabitation. Advantages and disadvantages can vary depending on the legal question at stake.

The fourth option represents another extreme position, aiming at equal treatment of cohabitation and marriage, thus reflecting the wish for uniform rules irrespective of choice (Agell, 1981). In this case legislators would not issue any separate rules on cohabitation, but instead would alter the rules on marriage in such a way that they would automatically apply to all persons living together on a long-term basis in circumstances resembling marriage – namely, to all married and cohabiting couples. Such a solution would bring about complete regulation of most couples. The main argument for this approach is that in formulating rules an effort would be made to avoid situations in which people are disadvantaged by marrying and gain by getting divorced or remaining in consensual unions. This solution, however, simply ignores that people have chosen cohabitation exactly because they do not want to have their relationship regulated according to the laws pertaining to marriage. Marriage is strongly encouraged simply by equating cohabitation to marriage. This approach would be practical from the point of view of legislation, but extremely difficult to control; each case would have to prove the existence of a consensual union.

The fifth option is to leave marriage law unchanged, and to regulate co-habitation on the basis of private contracts. Such contracts would specify each partner's expectations and responsibilities and regulate financial settlements at the time of termination, be it through death or dehabitation. In many European countries this option already exists. The old attitude that agreements on cohab-itation have no legal validity – being detrimental to public order and morality – has now been almost completely abandoned (van de Wiel, 1980). Unfor-tunately, very few cohabitants have taken the option to enter into their own legal contract (Wiersma, 1983). The reason is simple: if jurists have failed to define a reasonable set of regulations, this task becomes almost unsolvable for lay people. Moreover, establishing such a contract at a time when people are moving in together is often seen as sign of mistrust. Private contracts are not required by states before entering into a consensual union. While this option would, almost by definition, result in unequal treatment of comparable couples, it also strongly favors marriage as the preferred form of living together.

The sixth option involves a change in current marriage law. It proposes to regulate both relationships on the basis of private contracts. In other words, marriage would become more like cohabitation and not the other way around (Deech, 1980). The advantage of this solution would be that distinctions would no longer be made between marriage and cohabitation, aiming at an equal treatment of all couples. No preference to either type of relationship is expressed. However, all the disadvantages and limitations concerning private contracts mentioned above are applicable in this case.

The seventh option represents the most rigorous conceivable form of leg-islation. It considers only the individual and ignores the marital or cohabiting relationships when determining the legal position of individuals. In practice, one could gradually reduce the effects of marriage or simply abolish the rules on marriage altogether. This view is taken by Clive (1980) who argues that there is no need to legislate relationships with regard to dissolution, names, nationality, residence, or children.[7] Similar to Option 6, no major distinction is made between marriage and cohabitation and no preference is given to either relationship. This solution, however, is based on the assumption that there is no need for regulation in any situation, even when a definite need seems to exist (for example, possible payments at the time of divorce or dehabitation). Explicitly directed toward the individual, this option would probably discourage couples from forming families and having children.

The eighth option listed in *Table 3.2* was proposed by Straver *et al.* (1980). They recommend leaving marriage law unchanged and regulating cohabitation according to a so-called functional approach. They suggest identifying (unmarried) relationships according to the basic functions which the partners fulfill for each other, such as affection, housing, daily tasks, and care for the children. In a particular relationship, the two partners would have to specify their individual areas they would like to protect:

> If the partners want to enter into legal relationships with the authorities they would have to make clear which functions they fulfill and hence wish to have protected. In order to do so they should have to offer some formalities to those authorities; formalities that may differ in kind and scope according to the function. [Straver *et al.*, 1980]

This approach clearly takes into account the plurality of relationships found in today's societies. Cohabitants themselves can choose their legal position according to their requirements. Of course, the legal status associated with each possible function must be provided through clear legislation. Current marriage law includes and imposes all possible functions at all times. As a consequence, marriage and cohabitation are not treated equal – except if a cohabiting couple wants to have all possible functions fulfilled and regulated. Due to its legal flexibility, this regulation may encourage cohabitation, but marriage would remain the traditional social institution with its established legal treatment.

Finally, the ninth option would be a modification of the functional approach suggested in Option 8. Formally it aims at only one type of partnership – call it marriage, cohabitation, or something else – which is then regulated exactly as described in Option 8. Couples choose the number of functions and accordingly the number of legally protected measures and areas. Traditional marriage law would no longer be applicable, but a couple could chose to apply all possible functions to the relationship. This option clearly encourages the nuclear family.

No further distinction between marriage and cohabitation would be necessary. There is no inequality between the two types of partnership. Everyone would have to make a choice and hence would be encouraged to think about and openly discuss the functions, expectations, and responsibilities of the relationship. This would stimulate communication, avoid misunderstandings, and possibly increase union stability. More details concerning this legal proposal are given in Chapter 5. In addition, in this option homosexual unions would be protected by the same laws regulating heterosexual unions. As well this option may be expanded to include other types of living arrangements, such as students or more than one couple living together.

One issue needs to be added – namely, the social and legal position of children, in particular children of cohabiting and single parents. Tapp (1980, p. 437) writes:

> There is no evidence that, once adjustment is made for socio-economic status, the family created by cohabitation outside marriage performs the familial functions significantly less adequately than the family sanctioned by a legal marriage. Thus it is submitted that for the health of society equal protection and support should be given to all types of social groupings which provide the child's needs.

Not much can be added to this convincing statement. In theory, this opinion is fully recognized. As early as 1967 the United Nations issued a statement on "General Principles of Equality and Non-discrimination in Respect of Persons Born out of Wedlock." The Council of Europe took up this concern and established the "Convention on the Legal Status of Children Born Out of Wedlock" in 1975. In practice, however, a statement is insufficient without legislation to implement it. The objective of legislative and social policies should be to allow and encourage both parents to have a full and close relationship with the child so far as that is in the child's best interests (Tapp, 1980). This objective is most easily fulfilled in Option 9. In this case, parents are tied to legal responsibilities, independent of their status and relationship, and there is – by definition – no difference between children born inside and outside marital unions.

Equality is also achieved in Option 4, which applies uniform, traditional rules to all couples. The remaining options, those that do not provide equality but also those that are based on private contracts or on the individual, would have to be supplemented by separate legislation to protect children. Therefore, most authors agree that the maintenance and custody of children should be a separate matter.

In the next section we identify which government agencies in Europe have already taken legislative actions and discuss the options they have chosen.

3.5.4 Cohabitation law in Europe in the 1980s

Comparisons of all relevant laws and policies in all the European countries in this study and discussions on their impact on behavior are not possible because policy and laws concerning cohabitants and their children are changing rapidly. However, data on some countries are available. These countries have been selected for further study to provide some understanding of the situation.

This section focuses to a large extent on Swedish laws and policies (most of the information is from Agell, 1981). Information on the Netherlands, Germany, Austria, Italy, Norway, Great Britain, and Ireland is also included. It is instructive to look at the situation in Sweden because in this country consensual unions have increased more rapidly than elsewhere and the Swedish legislation has gone furthest in applying definite legal solutions to the problem (Agell, 1981).

Option 3, special laws on cohabitation in certain areas, is followed in Sweden. Consequently, its current legislation on cohabitation is unsystematic and confusing. According to Agell (1981), cohabitation is increasingly being equated with marriage, without any real discussion of the practical need for each particular question. If this is true, Swedish laws may become less confusing and more systematic, but, at the same time, they may totally ignore the needs of the people. Uniform rules, irrespective of choice, provide a solution but are not what one would expect from a progressive country.

Most European countries are slowly following Sweden's lead. They are beginning to implement special rules in certain areas. Current Dutch legislation, which continues to regard marriage as the most common form of living arrangement, is a good example. It only gives equal rights to marriage and cohabitation where it seems justifiable and necessary. In addition, the Dutch definition of cohabitation is valid only for specific regulations (van de Wiel, 1980). The legislation in Norway and Austria is in some areas like the Dutch legislation and in other areas like the Swedish legislation (examples are given below).

Legislation in Italy and Germany, however, has not progressed as far as it has in the previously mentioned countries. The German Basic Constitutional Law explicitly protects marriage and distinguishes between marriage and cohabitation (von Münch, 1985). Nevertheless, the constitution protects all families equally. In Germany consensual unions with children are given the status of family, while those without children are not. In consensual unions with children from former relationships a family exists only between the parent and child. In other words, children are protected in all unions.[8] Childless consensual unions are not given any legal status.

Certainly an extreme example in Europe is the Republic of Ireland. It has a policy that supports families founded on marriage. Irish family law buttresses the marital family with a variety of devices, such as preventing marriages that are vulnerable to breakdown and banning divorce. Preferences to the marital family include discrimination against unmarried fathers and mothers with regard to parental rights, discrimination against the children of unmarried parents with regard to inheritance, and discrimination against unmarried families with regard to privacy rights (Duncan, 1980). For example, the unmarried father is not recognized by the constitution, he is not a legal guardian of his child, and he cannot veto his child's adoption even if he wishes to play an active parental role. As well, not only is the child of unmarried parents denied intestate succession rights in relation to his or her father's estate, but his or her rights in relation to the mother's estate are lost if she has another child in a marital union. Also, contrary to the trend in most European countries, recent family legislation has deliberately refrained from extending the rights and duties that are given to married couples to cohabitants (Duncan, 1980).

Graue (1980) reports on attempts in the former Yugoslav Republic of Slovenia. In 1976, a "law on marriage and family relationships" was enacted under which unmarried men and women living in "long-term cohabitation" were to have the same rights as married persons unless there are grounds preventing them from getting married. Apart from the somewhat ambiguous definition of long-term cohabitation, this would come very close to Option 4 on uniform rules irrespective of choice. Sweden is also moving in this direction.

The legislation in Sweden classifies couples into three categories: currently married couples, cohabiting couples who have had children together or have been married to each other previously, and cohabiting couples without children. With regard to social and tax laws the first two types of couples are treated equally. Marriage law, which is increasingly having an impact on cohabitation, treats cohabiting couples with and without children equally.

The most interesting regulations concern children born "outside of wedlock."[9] Currently, the rules on children born to unmarried parents differ so slightly from the rules on children born to married parents that it is of little importance to a child's formal legal status whether or not the parents are married. In 1969, the full right of inheritance from both the mother and the father was introduced. In 1976, rules governing legal custody were changed in such a way that unmarried parents can request the court to grant joint legal custody, irrespective of whether or not they are cohabiting. In the case of a custody battle, however, cohabitation must be established for the father to build up enough social contact with the child; the court may then determine that the best interests of the child would be served if he had custody instead of the mother. Paternity of a child of an unmarried mother must be established by admission of the father or a court judgment; this investigation can be simplified if the mother cohabits with the father. Sweden's insurance scheme provides that either parent of a newborn may take up to nine months' leave from employment at nearly full salary and another three months' leave at partial salary. This rule is independent of whether or not a couple is married. Following the end of parental leave, Swedish parents have the right to hold their jobs part time (six hours per day) until their child is eight years old. The child of an unmarried mother is usually given the mother's family name, but cohabiting parents can notify the civil register that the child be given the father's surname instead.

To what extent liberalizing laws regarding children born out of marital unions might have contributed to the increase in long-lasting consensual unions with children is difficult to assess. The rules seem to be a logical consequence of the increase in the number of such unions. Some conclusions may be derived from looking at regulations in other European countries. Denmark and Norway, for example, have not introduced joint legal custody, as Sweden has done, even though the proportions of cohabitants are also very high in these two countries. Austria, with a much lower incidence of consensual unions than the Nordic countries, has regulations as liberal as those in Sweden (two years' parental leave after the birth of a child for either parent, independent of legal marriage), although joint legal custody for both unmarried parents was introduced ten years later. Either the liberal laws in Austria may lead to a significant raise in consensual unions in the decades to come or the regulations are rather a manifestation of the traditionally high proportion of children born out of marital unions in this country.[10]

In Sweden, a special act in 1973 dealt with the common dwelling of a cohabiting couple. Based on an existing statute on the right to the dwelling after divorce, it permits the cohabiting party with the greater need for the dwelling to retain it after dehabitation, even if the lease or the tenancy rights is held by the other party. In contrast to most countries, in Sweden the rules on alimony after divorce are equally applicable after dehabitation.

One event usually followed by a number of legal actions is the death of a spouse or a partner. Sweden has a two-tiered pension system consisting of a basic pension and an earnings-related supplementary pension. With regard to the basic pension, an unmarried woman cohabiting with a man at the time of his death is entitled to benefits if she has had children by him, or if she was earlier married to the deceased. There is no corresponding rule for supplementary pensions. The social security laws in most other European countries are more restrictive. In Great Britain widow's benefits and pensions, death grants, maternity grants, or invalid-care allowances are payable to married women only (Pearl, 1980). On the other hand, in some countries, such as the Netherlands, Norway, and Sweden, retired couples receive more benefits if they are not married (Brunborg, 1979).

The Swedish tax system also provides an interesting illustration of cohabitation laws. In the old tax system the income of married couples was subject to joint assessment, and this, with regard to the progression of tax with rising income, could provide an incentive for cohabiting couples to remain unmarried to reduce their income tax. In 1962 a law was introduced that treated cohabiting couples with children (or couples that had previously been married to each other) as married couples. In the new tax system, however, joint taxation was abolished altogether. Today, everyone's income is assessed separately without regard to the partner's income, irrespective of marital status and living arrangements. This new tax system can be seen as a step in the direction of a highly individualized society. A similar tax system has already been implemented in many European countries, such as in the Netherlands (van de Wiel, 1980). Pinelli (1992) predicts that in the 1990s all countries belonging to the European Union will adopt a system of individual taxation.

Those examples show that almost all European countries have selected Option 3 in one way or another and have introduced special rules on cohabitation. This option is probably the most unsystematic and confusing alternative. There seems to be a tendency toward uniform rules for all couples irrespective of living arrangement. None of the countries have addressed the question of how to legislate cohabitation in a more comprehensive manner. The conclusion must, therefore, be that the legal demands of today's couples are not being recognized.

Having argued that inappropriate legislation on marriage and the family was responsible for the changes in living arrangements we now take a closer look at the spread and distribution of consensual unions in the 10 countries in this study. Higher proportions of cohabiting couples, to some extent, indicate that marriage law has become inappropriate. But they also show that less restrictive policies are being adopted. If we look at some other variables, such as fertility trends, we can even see to what extent adjusted legislation serves the requirements of the people involved.

3.6 A Typology of Cohabitation

Given the scarcity of data on cohabitation a typology of the phenomenon seems particularly useful to understand past trends and to forecast future trends. This typology could, for example, help to determine whether developments in countries lagging behind are likely to follow the trends in leading countries. Typologies have been prepared by several authors already. In this discussion some of those existing typologies, their justifications and disadvantages, are reviewed and a new, more comprehensive typology is presented. This new typology may be considered a framework for further analysis, a framework that tries to get as much information as possible from the very limited data on cohabitation.

3.6.1 Existing typologies

In the 1970s Roussel and Festy (1978) argued that a global transformation of the matrimonial system in Europe was taking place and that the different developments of family formation in Europe might be considered separate stages of the same development. A considerable amount of new data has been released since the publication of their paper. Has their "evolution model" been confirmed by those data? Have other authors expressed similar theories?

In principle yes, but the explanations have not always been convincing. Virtually all cohabitation typologies are based on information about births outside marriage. The character of cohabitation has largely been defined by this information. As a consequence, the conclusions are very similar.

In the context of cohabitation and childlessness, Frinking (1988) distinguishes three situations in Western Europe. First, in countries such as Sweden and Denmark, the proportion of children born outside marriage is approaching 50 percent; cohabitation is becoming generally accepted and widely practiced. Second, several countries have increasing proportions of births outside marriage (between 15 and 20 percent); these countries include France, Great Britain, and Austria. Finally, in some countries most births still occur in marriage, with levels of births outside marriage below 10 percent; this group comprises Germany, Belgium, the Netherlands, and Switzerland. Frinking concludes that the observed and the expected rise of cohabitation is a major determinant for the increase in childlessness – except in Denmark and Sweden where the influence of cohabitation on fertility is negligible. He does not address the character of consensual unions, and he uses only one indicator – the proportion of births outside marriage.

Kiernan (1993), looking at all of Europe, also distinguishes three main groupings: countries where cohabitation is well established, countries where it is emerging as a significant form of living arrangement, and countries where it is rare or possibly undetected. In the first group, comprising Sweden, Denmark, and Iceland, cohabitation became evident during the 1960s. Premarital cohabitation is the norm, and couples frequently have their first and even second child in cohabiting unions. Marriage is losing its monopoly on partnerships. In the second group, comprising Austria, Finland, France, Germany, Great Britain, the Netherlands, Norway, and Switzerland, cohabitation emerged during the 1970s primarily as a child-free, transitional phase preceding marriage. In those countries cohabitation tends to be temporary. This second group appears to fall into two subgroups: those countries where births outside marriage are a significant minority and those where births outside marriage are relatively rare. The third group comprises the countries where cohabitation is seemingly rare: Southern Europe (Greece, Italy, Spain, and Portugal), Eastern Europe, and Ireland. Unfortunately, Kiernan does not deal with expected convergence or continued divergence between those groups, and she does not include any data analysis.

Lesthaege (1992) concentrates on fertility outside marriage, arguing that parenthood "changes the nature of cohabitation and converts it from a period of courtship into a union based on a firmer commitment." He distinguishes four patterns. The first group comprises all countries with already high or rapidly increasing proportions of births outside marriage and (relatively) high proportions of consensual unions: not only Sweden, Denmark, and Iceland, but also Norway, Great Britain, France, and Canada. In the second group of countries, cohabitation has risen considerably but it has also been accompanied by a slower rise of births outside marriage (Germany and the Low Countries). A third group of countries has high levels of births outside marriage given their reported incidence of consensual unions (Ireland, Australia, New Zealand, and the USA). The Mediterranean countries are still at the start of such developments. Quite correctly, this typology takes into account the relationship between levels of cohabitation and levels of childbearing outside marriage. Lesthaege offers a certain amount of data analysis. As one of the proponents of the notion of a second demographic transition, Lesthaege (1992) argues that lagging countries will follow the leading countries because of the irreversibility of the observed trends and the cohesiveness of the patterns. In contrast, Haskey (1991) argues that it is difficult to judge whether West European countries are following the lead set by Sweden or Denmark, or whether they are establishing a different pattern.

The most comprehensive family typology has been given by Roussel (1992). Looking not only at levels of cohabitation and proportions of births outside marriage, but also at levels of overall fertility and divorce, he determines four different combinations of indicators that also correspond to four geographical areas. Group south comprises Italy, Spain, Greece, and Portugal and has low levels of overall fertility, divorce, cohabitation, and proportions of births outside marriage. Group west includes France, Norway, Great Britain, and the Netherlands and has low levels of overall fertility and cohabitation, high levels of divorce, and moderate proportions of births outside marriage. Denmark and Sweden make up group north; these countries have high levels of divorce and cohabitation and relatively high levels of overall fertility and proportions of births outside marriage. Group center includes Germany, Austria, Belgium, Luxembourg, and Switzerland and has very low overall fertility rates, high divorce levels, moderate cohabitation rates, and low proportions of births outside marriage. While Roussel's typology is most comprehensive in its analysis, the results are partly surprising and deviate from other typologies. On the basis of the data presented by Roussel, the Netherlands should be part of the group center rather than the group west. The low level of cohabitation indicated for the group west has not been confirmed by the data. Western Europe is not homogeneous in demographic terms, but Roussel (1992) expects the differences to be substantially reduced in the future. There is a common pattern in all groups; changes that were first observed in the north, later became diffused through the south. As was the case with the first demographic transition, countries that are the last to be affected also tend to adopt the developments rapidly. Some demographers (particularly in Italy), however, strongly oppose the concept of "delay" for the explanation of recent changes (see Castiglioni and Zuanna, 1992).

The categorizations in the typologies seem in most cases justified, but the characteristics of cohabitation are not easily distinguishable between the different groups. These typologies are country typologies rather than cohabitation or family typologies. They tell us something about countries and differences between them, but they tell us only little – if anything – about cohabitation. One reason is that these typologies are, for the most part, based only on information on the proportion of births outside marriage.

The relationship between the proportion of cohabiting women at ages 15 and over and the proportion of births outside marriage is given in *Figure 3.2*.[11] A relationship certainly exists (the linear regression results in a significant correlation, R^2 equal to 0.70), but some countries fall outside, for example, Great Britain and the Netherlands. It is not easy to explain how a relatively large

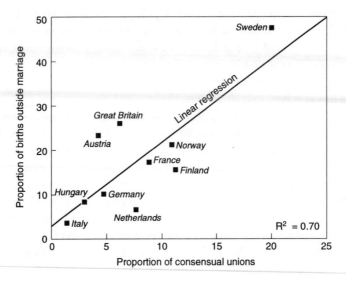

Figure 3.2. Relationship between cohabitation and births outside marriage in 1985.

number of cohabiting women and a low number of births outside marriage, as is found in the Netherlands, can be part of the same development.

It seems that the increase in fertility outside marriage reflects social acceptance of childbearing outside marriage, rather than the acceptance of consensual unions. Data on fertility in consensual unions (as compared with fertility of married and single women) would be useful in this discussion, but this information is not available for all countries involved in the study. Fertility among cohabiting women is discussed in Section 4.3.1.

Other important indicators are the average length of consensual unions (in particular, changes in duration over time), the stability of consensual unions, and proportions of women living in consensual unions among different subgroups of the population, such as the never-married and divorced groups.

The following section aims at describing a typology of cohabitation, based on a more comprehensive analysis of limited data and designed for a better understanding of past, current, and future trends in cohabitation. It defines several types or stages of cohabitation that are basically a consequence, or rather one element, of a global social transition. Countries are then assigned a position on the cohabitation continuum.

3.6.2   A new typology

Somewhat in line with the proposition of a global transformation of the matrimonial system in Europe (Roussel and Festy, 1978), in this study it is argued that we are witnessing a global social transition from patriarchy to partnership, in the following also referred to as *partnership transition*. As a consequence of the changing roles of men and women, we observe a transition from the traditional, patriarchal relationship to a modern relationship based on equal rights and partnership. But, what parts do cohabitation and marriage play in this transition?

In this study cohabitation is taken as a major indicator of the progress of the partnership transition. The spread of cohabitation in a given population is interpreted as a sign of the phase of the global social transition. Different stages and functions of cohabitation are identified that correspond to different stages of the partnership transition. In previous sections it was argued that people try to escape their traditional roles by choosing cohabitation over marriage; that cohabitation, due to the lower degree of institutionalization, allows a larger latitude and hence a better bargaining position, particularly for women, than marriage; and that cohabitation is more suited to the increasing heterogeneity of demands than marriage. Hence, during the course of the partnership transition the proportion of consensual unions is likely to increase, and the dominant pattern of cohabitation is likely to change. In short, cohabitation changes its character from being a deviant phenomenon to being a social institution and, within the latter, from being a prelude to marriage to being an alternative to marriage and to finally becoming a type of marriage. These different stages are largely identifiable through the spread of cohabitation in different age groups.

A hypothesis that provides a framework for further analysis is formulated and tested in Section 3.6.3. It is important to emphasize that the social transition hypothesis does not maintain that cohabitation is an *equal partnership* and marriage a *patriarchal relationship*. For many couples partnership transition takes place within a legal marriage. For an increasing number of couples, however, the partnership transition is expressed in the choice for cohabitation. This makes analyzing cohabitation relevant for understanding the patriarchy–partnership transition.

The basic idea of the typology is that the age pattern of cohabitation gives most of the information we need, with age- and status-specific fertility variables functioning as complementary knowledge. The advantage is that these simple variables are available for all 10 countries in this study.

Table 3.3. Age-related parameters for the new cohabitation typology: cohabitation sequence ratios and their equality in 1985.

Country	CSRs from age x to age $x + 1$				Gini coefficients of sequence ratios	
	15–24 to 25–34	25–34 to 35–44	35–44 to 45–54	45–54 to 55–64	15–64	15–54
Sweden	0.48	0.43	0.59	0.56	0.09	0.11
Finland	0.35	0.41	0.52	1.00	0.30	0.13
Norway	0.35	0.40	0.43	1.00	0.30	0.07
France	0.31	0.49	n.a.	n.a.	n.a.	n.a.
Netherlands	0.30	0.29	0.61	1.04	0.38	0.27
Great Britain	0.31	0.41	0.54	0.51	0.15	0.18
Germany	0.21	0.33	1.00	0.96	0.40	0.52
Austria	0.23	0.62	0.67	0.90	0.28	0.29
Hungary	0.61	1.15	1.00	0.98	0.15	0.20
Italy	0.71	0.66	0.89	1.22	0.18	0.10

Very significant differences exist between countries in the age pattern of consensual unions given earlier in *Table 3.1*. In Italy or Hungary cohabitation is somewhat equally distributed over all age groups. In all other countries cohabitation is very frequent at ages 15–24 (ranging from 19 percent among 20- to 24-year-old Austrian women living in a union to 93 percent among 15- to 19-year-old Swedish women), but rare at ages 40 and older. Particularly relevant is the difference in proportions cohabiting between subsequent age groups. Therefore, so-called cohabitation sequence ratios (s_x) are calculated; these CSRs give the fraction of cohabiting women at age $x + 1$ divided by the fraction of cohabiting women at age x (s_x is defined as the cohabitation sequence ratio from age x to age $x+1$).[12] These ratios are calculated for each pair of subsequent age groups, in this case resulting in a set of four cohabitation sequence ratios for each country (with x ranging from 15–24 to 45–54). Next, a numerical measure of inequality between the sequence ratios is calculated. This indicator is an overall measure of the age relation of cohabitation, but it can only be interpreted in connection with the set of sequence ratios. Adjusted Gini coefficients, which are briefly described in Appendix 1, are used as a measure of inequality.

Cohabitation sequence ratios and Gini coefficients for the 10 European countries are given in *Table 3.3*. Gini coefficients are calculated both for the age range 15–64 and for the age range 15–54. A Gini coefficient equal to zero means full equality between sequence ratios, while a Gini coefficient equal to one indicates maximum inequality between ratios.

The underlying hypothesis is the following: as long as cohabitation is a deviant phenomenon, such as it seems to be in Italy and Hungary, we expect relatively high and similar sequence ratios (close to one) and relatively low Gini coefficients, since we expect a somewhat uniform distribution of proportions in cohabitation over age. As a consequence, during this stage of development the mean age of the cohabiting population is hardly different from that of the married population.

When cohabitation becomes accepted as a social institution, it first appears as a prelude to marriage. In this case, sequence ratios should change rapidly and become dissimilar. They should be very low at young ages, reflecting the sudden decline in the proportion cohabiting at childbearing ages, and remain relatively high at older ages. The Gini coefficient should be large or even close to one.

Acceptance of cohabitation as an alternative to marriage could be concluded from Gini coefficients close to zero. If the proportion of consensual unions declines with age – which is the case partly due to transformations from cohabitation to marriage and partly because the phenomenon started as a prelude to marriage in most countries – then there is no reason why this decline should not be gradual. The desire for children, for example, should not increase the propensity to get married. Therefore, no sudden decline in proportions cohabiting should be seen at the childbearing ages. We should expect similar or equal sequence ratios. If sequence ratios are similar, that is, the Gini coefficients are close to zero, then higher sequence ratios indicate an advanced situation in which cohabitation is frequently observed at all ages. The stabilization of levels of cohabitation at all ages indicates the completion of the partnership transition, with cohabitation being accepted as a type of marriage.

At this point it is necessary to explain what is meant by cohabitation as a type of marriage as compared with cohabitation as an alternative to marriage, a distinction that was proposed in Prinz (1991b). An *alternative to marriage* means that individuals choose between two different living arrangements (marriage or cohabitation). A *type of marriage*, in contrast, means that cohabitation has gone beyond social acceptance. As marriage and cohabitation become indistinguishable, as a consequence of full gender equality, the partnership transition is completed.

In summary, the following trends can be expected: from being similar and close to one, sequence ratios should first become dissimilar, then they should gradually become more similar (but at a low level), and then they should

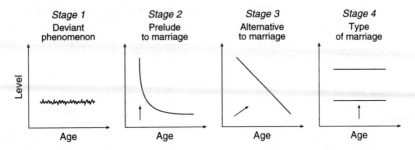

Figure 3.3. Four stages of cohabitation in the course of the partnership transition.

increase in a parallel manner. The last change would have a very limited effect on the overall level of inequality measured in terms of the Gini coefficient:

Stage 1	CSRs close to 1,	Gini ≥ 0,	no significant age dependency.
Stage 2	CSRs unequal,	Gini ≥ 1,	sudden decline after age 20–25.
Stage 3	CSRs very low,	Gini ≥ 0,	gradual decline with age.
Stage 4	CSRs equal to 1,	Gini $= 0$,	no age dependency.

The corresponding age patterns of cohabitation are presented in *Figure 3.3*. During the first stage, no significant age dependency can be observed. In the course of the partnership transition, we first expect a sudden decline after age 25 and then a gradual decline with age. In the final stage the age dependency again disappears.

Gini coefficients are calculated over two age ranges, 15–64 and 15–54, because data on proportions cohabiting in Finland and in Norway are only given for the age group 45–64. As a consequence, for these two countries Gini coefficients are overestimated for the age span 15–64 and underestimated for the age span 15–54. Gini coefficients corrected for the probable distribution within the age span 45–64 would be about 0.20 for Finland and about 0.15 for Norway. For the other countries, there is generally little difference between the two coefficients.

From *Table 3.3* we see that in 1985 Gini coefficients were lowest in Sweden (around 0.1); in this country, the first step toward cohabitation as a type of marriage – by reaching similar sequence ratios – will soon be completed. In a second step, all cohabitation sequence ratios are expected to increase.

Gini coefficients are relatively low in Norway, Finland, and Great Britain (between 0.15 and 0.20), suggesting that those countries have already reached the stage of alternative to marriage. In particular, sequence ratios from the 15–24 age group to the 25–34 age group are still clearly lower in these three countries than in Sweden. Since data for France are only available for 21–44 age groups, no Gini coefficients could be calculated. The difference between the first two sequence ratios (columns 1 and 2 in *Table 3.3*) for France is larger than the ratios for Norway, Finland, and Great Britain.

Gini coefficients are still significantly large in Austria (0.28–0.29), the Netherlands (0.27–0.38), and, in particular, Germany (0.40–0.52). Austria and the Netherlands seem to be in the transition from cohabitation as a prelude to marriage to cohabitation as an alternative to marriage, but the high coefficients for Germany clearly indicate the stage of prelude to marriage. As expected, Hungary and Italy have relatively low Gini coefficients (between 0.1 and 0.2), but the sequence ratios are higher at all ages than those of any other country.

A reasonable test of both the classification method and the hypothesis requires a set of time series of proportions cohabiting. Time series are not easily available, but some comparable statistics exist: census estimates for Norway and Sweden (both for 1980), a survey estimate for Great Britain (1979), and a recent micro-census estimate for Austria (1992). According to these statistics, Gini coefficients show declining trends in all countries: from 0.20 to 0.11 in Sweden, from 0.29 to 0.15 in Norway, from 0.32 to 0.18 in Great Britain, and from 0.29 to 0.21 in Austria. The speed of change is also similar. Sweden seems to be 5 to 10 years ahead of Norway and Great Britain and some 10 to 20 years ahead of Austria.

Chapter 4 includes discussions on a longer time series for Sweden (1975–1990), a projected time series for the period from 1990 to 2050, and the projected data rearranged according to birth. All are presented in the context of the cohabitation typology.

The crude typology obtained so far becomes more elaborate by considering the fertility-related variables given in *Table 3.4*. Again all data refer to the year 1985. In Sweden, every second child is born outside marriage (column 1). Below age 30, birthrates of unmarried women are 39 percent of the corresponding birthrates of married women (column 4), beyond age 30 even 75 percent (column 5); both rates are measured in terms of comparative fertility figures (CFFs) obtained from direct standardization.[13]

Childbearing outside marriage is unexpectedly high in Great Britain (25.5 percent) and Austria (23.2 percent). As shown in column 3 in *Table 3.4*, these figures are disproportionately high when compared with the respective proportions living in consensual unions (the unmarried births/consensual unions

Table 3.4. Fertility-related variables for the new cohabitation typology.

Country	Proportion of births to unmarried women			Age-standardized CFFs for unmarried women[a]		
	All ages	Ratio ages 15–24/35+	Ratio births/ Cons. unions	Below age 30	Age 30+	Ratio ages 30+/<30
Sweden	47.1	2.2	2.4	39	75	1.9
Finland	15.1	2.4	1.3	14	32	2.3
Norway	20.7	3.5	1.9	21	43	2.0
France	16.7	1.4	1.9	23	61	2.7
Netherlands	6.4	1.7	0.8	7	24	3.4
Great Britain	25.5	2.9	4.1	28	56	2.0
Germany	9.6	2.1	2.0	9	27	3.0
Austria	23.2	2.4	5.5	24	50	2.1
Hungary	8.2	0.6	2.8	14	54	3.9
Italy	3.3	1.3	2.4	4	21	5.3

[a]Direct standardization; married women equal 100.

ratio equals 4.1 in the Great Britain and 5.5 in Austria); this is, to some extent, due to childbearing outside marriage. In Austria, it is not uncommon to have a first child just before marriage. In contrast, childbearing outside marriage is disproportionately low in Finland and the Netherlands (the unmarried births/consensual unions ratios are equal to 1.3 and 0.8, respectively). In all other countries, the level of childbearing outside marriage more closely resembles the proportion of women living in consensual unions.

Childbearing outside marriage is a weak proxy for the social acceptance of cohabitation. Such acceptance is better mirrored by comparing birthrates of unmarried women with birthrates of married women.[14] Comparative fertility figures of unmarried women (columns 4 and 5) are generally highest in Sweden and lowest in Italy. British, Austrian, French, and Norwegian figures are also high, suggesting a high degree of social acceptance of cohabitation that goes beyond the stage of prelude to marriage. Again, the Finnish and, in particular, the Dutch figures are significantly lower than one would expect, with Germany being in between the two countries. In these three countries, the desire for children still seems to result in marriage. The proportion of married women in Hungary is very high in comparison with the other countries. Nevertheless, Hungary shows disproportionately high unmarried birthrates, in particular among women aged 30 and above. Childbearing outside marriage is rarest in Italy.

Column 2 in *Table 3.4* compares proportions of births outside marriage among 15–24 and 35 and over age groups, while ratios of comparative fertility figures (age 30 and above and below age 30) are compared in column 6.

Lower ratios in column 2 and higher ratios in column 6 correspond to higher occurrences of childbearing outside marriage at older ages relative to younger ages.

Hungary is the only country where childbearing outside marriage is more common at older ages than at younger ages (ratio of 0.6 in column 2), a fact that confirms the deviance of the phenomenon of cohabitation found for Hungary above. The low ratio for Italy (1.3) is a consequence of the deviance of cohabitation. In the other countries, where cohabitation can be regarded a socially accepted institution, we expect higher proportions born outside marriage at younger ages as a result of the age distribution of cohabitants. The low ratios found for the Netherlands (1.7) and in particular for France (1.4), corresponding to relatively higher proportions of births outside marriage at older ages, suggest a relatively large proportion of second unions in these two countries. The opposite is observed in Norway (the ratio equals 3.5).

On average, birthrates of unmarried women in relation to those of married women are two to three times larger at age 30 and above than below age 30. As expected, the ratios in column 6 are relatively higher in countries where cohabitation mostly functions as a prelude to marriage, such as Germany (3.0) or the Netherlands (3.4). In addition, the ratios are disproportionately high in France and in the Netherlands as a consequence of the high proportion of second unions in those two countries. The high unmarried birthrates in Austria and Great Britain at young ages result in low ratios in column 6 (about 2.0) in those two countries.

3.6.3 Summary of the new typology

In their typologies, Frinking (1988), Kiernan (1993) Lesthaege (1992), and Roussel (1992) classify European countries into three or four groups according to the role and function of cohabitation in the country. The classification of countries is straightforward, but the role of cohabitation in the respective groups is hardly – if at all – discussed. The advantage of the typology proposed in this study is that it is a typology of cohabitation rather than a typology of countries. On the basis of a typology of cohabitation, countries can easily be assigned a specific position on the continuum.

This cohabitation typology distinguishes four stages of development or four different stages of social transition from patriarchy to partnership. In the first stage, cohabitation emerges as a deviant phenomenon practiced by a small group of the population. Typically, this would be well-educated, often previously married, nonconformists living in urban areas. Protest against society and its authorities is a driving force during this stage. In the second stage, cohabitation becomes socially accepted as a prelude to marriage. It functions mostly as a trial marriage for young couples, and is transformed into marriage as soon as the desire for children arises. Cohabitation tends to be temporary rather than permanent. In the third stage, cohabitation becomes socially accepted as an alternative to marriage. It is a permanent alternative chosen because of its differences to marriage, such as increased independence and equality between the partners.[15] Childbearing is no longer restricted to marriage. Finally, in the fourth stage, cohabitation becomes a type of marriage or, rather, marriage becomes a type of cohabitation. Traditional marriage vanishes; marriage and cohabitation increasingly converge with regard to lifestyle; and the responsibilities between the partners are distributed equally. The partnership transition is completed with a new form of nuclear family; when this occurs the distinction between marriage and cohabitation is meaningless. In this fourth stage the couples' desires for mutual commitment and their demands for legal regulations remain just as strong as they are today.

The different stages vary in length, and it is difficult to assess at what time and to what extent the final stage will be reached. Once a country has reached a certain stage, it is impossible to return to a previous stage. Also, once a certain stage has been reached, all previous types of cohabitation can and do exist in the country in parallel.

It is possible to assign each country in this study to a specific stage of development within the partnership transition. Indeed, it is useful and even necessary to describe each country's position separately.

In this discussion, the countries are taken sequentially starting from the least progressive country in partnership transition and ending with the most advanced country. The sequence begins with Hungary, which has not reached the first stage of transition. Cohabitation certainly is a deviant phenomenon, but not yet in the form described in stage one. Hungary is still in the pre-transition stage. Cohabitation is almost uniformly distributed over all age groups, which is documented by cohabitation sequence ratios close to one; the mean age of cohabiting women is almost identical to the mean age of married women. Childbearing outside marriage is relatively frequent, but, contrary to what we expect, it occurs regularly at older childbearing ages.[16] Indeed, Carlson and Klinger (1987) have shown that cohabitation in Hungary is completely different from that in other countries. Cohabitation is by far most widespread among people with little education. Only 13 percent of all cohabiting couples consist of two never-married individuals, while this group in other countries usually constitutes two-thirds of all cohabitants (see, for example, Eichwalder, 1992, for Austria; Leridon and Villeneuve–Gokalp, 1989, for France). One-fourth of all cohabiting couples involves at least one currently married person. The conclusion is obvious: cohabitation in Hungary, where larger proportions of the population are married than in any other European country in the study, is to a large extent practiced by people who cannot get married for socioeconomic reasons or because they cannot get divorced. Although Hungary, as well as perhaps other Central European countries, has not yet started the transition, it might begin it very soon. However, the current economic and political situations in Hungary and all of Central Europe make any predictions about the near future difficult.

Italy is a perfect example of a country in the first stage of the partnership transition. Cohabitation is still a deviant phenomenon practiced by a very select population. The distribution over age is relatively flat, but cohabitation sequence ratios clearly show an increase with age. The lowest proportions of consensual unions are found at those ages with high proportions of the population living with a partner (ages 30–50), while somewhat higher proportions are found at younger and older ages. Childbearing outside marriage is low, which corresponds to the low proportion of consensual unions. A relatively rapid increase in cohabitation is expected in the future.[17] Between 1985 and 1990, the proportion of births outside marriage increased from 3 to 6 percent. Italy could reach a stage of social acceptance of cohabitation (stage two) in the near future.

Germany, next in the sequence, is a good example of a country in the second stage of the transition. Cohabitation is socially accepted, but only as a prelude to marriage by young couples. This is best demonstrated by the very low cohabitation sequence ratios at young ages, and the sequence ratios equal to one at older ages, that is, strong inequality between the ratios. The low unmarried birthrates in this country are also a sign of the acceptance of cohabitation as a prelude to marriage. When children are desired, consensual unions are transformed to marriage.

In the Netherlands, cohabitation has recently gone beyond the stage of acceptance as a prelude to marriage: cohabitation in this country is significantly more frequent than in Germany, in particular at ages 25 to 35, and cohabitation sequence ratios are more similar. Childbearing outside marriage has increased disproportionately slowly; hence, the mean age at childbearing increased more than in other countries. However, due to a recent rapid increase, by 1990 the proportion of births outside marriage in the Netherlands surpassed the respective proportion observed in Germany.

Next in the sequence is Austria, a most irregular country. Given the high unmarried birthrates and, hence, the large proportion of births outside marriage in relation to proportions cohabiting, Austria has gone beyond stage two. Eichwalder (1992) finds that the underestimation of cohabitation in the Austrian micro-census is particularly large. Most striking is the very low cohabitation sequence ratio from the 15–24 age group to the 25–34 age group, which is a characteristic of the stage of cohabitation as a prelude to marriage by young couples. This could mean that the underestimation of consensual unions varies greatly with age. Judging from Gini coefficients of sequence ratios in 1985 and their significant decrease in 1992, cohabitation in Austria is expected to be closer to the alternative-to-marriage stage.

France, Finland, Great Britain, and Norway – in exactly this order – are at the stage where cohabitation is considered an alternative to marriage. Inequality of sequence ratios is largest in France.[18] Also the age distribution of childbearing outside marriage is atypical in this country: the proportion of births outside marriage at older ages is almost as high as the proportion at young ages. This is a consequence of the unusual high proportion of divorced cohabitants. Recently, France experienced a very substantial increase in proportions of children born outside marriage; this can be inferred as an increase in the popularity of cohabitation.

The proportion of consensual unions is higher in Finland than in France or Great Britain; it is almost as high as the proportions in the other Scandinavian countries. On the other hand, unmarried birthrates, and hence childbearing outside marriage in relation to cohabitation, are disproportionately low. In Finland, cohabitation is obviously more popular than its degree of acceptance by the society would imply – perhaps because of its proximity to Sweden.

Cohabitation in Great Britain is very low compared with the other two countries – slightly more than half of the proportions observed in Finland. However, cohabitation sequence ratios are already quite low at older ages, and unmarried birthrates are particularly high, almost as high as in Sweden; both are signs of high social acceptance of cohabitation in Great Britain.

Norway is the best example of a country that is at the stage of cohabitation as an alternative to marriage. Both cohabitation and childbearing outside marriage occur often, and equality of cohabitation sequence ratios is already high. Indeed, in recent years the relative birthrates in Norway have been rapidly approaching those in Sweden. Within only a fews years, the proportion of births outside marriage increased from 26 percent (in 1985) to 43 percent (in 1992).

In 1985, Sweden was the only country that had gone beyond stage three; it is slowly approaching a situation in which cohabitation becomes a type of marriage. The proportion of cohabiting couples is very large; there is almost full equality between cohabitation sequence ratios, which also show an increasing trend. Half of the children are born outside marriage, and at ages 30 and above unmarried birthrates are equal to married birthrates. In Chapter 4 we learn more about Sweden including its trend toward completion of the proposed partnership transition.

3.7 Expected Future Developments

In the past the proportion of men and women living in unions has not changed dramatically. *Table 3.5* shows the changes in the proportion of married women and changes in the proportion of women living in either marital or consensual unions between 1960 and 1985, both for the total adult population and for the age group 20 to 40. The underlying assumption is that in 1960 all unions were marital unions. This assumption seems reasonable since even in Sweden the proportion of consensual unions among all unions at the beginning of the 1960s was estimated to be less than 1 percent (Trost, 1985).

While the proportion of married women declined remarkably – on average, 7 percent for all ages and 14 percent among young adults – the proportion of women living in unions changed only marginally. In most countries the decline in marriage was somewhat compensated by the increase in cohabitation. For France, Leridon and Villeneuve-Gokalp (1989) have shown that until 1981–1982 cohabiting unions compensated completely for the decline in marriage, but the proportion of all unions declined somewhat afterward.

Apart from the fact that the nuclear family does not seem to be threatened (that is, unions are not expected to decline much) two developments have been stressed in this chapter: a continuation of the trend toward larger proportions living in consensual unions in all countries and a catching-up process in those countries with low levels of cohabitation.

The reason for the emergence of and increase in cohabitation is that current legislation is inappropriate because of the changing gender roles of men and women. Gender roles will certainly continue to change since gender equality has not been reached in any country. Both economic independence of women and changes in social norms and attitudes toward women and motherhood will continue to increase. As precisely pointed out by Pinelli (1992, p. 21):

Table 3.5. Changes in proportions of women living in marriage and women living in unions from 1960 to 1985.

	Changes in proportion of women living in marriage (percentage points)		Changes in proportion of women living in unions (percentage points)	
	Adult pop.	Ages 20–40	Adult pop.	Ages 20–40
Sweden	−20.3	−41.2	−0.4	−5.5
Finland	−7.0	−16.8	5.0	2.7
Norway	−9.8	−19.1	1.1	−0.2
France	−4.6	−15.2	4.6	−1.1
Netherlands	−9.1	−12.2	−1.7	1.1
Great Britain	−11.3	−18.8	−5.4	−8.2
Germany	−6.1	−15.4	−1.5	−7.1
Austria	−3.0	−10.2	1.6	−3.6
Hungary	−2.8	−3.0	0.1	−0.3
Italy	4.4	9.4	5.9	11.2
Unweighted average	−7.0	−14.3	0.8	−1.1

> It would appear that the major success has been obtained in the area of respect for and protection of "difference" rather than in the area of "equality," and various symptoms suggest that further progress towards gender equality might be made by modifying male patterns of behavior, rather than seeking to "masculinize" female patterns.

Indeed, gender equality has not yet been achieved even in Sweden. Hoem and Hoem (1988) give a few examples for continued inequalities. For example, although women's labor-force participation rates are very high in Sweden, part-time work is common among women with young children: while 60 percent of women with at least one preschool child worked less than 35 hours per week in 1986, the corresponding figure for men was only 4 percent.[19] Citing their colleague Eva Bernhardt, Hoem and Hoem (1988, p. 410) state, "Part-time work and absence from work are important features in a Swedish woman's 'combination strategy' to reconcile her occupational and family roles." B. Hoem (1992) concludes that the greatest barrier to increased gender equality in Sweden may be the erroneous belief that it has already been achieved.

The typology suggested claims that a great social transition is under way; one that moves from a traditional patriarchal relationship to a modern partnership based on equal rights – a development that is also characterized by a changing role of cohabitation (from a deviant phenomenon to a social institution, and within the latter from a prelude to marriage to an alternative to marriage and eventually to a type of marriage). This transition is mainly driven by the fact that the changing roles of women and men have made the current laws on marriage inappropriate. When equality between men and women is reached, the transition will be completed. Similar to the theory on the second demographic transition (Lesthaege, 1992; van de Kaa, 1987), this development is irreversible and inevitable. The partnership transition theory postulates that developments will happen rapidly in countries that are the last to be affected (see discussion on the delay theory in Roussel, 1992); it is, therefore, to be expected that the differences that exist at present will become less marked in the future.

Notes

[1] According to the census definition the cohabitants must share a household and both cohabitants must declare that they live in a consensual union.

[2] A micro-census is a survey of 1 percent of the population carried out annually or even quarterly. Eichwalder (1992) finds that micro-census data underestimate cohabitation at least to the same degree as census data. In Austria, for example, the 1986 micro-census counted even fewer consensual unions than the 1981 census (75,000 compared with 82,000), even though the phenomenon certainly increased over that period. As a consequence, data for the three countries may be unreliable compared with the survey data for the other countries.

[3] The 1985 census reported 18 percent fewer consensual unions than the Survey of Living Conditions; the former is used in this study.

[4] Drawing on crude estimates of cohabitation in Southern and Central Eastern Europe, it seems likely that Italy and Hungary are good examples of the respective regions. Only Portugal, Slovakia, and the Czech Republic show a higher prevalence of consensual unions.

[5] The seminar was held in Rome, 27–30 January 1992; it was organized by the International Union for the Scientific Study of Population (IUSSP) Committee on Gender and Population.

[6] Among those damages and expenditures would be financial disadvantages incurred by giving up or altering one's professional career for the sake of living together or by spending money regularly on the partner's meals, rent, and so on (see von Krbek, 1980).

[7] Clive (1980, p. 71) is not attacking the social institution of marriage. He is only concerned "with the legal concept of marriage, a technical matter which has no necessary relationship to the social institution.

[8] This does not automatically imply that differences between children born in marital unions and out of marital unions are entirely removed from all issues.

[9] The terms "within wedlock" and "outside wedlock" were eventually removed from the statutory text in 1976. The terms "legitimate" and "illegitimate" were dropped in the 1910s.

[10] Lodrup (1980) describes an interesting early attempt to deal with determining paternity in Norway. The legislature proposed that paternity should be decided for every child either by the father's acknowledgment or by the court in order to achieve the greatest extent of equality. This proposal was, however, strongly criticized – particularly in Norwegian newspapers – as it was seen as an attack against marriage as a social institution.

[11] This figure gives the situation in 1985. It should be emphasized that since then the proportions of births outside marriage and, presumably, cohabitation have increased rapidly. By 1992, for example, the proportion of birth outside marriage had increased to 43 percent in Norway, 33 percent in Great Britain, 29 percent in Finland, and 25 percent in Austria.

[12] Since data on cohabitation are for most countries available only for one or two calendar years, these sequence ratios are calculated on a synthetic cohort (period) basis. Very large, 10-year age intervals are chosen in accordance with the data available for Finland, Norway, and Germany. Age groups beyond age 65 are not considered, because of both the small number of cases at that age and the bias resulting from quite different proportions of widows in different countries. Real cohort-specific data are available only for Sweden. These cohort-specific results confirm the period-specific results obtained in this section.

[13] In these figures the unmarried population comprises cohabiting and single women. If we measure the comparative fertility figure of cohabiting women this would result in a figure above 100 for ages 30 and over.

[14] Of course, birthrates of cohabiting women would be preferred if they were available.

[15] Again, this does not necessarily imply inequality and dependence in marital unions.

[16] Hungary has a tradition of childbearing outside marriage that is similar to the pattern in Austria.

[17] This view is shared by Roussel. He expects changes to occur even more rapidly in countries lagging behind.

[18] Unfortunately, French data only refer to the 21 to 44 age group.

[19] Fathers as well as mothers with children up to age eight have the legal right to reduce their working hours.

Chapter 4

Union Status: Cohabiting, Married, Single

Cohabitation has been identified as a major element in the transition from traditional marriage to modern partnership. Different countries have reached different stages within this transition, but the trend toward increasing proportions living in consensual unions is expected to continue in all countries. The analysis of union status becomes increasingly problematic if cohabitation is disregarded as a separate status. Information on legal marital status is biased in many respects, such as with regard to fertility.

This chapter deals with the analysis and projection of union status as defined in Section 1.5. It complements the analysis of marital status and, more importantly, demonstrates a number of hitherto unknown developments. Of special relevance are union-status-specific fertility and mortality analyses and union-status population projections that have not been undertaken thus far for any European country. The differences in the marital-status analyses and projections are compared in detail in Chapter 5.

For practical reasons, most of the analysis in the chapter is based on Sweden. Information on the other countries is added occasionally. Sweden, however, is the only country for which detailed data at the union-status level are available, including information on fertility, mortality, and couple formation and dissolution (see Section 4.1). Such detailed data sets exist for three time periods (corresponding to the last three censuses in Sweden): 1980, 1985, and 1990. Sweden is also the country that has advanced furthest in the proposed partnership transition; hence, a study on Sweden is relevant for all European countries.

The first section of this chapter looks at data issues; in particular, the Swedish data are described. Next, Swedish population structures by union status are analyzed for the period 1975 to 1990 with particular emphasis on the 1989 marriage peak. In an extensive section, demographic differentials by union status are discussed, looking successively at fertility, mortality, couple formation, and couple dissolution. This comprehensive analysis of differentials is followed by a theoretical section on union-status modeling. Eventually, the union-status model is applied to the population of Sweden in 1985 (the reason for choosing this year as the starting year is given in Section 4.5). A number of alternative scenarios are specified for the period 1985–2020.

4.1   Data on Union Status

As already mentioned in Section 3.2, most research on cohabitation and on union status suffers from the lack of adequate data. Data on population stocks are usually taken from population censuses, but consensual unions are usually not reported in censuses; of the countries in our sample, only Sweden and Norway report these data separately. As a consequence, stock information is difficult to obtain and must generally be derived from surveys. (Problems with survey data in general and survey data on cohabitation in particular are discussed at length in Section 3.2.)

While it is possible, although difficult, to estimate or approximate stock information on union status, at least for some European countries, it is almost impossible to get an estimate of union-status dynamics. For this purpose, the ideal situation would be a continuous registration system that records both the type of event (including the formation and dissolution of consensual unions) and its time of occurrence. Such a system does not exist in any country. However, for Sweden data sets have been prepared that include all the properties of such a registration system.[1] These data sets are exceptional for the following reasons: they give information on the total population and thus avoid any sample bias; there are no numerator/denominator inconsistencies or memory biases; and emigration and mortality are accurately recorded.[2]

The data for these data sets stem from four different sources: the population censuses, which classify people according to marital status and union status (information on stocks); the register of marriages; the register of internal migration; and the register of deaths. Linking the registers together to obtain the information on union-status dynamics has been possible because of the Swedish system of personal identification numbers. To study couple formation the census register was updated with information on marriages and internal migration in the year before the census, and to study couple dissolution the census register was updated with information on internal migration and deaths in the year after the census. Thus, the data sets give unique information on formation and dissolution flows of consensual unions and detailed data on mortality by actual living arrangements.[3] This method is not a continuous registration system itself, but by linking the respective registers it has all the features of such a system. Similar registration systems, including personal identification numbers, exist in several countries, but nowhere have those registers been linked together as they have in Sweden.

The Swedish data sets provide stock and flow information on the following states:

- Single persons (not living in a union) by legal marital status and marriage order.
- Cohabiting persons (living in consensual unions) by legal marital status and marriage order.
- Married persons (living together or separate) by marriage order.

In addition, for the first time age-specific fertility rates of single, married, and cohabiting women were estimated for 1985 and 1990. The estimation procedure is, in principal, the same as above. Births, taken from the birth register, are linked – using personal identification numbers – to the mothers in the census register. The latter register gives the required information about the mother's union status, union duration, and parity. In this case, however, a number of problems arise. First, the census register only includes the population in private households (which includes approximately 98 percent of the total number of women in childbearing ages). Second, only women who answer the census form are included (the rate of nonresponse in 1990 was 3.7 percent). However, since both the numerator and the denominator miss the same 5 to 6 percent of the population, the calculation of birthrates is not significantly affected. The only serious problem is the following: we only know the mother's union status at the time of the census; we do not know her status at the time she gave birth. A number of women, however, will have changed their union status during the period between the census and the birth from single to cohabiting. As a consequence, a large number of all births are counted as if occurring to a single mother: fertility rates among single women are overestimated, and those of cohabiting women are underestimated. The corresponding bias is small, however, since all births that occurred six months before and six months after the census are considered. Couple formations and couple dissolutions during these periods largely cancel each other out. It should be noted that these union-status-specific fertility rates should be used with caution, but it is safe to assume that differentials between statuses measured in this way are valid and reasonable.

4.2   Population Distribution by Union Status

Union-status structures differ from marital-status structures discussed in Chapter 2 for a number of reasons. First, cohabiting couples, which form a significant part of the legally never-married and divorced subpopulations, are considered a separate group. Second, the married subpopulation differs as a small share of legally married couples lives apart – some as legally married singles and others in consensual unions. It is not straightforward to match marital- and union-status population distributions except if both types are considered simultaneously.

In the following subsections, Swedish population structures are analyzed, with special emphasis on trends over the period from 1975 to 1990. Section 4.2.1 takes a look at the unexpected marriage peak, which occurred in December 1989 and resulted in a number of abrupt trend reversals. Section 4.2.2 discusses the general trend since the mid-1970s.

4.2.1   The 1989 marriage peak

In Sweden a surprisingly large number of women and men married in December 1989. This increase is connected with the reform of the national widow's pension, which went into effect 1 January 1990. The transitional provisions of the reform made it advantageous for many women to marry before the end of 1989. The number of marriages increased from 44,229 in 1988 to 108,919 in 1989, and dropped to 40,477 and 36,836 in 1990 and 1991, respectively. The *excess* marriages registered in 1989 were all contracted in November and December; there is no indication of rise during the months before. It is estimated that 98.5 percent of the excess marriages were contracted by cohabiting couples.

With the latest pension reform a woman's right to the national widow's pension upon the death of her husband, previously granted to all married women regardless of income, was abolished. Since then, Swedes have been expected to support themselves by their own labor. One assumes that when they reach retirement they will receive a personal old-age pension generated through their own previous earnings (J. Hoem, 1991). The reason why so many people married before the end of 1989 was that a transitional provision was set up in the reform to protect specific groups of women. However, it was not clear which groups would actually benefit from getting married. J. Hoem (1991, p. 129) writes, "The transitional provisions are rather complicated and difficult to grasp, and they differ for different categories of women."

Table 4.1. First marriage rates per 1,000 women, by age: 1988 equals 100.

Year	20–24	25–29	30–34	35–39	40–44	45–49
1988	100	100	100	100	100	100
1989	152	200	355	589	729	747
1990	98	98	87	84	84	84

The transitional provision states that women aged 45 and older (born in or before 1944) could more easily gain rights to a national widow's pension by marrying before the end of 1989. In particular, unmarried women among these cohorts could have an economic reason for marrying if they were single or lived with a man they did not have children by. Younger women, if they had a child or at least legal custody of a child, could gain by marrying the child's father. For some other groups of women certain parts of the transitional provisions would also apply, however, irrespective of whether they married by the end of 1989. For most women, the amount they would gain at the time of death depended on their husband's previous income.

Due to the complexity of the issue, it seems unlikely that many women could easily calculate whether and how much they would gain by marrying. The unclear situation is probably responsible for the increase in marriage rates at all ages. *Table 4.1* gives age-specific first marriage rates per 1,000 unmarried women for 1989 and 1990, relative to the 1988 rate.

Among women aged 25 to 29 marriage rates doubled in 1989, even though the incentive to marry generated by the pension reform was small for this age group. Women at older ages had more reasons for marrying, and marriage rates for this age group increased more than sevenfold in 1989. J. Hoem (1991) found that marriage rates increased twentyfold among never-married cohabiting women in the two oldest age groups. Data on marriages by marriage order show that first marriage rates were affected most, and that the impact of the new provision on marriage rates declined as marriage order increased.

When analyzing the large and unexpected number of marriages several questions arise. Why didn't these women marry earlier? Before the law was changed, many of the women who eventually married in December 1989 would have received a higher widow's pension if they were married rather than cohabiting at the time of their partner's death. If this fact did not play an important role before the reform, what made so many couples decide to marry in 1989? After all, 62,000 additional marriages among cohabitants means that almost 15 percent of all women cohabiting at that time married within only one month. A legitimate question in this context, posed by J. Hoem (1991), is "Why did some eligible women refrain from marrying before 1

January 1990?" The unforeseen marriage peak in Sweden in December 1989 seems to give some hints of the perception of marriage and cohabitation in Swedish society. The explanation given by J. Hoem (1991, p. 132) is that the marriage peak "clearly confirms how lightly Swedes in general have taken the choice between cohabitation and marriage. Many cohabiting couples cannot have paid particularly great attention to the legal form of their life together." B. Hoem (1992, p. 17) suggests, "Many people live as cohabitants without seriously informing themselves about the consequences of not marrying." To prove this statement she mentions the low incidence of (private) contracts between cohabitants. While these interpretations sound reasonable, they do not determine whether these marriages were indeed caused by the specific change in legislation itself, by the fact that many cohabitants were stimulated to think about marriage more consciously, or just by imitating a fashionable trend.

The marriage peak could have been caused by other factors, as well. If one thinks in terms of the cohabitation typology introduced in Chapter 3, and the advanced status of Sweden in the proposed partnership transition, the large number of marriages could indicate a change in the marriage trend. For those most advanced in the partnership transition, cohabitation and marriage could have reached the stage of being indistinguishable, hence relatively small incentives might influence their decision to marry. On the other hand, being aware of the heterogeneity of consensual unions, particularly in Sweden, the opposite conclusion might hold; those couples still in the early stage of the partnership transition – that is, before the stage at which cohabitation is fully accepted as a true alternative to marriage – might have been influenced by the attention that the reform provision received in the national media. To address these two, not necessarily exclusive, interpretations, one must know more about the very characteristics of those cohabitants who married in December 1989 as compared with those who did not, particularly about their union duration, union stability, and fertility.[4] Some of this information can be indirectly derived from the analysis of demographic differentials and their development over time which follows in Section 4.3.

In addition, the 1989 marriage peak had a number of consequences. For example, the cohabiting population given in the 1990 census is certainly quite different from what it would have been without the marriage peak, and probably also quite different from the 1985 population. One can expect some trends that were apparent between 1975 and 1989 to have reversed or possibly even accelerated. Obviously, the proportion of cohabitants in the 1990 population is smaller than expected. Whether their fertility rates, their mortality rates, and their rates of dehabitation are smaller or larger than envisioned largely depends on the composition of the subgroup of cohabitants that chose to marry. This is examined more closely in Section 4.3.

4.2.2   Population structures from 1975 to 1990

Sweden is fortunate to have excellent data on population structures by union status. The last four censuses (1975, 1980, 1985, and 1990) include information on legal marital status and union status. The censuses provide a detailed and relatively long time series on cohabitation.

A number of points can be made regarding the precision of the estimates of cohabitation in the censuses. First, the definition of cohabitation is relatively strict.[5] The regularly taken Surveys on Living Conditions (SLC) give estimates of consensual unions higher than those derived from the census.[6] The SLC estimates were 12, 19, 18, and 32 percent higher than the census estimates for 1975, 1980, 1985, and 1990, respectively. Changes in differences over time have been analyzed in Nilsson (1992). The upward shift from 1975 to 1980 was obviously due to changes in the method used in the SLC. The significant upward shift in 1990 is particularly difficult to explain. Part of the answer is an unprecedented increase of nonresponse in the 1990 census; this, however, cannot explain the entire increase in the difference between the SLC and census estimates. The marriage peak in December 1989 must have had different effects on the two estimates. In any case, the 1990 census estimates have to be interpreted cautiously, as a consequence of both the 1989 marriage peak and the increased rate of nonresponse.

In this section we not only look at observed population structures for the years 1975 to 1990 but also discuss forecasts of the 1990 population distribution obtained from projecting the 1985 population into the future. Details on the projection model and its parameters are described in Section 4.4.[7] By including the 1990 forecast of the population's union-status structure we are able to estimate the demographic consequences of the 1989 marriage peak. What would the Swedish population structure have looked like in 1990 if the widow's pension reform had not been enacted? The low estimate of consensual unions in the 1990 census makes alternative estimates particularly valuable.

The following analysis focuses on the three main statuses – cohabiting, married, and single – and on the share of cohabitants among different groups of the population, for example, the total population living in unions or various legal marital-status groups of the population. Whenever necessary, men and women are discussed separately, but the focus is generally on women. Three

Table 4.2. Proportion of cohabiting, married, and single women, by age group, in Sweden, 1975–1990.

Population	Age group	1975	1980	1985	1990	1990 forecast
Proportion cohabiting	15–24	20.4	18.7	18.7	18.0	18.0
	25–39	10.4	16.4	22.0	20.8	28.4
	40–59	2.9	4.5	6.9	7.6	9.8
Proportion married	15–24	13.0	6.9	4.6	5.4	4.1
	25–39	68.9	60.8	52.3	51.0	44.4
	40–59	76.5	73.9	70.3	68.1	67.0
Proportion single	15–24	66.6	74.3	76.7	76.6	77.9
	25–39	20.7	22.8	25.7	28.2	27.3
	40–59	20.5	21.6	22.8	24.3	23.2

large age groups are considered: young couples/women (15 to 24 years), women in their main childbearing ages (25 to 39 years), and middle-aged couples/women (40 to 59 years). Age groups beyond age 60 are not included for two reasons: the proportion cohabiting is very small at that age and in those age groups marital status is strongly influenced by mortality. In all cases, census estimates for the years 1975, 1980, 1985, and 1990 and the 1990 forecast without the marriage peak are compared.

Table 4.2 gives the proportions of women in the three union statuses by large age groups. The proportion of single women has gradually increased over the whole period. The increases range from 10 percentage points among the youngest group to 4 percentage points among 40- to 59-year-old women. That is, the proportion of women living in unions has steadily declined at all ages. More precisely, the proportion of married women has declined substantially, from 69 percent among the 25- to 39-year-old women in 1975 to only 51 percent in 1990. The proportion for cohabiting women has more than doubled in the 25–39 and 40–59 age groups, but it has decreased for the youngest age group. The increase in the proportion living alone among young adults seems to result from a voluntary choice of people who can afford this living arrangement or, in other words, an active expression of individualism. (For more on the contribution of changes in couple formation and dissolution rates see Section 4.3.)

If there had not been a marriage peak in 1989, all the trends would have continued into 1990. Due to the peak, however, a number of trends were reversed or their pace was at least slowed. Comparing observed and forecasted values for the year 1990 we see that proportions of single women were hardly affected by the marriage peak.[8] On the other hand, the large number of

Table 4.3. Proportion of cohabiting women among selected groups, by age group, 1975–1990.

Population	Age group	1975	1980	1985	1990	1990 forecast
Share among women	15–24	61.1	73.0	80.3	76.8	81.4
living in unions	25–39	13.1	21.3	29.7	28.9	39.0
	40–59	3.7	5.7	9.0	10.1	12.8
Share among never-	15–24	23.4	20.1	19.6	19.0	18.8
married women[a]	25–39	33.3	47.6	51.0	46.2	54.8
	40–59	12.5	16.5	25.8	29.1	36.7
Share among	15–24		31.1	28.7	26.4	27.4
divorced women	25–39	n.a.	32.1	33.3	29.4	30.5
	40–59		21.2	25.6	23.9	26.3

[a]Figures for 1975 refer to the total unmarried population.

cohabiting women above age 25 who chose to marry in December 1989 is clearly reflected in *Table 4.2*. With couple formation and dissolution rates constant as of 1985, the proportion of cohabiting women aged 25–39 was forecasted to reach 28.4 percent in 1990 – a substantial increase since 1985. The observed proportion is much smaller: 20.8 percent, even smaller than the 1985 figure. Hence, the proportion of cohabiting women among all women below age 40 living in unions declined between 1985 and 1990 contrary to what was expected on the basis of 1985 data.

Table 4.3 shows that among the youngest group of women, cohabitation as an alternative to marriage was widespread even in 1975. Its popularity has since increased in all age groups.

In 1985, every second never-married woman between ages 25 and 39 lived in a consensual union; the respective share among legally divorced women was somewhat lower, one-third only. Among the youngest group, cohabitation is naturally more common among divorcées, as a large number of never-married women at that age have not yet left their parents' household. The largest relative increase in cohabitation is found among 40- to 59-year-old never-married women. Among men, developments were almost the same except at older ages.

Figure 4.1 gives consensual unions as a proportion of all unions for women by five-year age groups. Here, the increase in the proportion at all ages, most particular at ages 25 and over, is evident. The 1989 marriage peak had an immense effect: it reversed the trend for women below age 40 and slowed the trend for women aged 40 and over. However, even the 1990 forecast shows a leveling off and even a moderate decline in the proportion cohabiting at ages

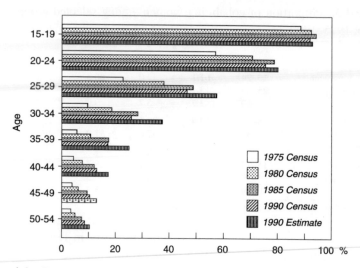

Figure 4.1. Proportion of women in consensual unions among all women living in unions, by age.

20–24 and 15–19, respectively. As concluded in Nilsson (1992), if new patterns or lifestyles are created by young people, this recent decline might form a new trend. The partnership transition introduced in Chapter 3, however, suggests that proportions cohabiting stabilize at young ages first, before reaching stable levels at older ages.

These data are used in the calculations introduced in Chapter 3 (Section 3.6.2) to compute cohabitation sequence ratios and their equality, the latter measured in Gini coefficients. The concept of cohabitation sequences over age and of Gini coefficients to measure differences between the sequence ratios was introduced to estimate the function or role of cohabitation and to establish a typology of cohabitation.[9] It was postulated in Chapter 3 that over the course of the partnership transition the role of cohabitation gradually shifts from a deviant phenomenon to a social institution and that, when considered a social institution, cohabitation changes from being a prelude to marriage to being an alternative to marriage and eventually to being a type of marriage. During this shift, cohabitation sequence ratios generally converge; hence, Gini coefficients approach zero. The extent to which this hypothesis holds for Sweden can be derived from *Table 4.4*. For the year 1990, the table again gives two values: an observed figure and a forecasted figure.

Table 4.4. Partnership transition between 1975 and 1990: sequence ratios of proportions cohabiting and resulting Gini coefficients.

Indicator	1975	1980	1985	1990	1990 forecast
Minimum sequence ratio	0.40	0.49	0.58	0.56	0.65
Maximum sequence ratio	1.00	0.91	0.90	0.86	0.86
Mean sequence ratio	0.78	0.74	0.74	0.75	0.75
Gini coefficient	0.132	0.096	0.068	0.061	0.038
Index of Gini coefficient	100	73	52	46	29
Proportion of cohabiting couples among all couples	11.2	15.0	18.9	18.5	23.0

As expected, minimum sequence ratios increase, while maximum ratios decline. The resulting Gini coefficient declines from 0.132 in 1975 to 0.061 in 1990. One could have expected a much lower Gini coefficient for 1990: 0.038, which would have reflected a continuation of the trend observed between 1975 and 1985. In this case, by 1990 the proportion of cohabiting couples, which is also given in *Table 4.4*, would have increased to 23 percent. But even with the unexpected marriage peak in December 1989, the 1990 Gini coefficient is below the 1985 value, which confirms the progress of the partnership transition.

Analyzing the behavior of Swedish birth cohorts is an important and useful supplement to period analysis. Some of the changes over time might be due to cohort behavior. Since the time series from 1975 to 1990 is still very short, a cohort rearrangement of cohabitation data is given in Section 4.5 in the context of cohabitation projections. By projecting future patterns, an extended birth cohort time series can be constructed and the explanatory capability of cohort analysis is strongly improved. In short, the period trends described above are clearly confirmed through a cohort analysis.

At this point, a brief outlook into the future should be given. The unforeseen marriage peak should not be interpreted as a reversal of the trend toward increasing proportions of couples choosing to live together without getting married. Rather, the unexpected peak is a delay of the process. More recent estimates of cohabitation could confirm this statement. An indication of the delay, rather than a trend reversal, is found in birth data. Having increased for several decades, in 1990, as a consequence of the marriage peak, the proportion of children borne by unmarried mothers dropped from 52 to 47 percent. However, it has increased since 1990.[10] If one takes this development as an indication of delay, and if one interprets the stabilization in the proportions of cohabiting 15- to 24-year-old women mentioned above as the highest level (90 percent for ages 15–19, 80 percent for ages 20–24), one could envisage a very different future. Cohabitation sequence ratios might increase to 0.88 (0.8/0.9) at all ages, resulting in about 50 percent of all couples living in consensual unions. This maximum level could, however, be very different if societal or legislative factors (for example, the pension reform of 1989) changed drastically. This is a qualitative view on possible future developments. Future union-status distributions are discussed quantitatively on the basis of an elaborate projection model in Section 4.5.

4.3   Demographic Differentials by Union Status

This study is one of the first systematic analyses of demographic differences between marriages and consensual unions. Comparable data are rare, but they generally indicate that cohabiting couples have lower fertility and higher dissolution rates than married couples. Fertility and mortality levels of cohabitants are useful indicators of the function of cohabitation, in particular in the context of the proposed partnership transition. Information on union-status differentials is a valuable supplement to the analysis of marital-status differentials given in Chapter 2. Indeed, some of the changes in marital-status differentials can only be explained through knowledge on levels of and changes in union-status differentials. In the following we successively look at levels of fertility, mortality, couple formation, and couple dissolution by union status.

4.3.1   Fertility

A major finding of the analysis of marital-status-specific fertility differentials in Chapter 2 (Section 2.3.1) is the enormous increase in fertility among unmarried women relative to their married counterparts. In Sweden, for example, the relative fertility rate of unmarried women increased from 16 in 1963 to 55 in 1985 (the rate of married women equals 100), an increase of 243 percent. During the same period the proportion of children born to unmarried women increased from less than 15 percent to more than 45 percent. In Chapter 3 it is speculated that this huge increase must be due to an ever-increasing proportion of unmarried women living in consensual unions. Hoem and Hoem (1988, p. 397) state: "It is important to note that even though almost half of all children are now born outside of marriage in Sweden, nearly all children are born to parents who live together in a marital or non-marital union." In this section we learn more about fertility levels and changes among both cohabiting and single women in relation to married women, particularly in Sweden.

Surprisingly little information on fertility among cohabiting women can be derived from the literature. This is obviously due to a lack of extensive surveys that contain complete marriage/cohabitation and childbearing histories. However, some findings are available for various countries. Looking at the group of 20- to 34-year-old cohabiting French women, Leridon (1990a) found that fertility increased from 42 percent of the level of married women between 1974 and 1979 to 56 percent, between 1980 and 1984.[11] Fertility among cohabitants and the proportion cohabiting increased simultaneously. Leridon also found that fertility differentials are more pronounced – that is, fertility among cohabitants is relatively low – when union duration is incorporated or when only first births are considered.

The Dutch Central Bureau of Statistics (CBS, 1991) noted a significant increase in mean parity of never-married cohabiting women between 1982 and 1988 (for example, from 0.11 to 0.31 among 30- to 37-year-old women). During the same period mean parity of married women of the same age declined from 1.90 to 1.88. For Norway, Ostby (1988) found very low levels of rates of first birth for cohabiting women, albeit considerably higher than among single women.[12] In 1977, rates of first birth in marital unions were three to six times higher than within consensual unions. Hoem and Rennermalm (1985), in their study of birth cohorts in Sweden from 1936–1940 to 1956–1960, found surprising stability in the rates of first birth for each status (single, cohabiting, and married women).[13] On average, the rates for single women have been about 10 percent of the rates for cohabiting women.

None of the studies, however, gives a very clear picture of actual fertility differentials by union status. The following fertility analysis focuses on Sweden, making extensive use of the fertility data described in Section 4.1. Status-specific fertility rates are analyzed not only by age, but also by parity and union duration. The data refer to two years: 1985 and 1990. The 1990 data are obviously affected by the 1989 marriage peak. One hypothesis would be that marriagelike consensual unions (that is, cohabiting unions with high potential fertility) were transformed into marriages during December 1989. Fertility trends between 1985 and 1990 must be interpreted with caution. Relative increases or decreases cannot easily be explained or be taken as proof for convergence or divergence in behavior of married and cohabiting couples.

Figure 4.2 gives age-specific fertility rates for single, cohabiting, and married women. Fertility rates differ significantly among these groups. Marital fertility exceeds consensual-union fertility; after age 30, however, the situation is reversed. Fertility rates among single women are consistently at the lowest level. Based on these age- and status-specific fertility rates the following

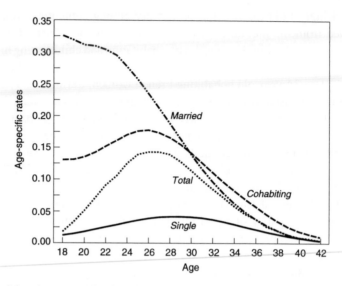

Figure 4.2. Age-specific fertility rates for cohabiting, married, and single women in 1990.

summary indicators have been calculated and compared: age-standardized comparative fertility figures (CFFs) obtained from direct standardization,[14] specific total fertility rates (TFRs) with the population at risk in the denominator, and ratios calculated on the basis of these two indicators. These indicators are calculated not only over all age groups (18–45), but also over two sub-strata groups – women below age 30, and women aged 30 and above – to overcome problems of biases with single summary indicators.

Results for 1990 are given in *Table 4.5.* CFFs measure the fertility level relative to the standard level; TFRs give the hypothetical average number of children born to each woman in a particular status. The ratio to marital fertility is given in square brackets. Overall, fertility in consensual unions is lower than in marital unions. With the extreme TFR measure, which gives equal weight to all age groups, cohabiting fertility is 77 percent of marital fertility (4.3 versus 3.3 children); however, the more appropriate age-standardized CFF measure is 88 percent (CFF of 114 versus 101). Fertility among single women amounts to about one-fifth of marital fertility and about one-fourth of consensual-union fertility.

Among women aged 30 and over consensual-union fertility is approximately 27 percent higher than marital fertility. Consensual-union fertility

Table 4.5. Fertility differentials by union status in 1990.

Age group	CFF[a] [ratio to married]			TFR [ratio to married]		
	Cohabiting	Married	Single	Cohabiting	Married	Single
18–29	89	126	18	2.14	3.39	0.37
	[0.71]	[1.0]	[0.14]	[0.63]	[1.0]	[0.11]
30–45	120	95	37	1.19	0.95	0.36
	[1.27]	[1.0]	[0.39]	[1.26]	[1.0]	[0.38]
18–45	101	114	25	3.33	4.34	0.73
	[0.88]	[1.0]	[0.22]	[0.77]	[1.0]	[0.17]

[a] Direct standardization; the sum of the married and the cohabiting populations was taken as the standard age distribution.

between ages 18 and 29, on the other hand, is only two-thirds of marital fertility in these age groups. Similarly, relative to the other groups, fertility among single women increases with age. Changes in fertility differentials between 1985 and 1990 are not given in a table; however, keeping all the limitations described above in mind, they can be summarized in two sentences. In Sweden, 1985–1990 was a period of rapid and substantial fertility increase; fertility increased at all ages and in all union statuses. Relative to marital fertility, fertility among both cohabiting and single women increased at younger ages (age group 18–29), but remained unchanged at ages 30 and above. If, indeed, the marriagelike cohabitations were transformed into marriages during December 1989, the small increase of 7 percent in fertility rates of cohabiting women between 1985 and 1990, relative to the fertility rates of married women over the same period, might underestimate the real fertility change that occurred in the group of cohabitants that did not marry during the marriage peak.

Recent literature on fertility analysis of modern societies where contraceptives are commonly used increasingly rejects age as the exclusive variable in determining reproduction. Further insights are gained through the analysis of status-specific fertility differentials by union duration and by parity. *Table 4.6* gives age-standardized comparative fertility figures for married and cohabiting women by duration (in years) of the respective union in 1990. For reasons of data reliability only the ages between 25 and 40 are considered. The CFFs of married women exceed those of cohabiting women at all union durations, but excess marital fertility declines with increasing union duration (for example, a ratio of 0.75 at durations 0–4 years and a ratio of 0.98 at durations 10 or more years). Summarized over all union durations, however, consensual-union fertility exceeds marital fertility.[15] The explanation is simple and can be derived from the last two columns of *Table 4.6*: a much higher proportion of cohabiting women belongs to the group with relatively high fertility rates,

Table 4.6. Fertility differentials and population distribution by union duration in 1990, ages 25–40.

Union duration	Age-standardized CFFs[a]			Population distribution (in %)	
	Cohabiting	Married	Ratio of Coh/Mar	Cohabiting	Married
0–1 year	145	188	0.77	15	2
1–2 years	134	177	0.76	13	4
2–3 years	129	176	0.74	11	4
3–4 years	117	157	0.75	9	5
4–5 years	117	137	0.85	9	5
5–6 years	107	128	0.83	8	6
6–8 years	97	108	0.91	12	12
8–10 years	85	86	0.99	8	12
10+ years	64	66	0.98	16	50
All durations	106	102	1.04	100	100

[a]Direct standardization; married and cohabiting women of all durations equal 100.

namely, those unions with short durations. For example, 39 percent of all cohabiting women but only 10 percent of all married women live in unions of durations under three years.

Obviously, a major reason for the high fertility rates among cohabiting women is that these unions are relatively *new*. This is also a major reason for higher fertility rates among cohabiting women above age 30 (see *Figure 4.2*). Short union duration is important with regard to not only union dissolution, but also fertility. Compared over different durations, *Table 4.6* shows that consensual unions with durations of one to three years have approximately the same fertility propensity as marital unions with durations of four to six years .

There is also a correlation between union duration and parity; the more recent the union, the more likely women are at parity zero or one and at this parity another birth is much more likely. Status-specific fertility information by parity is given in *Table 4.7*, for 1990 considering only ages 25 to 40. The conclusion drawn from *Table 4.7* is similar to that from *Table 4.6*. Cohabiting women have a totally different distribution over parity, with 66 percent belonging to the groups of parity zero or one, as compared with only 28 percent of all married women belonging to these groups. Therefore, the relatively high fertility rates among cohabiting women are partly explained by their lower parity and hence higher probability of a birth for a large part of this subpopulation. For single women, fertility does not depend on parity. Age-standardized comparative fertility figures among single women are highest at parity four or more.

Table 4.7. Fertility differentials and population distribution by parity in 1990, ages 25–40.

| Parity | Age-standardized CFFs[a] | | | | | Population distribution (in %) | | |
	Cohabit.	Married	Single	Ratio Coh/Mar	Ratio Sin/Mar	Cohabit.	Married	Single
0	153	199	30	0.78	0.19	38	10	61
1	148	192	55	0.77	0.28	28	18	18
2	60	63	40	0.95	0.64	26	46	15
3	55	50	46	1.09	0.93	7	21	5
4+	72	72	70	1.00	0.97	2	6	1
All parities	106	104	36	1.02	0.34	100	100	100

[a]Direct standardization; married and cohabiting women at all parities equal 100.

For most couples in modern societies the number of children already born is a major factor in the decision for an additional birth. Therefore, parity-specific fertility analysis becomes increasingly important. For the analysis of cohorts beyond childbearing age no difficulties arise if relevant data are available. From a period-perspective, however, only age- and parity-specific birth intensities can be measured. The summation of such rates is not possible; since not all women experience all possible parities, these rates refer to very different risk populations. Specific models have to be constructed for the analysis of period data. A valuable model, suggested by Chiang and van den Berg (1982) and modified by Feichtinger and Lutz (1983) is the parity-specific period fertility table. Such tables are similar to life tables, except that age is replaced by parity. They are a useful tool in measuring the timing and intensity of reproduction in the context of the family life cycle. In particular, the birth-order distribution, or the concentration of childbearing, can be derived from this method. A brief description of the sequence of calculations found in Lutz and Feichtinger (1985) is given in Appendix 2.

A serious question involves the age span covered in the parity-specific fertility table. Age 45 or age 50 is usually taken as the maximum childbearing age, $x(w)$; results are significantly different depending on which age is chosen. Another important value is $x(0)$, the beginning of the risk period. According to Lutz (1989), fertility table results are more sensitive to the $x(0)$ selected than to the $x(w)$ chosen. In fertility tables for all women, age 15 is usually taken as $x(0)$. The general rule for the fertility table based on parity is that the risk population covered in the empirical parity-specific fertility rates has to correspond to the risk population in the life-table model.

Table 4.8. Results from a parity-specific period fertility table for all women in 1990.

Parity i	Mean age at birth order i, $x(i)$	Parity-spec. fert. rate, $r(i)$	Parity-progres. ratio, $p(i)$	Women at parity i or more, $l(i)$	Women remaining at parity i, $d(i)$	Completed parity distrib., $c(i)$
0	18.0	0.0793	0.860	100,000	14,009	14.0%
1	26.2	0.1645	0.833	85,991	14,362	14.4%
2	28.5	0.0460	0.464	71,629	38,426	38.4%
3	31.2	0.0325	0.323	33,204	22,478	22.5%
4	33.0	0.0418	0.351	10,726	6,960	7.0%
5+	34.8			3,765	3,765	3.8%

Mean completed parity 2.05

In *Table 4.8*, results obtained from a parity-specific period fertility table for all Swedish women in 1990 are presented. In this application $x(0)$ is age 18, since births below this age are very rare in Sweden and $x(w)$ is 45. The fertility table for Swedish women between ages 18 and 45 implies that the fertility pattern in 1990 would result in 38 percent of all women having two children, 14 percent remaining childless, another 14 percent having one child, and 34 percent having three or more children. The resulting mean family size is 2.05 children per woman.[16]

It would be particularly interesting to compare the birth-order distribution of cohabiting women with that of married women. In the construction of fertility tables for subgroups of the population, and in particular for interacting subgroups, a number of problems arise. The construction of marital fertility tables is quite common; however, two difficulties must be overcome. First, there is no clearly defined age minimum for $x(0)$, the beginning of exposure. This problem is usually solved by taking the mean age at marriage as $x(0)$. In the case of Sweden, however, the majority of marriages are entered after a period of cohabitation. Under such circumstances the mean age at union formation (taking all direct marriages and formations of consensual unions together) seems a more appropriate approximation of $x(0)$ than the mean age at marriage. Second, the table only includes marital-union births. Premarital births to women who are later married do influence the actual completed parity distribution of married women but cannot be included in the marital parity table. This problem cannot be resolved and must be kept in mind when interpreting results.

Similar difficulties arise when constructing a consensual-union parity table. The mean age at cohabitation can be taken as $x(0)$ to solve the first problem. A large fraction of cohabiting women eventually marry, hence they contribute to

Table 4.9. Results from a parity-specific period fertility table for married and cohabiting women in 1990.

Parity i	Mean age at birth of order i		Parity-specific fertility rates		Parity progression ratios		Completed parity distribution (in %)	
	Cohabit.	Married	Cohabit.	Married	Cohabit.	Married	Cohabit.	Married
0	25.0	26.3	0.1817	0.2392	0.801	0.877	19.9	12.3
1	25.6	27.9	0.1865	0.2199	0.856	0.839	11.6	14.4
2	27.7	29.1	0.0617	0.0469	0.565	0.454	29.8	40.2
3	30.5	31.4	0.0480	0.0319	0.435	0.315	21.9	22.9
4	32.6	33.0	0.0541	0.0419	0.434	0.351	9.5	6.8
5+	34.8	34.8					7.3	3.7

the completed parity distribution of cohabiting women but eventually they are no longer part of this group. Obviously the interpretation of such consensual-union and marital parity tables is mostly of a theoretical nature: these tables can only show the birth-order distribution implied by the current parity-specific (period) fertility rates for married and cohabiting women, but they do not show the true eventual birth-order distribution of married or cohabiting women. Nevertheless, even the theoretical interpretation has some analytic value.

Results obtained from fertility tables based on parity-specific period fertility rates for married and cohabiting Swedish women are given in *Table 4.9*. There are remarkable differences between the two groups. According to 1990 fertility rates, only 12 percent of all married women but 20 percent of all cohabiting women would remain childless.

However, once having proceeded to parity one, cohabiting women are more likely to have an additional birth, in particular at higher birth orders (compare the parity progression ratios in *Table 4.9*). Consequently, the completed parity distribution is significantly higher for cohabiting women at birth order four or more than for married women at the same order (16.8 percent versus 10.5 percent). On the other hand, no difference in the quantum of fertility appears: the mean family size of the two groups is identical, 2.1 children per woman.

Given these parity-specific fertility patterns, childlessness in Sweden might be expected to increase at the expense of the typical two-child family, if it is accepted that cohabitants are the forerunners in fertility trends. This tendency could be accentuated if the trend of women remaining single increases, since single woman have a much larger probability of remaining childless; child-lessness of about 60 percent could be expected on the basis of a single women parity table for 1990. However, during the second half of the 1980s Sweden experienced a remarkable fertility increase. The increase was not due to com-positional changes in union or marital status or to an overproportional increase in fertility among cohabiting women; it had other socioeconomic reasons that have not been analyzed in this study. Between 1985 and 1990, union-status-specific fertility differentials were quite stable; and consensual-union fertility did not lag far behind marital fertility. Due to the increasing average duration of consensual unions, in the future overall fertility among cohabiting women could actually be expected to decline relative to that of married women.

4.3.2 Mortality

The analysis of marital-status-specific mortality differentials in Chapter 2 (Section 2.3.2) shows a number of interesting results and raises a number of questions. First, mortality differentials and changes in differentials over the past two decades are found to be amazingly similar in the 10 European countries in this study, notwithstanding quite significant differences in, for example, marital-status distributions and changes, health-care systems, disease patterns, or socioeconomic conditions. Second, in all countries the excess mortality of the unmarried population has increased, although at the same time the proportion of this group has also generally increased. Third, differences between the never-married and the divorced subpopulations are not very significant.

These findings do not add much support for the selection theory, which poses that healthier individuals are selected for marriage. Rather, selection effects seem to play a minor role. The protection theory, which claims that being married is a protective factor, particularly in relation to stress (through social support and the socially accepted and expected role), is not necessarily supported by the data either. The significant increase in the proportion of cohabiting couples among the unmarried population in practically all countries would lead us to expect a decline in excess mortality of the unmarried population. Does protection also play a minor role?

Obviously, marital-status-specific mortality analysis gives an amazing contradiction in findings. The debate between selection theory and protection theory continues. Union-status-specific mortality analysis sheds some light on the contradictory findings presented in Chapter 2, and can partly solve the selection/protection conflict. However, adding mortality rates of cohabitants to the discussion complicates the issue and raises additional questions. Do protection and selection effects apply to cohabitants as they do to married people? Or, should we expect significant differences between marriage and cohabitation with regard to their selective and/or protective role?

The role of cohabitation varies from country to country, which is also reflected in the particular stage of the partnership transition (see Chapter 3).

Therefore, we should expect significant differences in mortality rates of cohabitants in relation to their married counterparts between countries. Unfortunately, mortality rates by union status are only available for Sweden; so a comparison of the countries is not possible.

In the literature, the issue of mortality among cohabitants is almost completely ignored. Joung *et al.* (1992) undertook a very interesting study on morbidity differences by marital status and by living arrangement. The latter study investigates two types of living arrangements: living alone (single) or living as a couple. Looking at a Dutch community, their conclusion was that not all health differences by marital status can be explained by differences in living arrangement. More importantly, their results suggest that marital status and living arrangement have separate effects on health status. However, this study has a number of shortcomings. First, they were using self-reported health measures (perceived general health, subjective health complaints, chronic conditions during the past year, and work disability benefit) to determine health status. Second, nonresponse (with a nonresponse rate of 30 percent) was selective and resulted in a peculiar, not representative, status distribution of the sample with extremely high married proportions. It should be noted that morbidity differences are not necessarily equivalent to the differences in mortality.

In Sweden, the age-standardized comparative mortality figures (CMFs) for men and women at ages 20 and above are given in *Table 4.10*.[17] In contrast to Chapter 2, ages 60 and over are not discussed separately, because the proportions of cohabitants are still very low at these ages. The data in *Table 4.10* show differences between men and women. Among single men, age-standardized comparative mortality figures are very high; excess mortality of single men over married men is at least twice as high as excess mortality of single women over married women. Among cohabitants the situation is the opposite; age-standardized comparative mortality figures and, hence, excess mortality are clearly higher among women. Indeed, excess mortality of cohabiting women differs insignificantly from that of single women, while among men the mortality level of cohabitants is much closer to that of their married counterparts. Among both genders, married persons have by far the lowest mortality rates at all points in time.

Time trends between 1980 and 1990 indicate the following: age-standardized comparative mortality figures increased among singles, remained constant among cohabiting men, and decreased among married men and women and among cohabiting women. Consequently, over a period of only 10 years, excess mortality of singles (over that of married people) has indeed increased significantly. Excess mortality of cohabitants, on the other hand,

Table 4.10. Mortality differentials by union status in 1980, 1985, and 1990, at ages 20 and above.

Gender	Year	Age-standardized CMF[a]			Ratio of CMF to married women and men	
		Cohabiting	Married	Single	Cohabiting	Single
Women	1980	122	95	112	1.29	1.18
	1985	109	91	116	1.20	1.28
	1990	115	88	118	1.31	1.35
Men	1980	102	88	135	1.15	1.53
	1985	100	86	139	1.16	1.62
	1990	102	84	142	1.21	1.68

[a]Direct standardization; total population equals 100.

declined between 1980 and 1985 among women and increased somewhat between 1985 and 1990 among both sexes. The latter increase is most probably again a consequence of the marriage peak in December 1989.

A major characteristic of the change during the 1980s is the decline in age-standardized comparative mortality figures of married men and women. Heterogeneity of couples has obviously increased. From Section 4.2 we know that a growing number of couples refrain from marriage and sometimes choose long-lasting cohabitation. There seems to be a major difference in lifestyle between married and cohabiting couples. Those cohabiting couples that do not significantly change their lifestyle with their new living arrangement, or, in other words, that keep their individualistic lifestyle (often because they have, on average, fewer children), are those that do not marry. Protection seems to have different meanings for married and cohabiting couples. This difference would explain not only the higher age-standardized comparative mortality figures of cohabitants but also the decline in these figures for the married population. Selection, on the other hand, plays an insignificant role, in particular since the overall proportion of couples has slightly declined.

The selection theory does not provide an explanation for the fact that the proportion of singles and their respective excess mortality increase simultaneously. Indeed, increasing excess mortality of singles is also largely a consequence of the fact that most less protected couples no longer marry. More than half of the increase in the ratios in the last column of *Table 4.10* is due to the decline in age-standardized comparative mortality figures of married men and women, which is caused by the growing heterogeneity of couples. The remaining, albeit small, increase in age-standardized comparative mortality figures of singles is most likely due to changes in lifestyle of this group of the population. The growing single population is increasingly dominated by individuals who choose to remain single.

Figure 4.3 gives smoothed relative mortality rates by five-year age groups for men and women in Sweden in 1990. Between ages 20 and 59, when death rates are generally at a low level, mortality of cohabitants is far below that of singles and clearly closer to that of married persons – particularly for age groups 20 to 34, the ages at which cohabitation is widespread.

At age 40 among women and age 50 among men mortality of cohabitants surpasses the value of 100 which represents average mortality at each age. Beyond age 60, overall death rates increase rapidly and status differentials in mortality decrease. The mortality level of cohabitants approaches the level of singles, and for women beyond age 70 it even surpasses this level. Since the great majority of all deaths occurs above age 65, overall age-standardized comparative mortality figures are clearly dominated by differentials at higher ages. Regarding the very high mortality level of cohabitants above age 65, we should remember that at this age only 2 percent of the population is living in consensual unions. In the future, with increasing numbers of elderly cohabitants, excess mortality of cohabitants is likely to decrease.

A different measure of overall mortality are life expectancies derived from ordinary period life tables. These indicators are shown in *Table 4.11*, calculated for each union status separately as if one lives in one state throughout his or her life. Two age spectra are considered: life expectancy at birth and life expectancy at age 60. In general the figures in *Table 4.11* confirm the results obtained from the analysis of age-standardized comparative mortality figures. On the basis of life expectancy, union-status-specific mortality differentials appear to be more pronounced among men than among women (for example, the difference between single life expectancy and married life expectancy at birth is 6.2 years for men and 2.4 years for women). Life expectancy of cohabiting men is much closer to that of married men; among women at age 60 life expectancy of cohabitants is below that of singles.

Percentage changes in status-specific life expectancies provide additional information. First, during the 1980s life expectancy increases were significantly larger at age 60, irrespective of status and gender. Second, increases during the 1980s were largest among those cohabiting, and by far smallest among the single population. The explanation lies again in compositional changes of these groups. The cohabiting population is growing and, hence, covers a more representative group in 1990 than in 1980; as a consequence, the mortality rate of this group fell to an overproportionate extent. The 1990

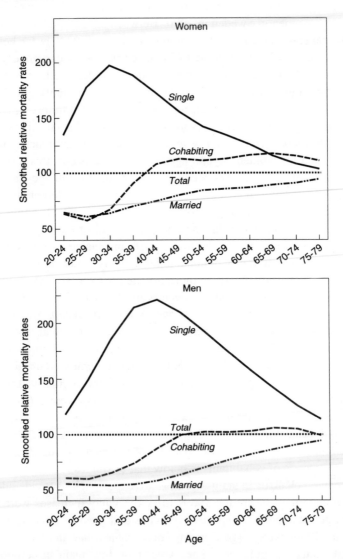

Figure 4.3. Relative mortality rates by union status for women and men in 1990.

Table 4.11. Life expectancy at birth and at age 60 by union status.

| | Life expectancy in 1990 | | | | Percentage increase in life expectancy between 1980 and 1990 | | | |
| | At birth | | At age 60 | | At birth | | At age 60 | |
Status	Men	Women	Men	Women	Men	Women	Men	Women
Cohabiting	76.5	81.0	20.0	23.5	3.0	3.4	9.5	8.7
Married	78.0	82.5	20.5	24.5	2.6	1.9	7.0	6.1
Single	71.8	80.1	17.7	23.6	2.5	1.2	3.1	2.8

single population consists of a larger proportion of voluntary singles with presumably higher risk behavior and, hence, higher mortality rates than the 1980 population; this change causes an underproportional decline in mortality rates. The 1990 married population is more homogeneous than the respective 1980 population and therefore their mortality decline is also remarkable.

4.3.3 Couple formation

The analysis of marriage rates and their development in recent years gives very little information about trends in actual couple formation, particularly in a country such as Sweden (see Chapter 2). The demographic literature also contributes very little to this topic; for most countries we do not know to what extent shrinking marriage formation rates have been compensated by rising rates of consensual union formation. The few available articles on actual couple formation are mostly on Sweden.[18]

Hoem and Rennermalm (1985), for example, analyzing the 1981 Swedish Fertility Survey, found that marriage without prior childbearing or cohabitation must have been less popular than previously thought. They estimated that already in the 1936–1940 birth cohort only about half the women ever married in this manner. For the 1951–1955 birth cohort, the respective proportion declined to only 6 percent.

Using the same survey, Hoem and Hoem (1988) estimated that among those women between ages 20 and 29, who married for the first time in 1965, 4 percent had lived in consensual unions for at least three years before marriage (not necessarily with their later spouse). By 1980, 45 percent had lived with a partner for more than three years before marriage.

On the basis of the 1981 Women in Sweden Survey, Blanc (1987) studied the formation and dissolution rates of second unions. She found that women who have dissolved a consensual union enter another union sooner than women who have dissolved a marital union and that, while the overall tendency to initiate

Table 4.12. Age-standardized comparative couple formation figures by union status in 1980, 1985, and 1990. The first marriage rates of singles are set to 100.[a]

Type of couple formation	Women			Men		
	1980	1985	1990	1980	1985	1990
Marriage rates						
Single, never married	99	107	120	85	89	100
Single, divorced	140	156	189	233	236	221
All singles	100	100	100	100	100	100
Transformation rates						
Cohabiting, never married	388	371	243	482	435	295
Cohabiting, divorced	613	629	416	757	640	499
All cohabitants	431	419	273	529	487	325
Cohabitation rates						
Single, never married	518	589	421	539	595	422
Single, divorced	752	820	552	1,097	1,111	797
All singles	583	663	460	618	681	475

[a]Direct standardization; total single population is taken as standard age distribution.

a second union has not changed much, the type of union women choose to enter has shifted significantly toward cohabitation. It seems that post-marital cohabitation is replacing remarriage to an even larger extent than cohabitation is replacing first marriage.

This type of information can only be derived from life history surveys. The data set analyzed in this study is of a different nature. We cannot follow single individuals; instead we have detailed information on couple formation for all different union statuses and, most importantly, for the total population. In the following, couple formation rates by union status from the 1980, 1985, and 1990 censuses are compared. To measure differentials, again direct standardization is used. In this case, the total single population is taken as standard;[19] all age groups, 20 and over, are taken together. Resulting age-standardized comparative couple formation rates are given in *Table 4.12*.

The table shows that among women in 1980 and 1985 transformation rates (that is, marriage rates of cohabitants) are four times larger than first marriage rates of singles; among men transformation rates are five times larger. Direct marriage rates of singles are so low because their cohabitation rates are so high – even higher than the transformation rates of cohabitants. In all instances – that is, for marriage, transformation, and cohabitation – the propensity to form a union is significantly higher among those divorced than among the never-married population (between 40 and 70 percent for women and between 50 and 170 percent for men). Cohabitation rates of divorced single men are

Table 4.13. Percentage changes in age-standardized comparative couple formation rates between 1980–1985 and 1985–1990.

Period	Women			Men		
	Marriage	Transform.	Cohabit.	Marriage	Transform.	Cohabit.
1980–1985	–7	–10	3	–4	–12	6
1985–1990	31	–14	–7	29	–12	–8

12 times higher than direct marriage rates of never-married single men. It seems that the population consists of different subgroups: those that form (and dissolve, see Section 4.3.4) unions easily, such as the divorced subpopulation, and those that do not. Unfortunately, the data do not distinguish consensual unions according to their order.

The data for 1990 show some unexpected trend reversals; this is mainly due to the marriage peak in December 1989. At this time the respective transformation rates were suddenly much lower relative to direct marriage rates of single men and women (although still about three times higher). This, however, is a statistical artifact caused by the time periods chosen for the calculation of couple formation rates. For the estimation of direct marriage rates, the one-year period before the 1990 census was taken as reference. The 1989 marriage peak falls into this period; hence, direct marriage rates increased during this period. For the estimation of transformation rates, on the other hand, the one-year period after the 1990 census was considered. Here, the marriage peak of 1989 is not included. In this period the number of transformations is disproportionately low. Therefore, because of the way these marriage and transformation rates were obtained and because of the impact of the marriage peak itself, the data for 1990 are not comparable.

Changes in age-standardized comparative couple formation rates between 1980–1985 and 1985–1990 are given in *Table 4.13*, but only for the union-status aggregates. Between 1980 and 1985, the popularity of cohabitation increased at the expense of marriage: direct marriage rates and transformation rates declined, the latter more rapidly, and cohabitation rates increased. The decline in transformation rates, which was particularly strong before the 1980s (see Nilsson, 1992), is a consequence of the longer average duration of consensual unions and of the still rising acceptance of permanent cohabitation.

Between 1985 and 1990, however, these trends did not continue, because of the marriage peak in 1989. Some formations of new consensual unions were replaced by direct marriages; the rate of the former declined by some 7 and 8 percent while that of the latter increased by some 30 percent. It should be noted that in absolute figures these two percentages exactly compensate each other, that is, the total number of couple formations among singles did not change. This very significant increase in direct marriage rates is surprising, as it was estimated that some 98.5 percent of the marriages contracted in December 1989 were of cohabiting couples. Either the number of direct marriages contracted during the peak period has been underestimated or the popularity of marriage without cohabitation has indeed increased.

The declining trend in the transformation rate, however, continued until 1990, mostly due to the increasing average duration of consensual unions. Because such a large number of cohabiting couples married in December 1989, we expect a smaller number of transformations after the census period (those cohabiting couples that intended to marry should have done so in December 1989). The fact that the decline in the transformation rate during the period 1985–1990 was not stronger than the 1980–1985 trend, but rather just a continuation of it, might indicate a slowing in the rapid decline of the transformation rate. This could, however, be temporary. From the analysis of the figures in *Table 4.13*, two almost contradictory trends seem possible: a revival of direct marriage among singles and a tendency toward permanence among established consensual unions. The latter trend is particularly strong among those 40 and over. Since cohabitation rates are still almost five times larger than marriage rates (see *Table 4.12*), this does not mean that cohabitation will be less frequent in the future. Possible consequences of these trends are analyzed in Section 4.5.

An interesting question is whether couple formation during the 1980s, irrespective of marital status, is different from couple formation, say, in the 1960s. No reliable data on couple formation prior to 1980 exist; however, we know that before 1960 only very small numbers of cohabitations were observed and that these cohabitations were of short duration. It is interesting therefore to compare the overall marriage rate in 1960, which was a fairly good estimate of couple formation at that time, with total couple formation rates – that is, the sum of direct marriage and the cohabitation rates – in the 1980s (see Nilsson, 1992).

Table 4.14 gives age-specific rates for Swedish women. Among young women (between ages 15 and 29) there was very little change in couple formation intensities; marriage rates in 1960 are at about the same level as couple formation rates in the 1980s. A remarkable increase in couple formation occurs at ages 30 and over; at these ages today's couple formation rates are notably higher than marriage rates of 1960. A major reason for this change is the high union dissolution rates, which lead to a large number of second and third unions.

Table 4.14. Couple formation rates per 1,000 single women in 1960, 1980, 1985, and 1990.

| Age group | Marriage rate in 1960 | Couple formation (marriage + cohabitation) rate in | | | Average 1980–1990 (1960 set to 100) |
		1980	1985	1990	
15–19	38	41	38	31	96
20–24	185	207	196	193	108
25–29	186	190	187	188	101
30–34	97	127	136	135	137
35–39	55	85	95	91	164
40–44	32	63	73	66	208
45–49	19	45	55	51	263
50–54	9	26	32	32	333

4.3.4 Couple dissolution

The analysis of divorce rates and trends in Chapter 2 gives only partial information about trends in actual couple dissolution. For a country such as Sweden, where one-fifth of all couples (and a much larger fraction at younger ages, at which couple dissolution is much more frequent) choose to cohabit, this limited analysis is particularly problematic. Chapter 2 points out that divorce rates have rapidly increased, particularly in Sweden. This is remarkable since marriage formation has become progressively more selective and concerns ever fewer groups that have traditionally had relatively high divorce risks (fewer teenage marriages and forced marriages due to unplanned pregnancies, see Hoem and Hoem, 1988). The continued increase in divorce with still falling marriage rates gives the appearance of a contradiction at first glance. Leridon (1990a) rightly argues that these trends are two aspects of the same phenomenon, the weakening of marriage as an institution. Legal marriage is increasingly regarded as no longer necessary (hence the reduction in nuptiality). In addition, it is considered unnecessary to continue a marriage when there are difficulties (hence the rise in divorce). Sweden has one of the highest rates of family dissolution in the industrialized world. Popenoe (1987, p. 178) says: "Family dissolution is one of the few classically defined social problems that is getting worse in Sweden."

An understanding of the stability of consensual unions will extend our knowledge on the roles such unions play. In the study of couple dissolution a number of methodological and theoretical problems arise because consensual unions are often associated with marital unions. For example, transformation of consensual unions into marriages is very frequent, and almost all marriages are preceded by cohabitations of varying length. When we compare divorce and dehabitation rates we are also comparing different types of unions of very different average durations. In the study of duration-specific divorce rates it is not clear whether duration since marriage or rather since entry into the union should be considered. Considering marriages and cohabitations with similar characteristics is useful; however, survey data on consensual unions with long durations or with children present are limited. The data set used in this study gives little information about union duration and order.

A hypothesis of the impact of premarital cohabitation on the future of divorce rates was formulated when cohabitation was first regarded as a social phenomenon. Cohabitation was thought to serve as a screening process for potential long-term partners. In the literature this hypothesis is referred to as the "weeding-out hypothesis" (Manting, 1992). Less stable unions are weeded out before marriage during the period of cohabitation. The consequence of the weeding-out process is that, of those that cohabit, only the stable couples marry. For those that do not cohabit prior to marriage, the weeding-out process is assumed to start at the time of marriage; therefore, it was believed that couples that married after having lived with their partner in a consensual union have a lower risk of divorce than couples that married without cohabiting. Empirical findings for several countries, however, do not support this hypothesis. Rather, cohabiting couples have a higher risk of divorce than noncohabiting couples (see, Hoem and Hoem, 1988, for Sweden; Leridon, 1990a, for France; and CBS, 1991, for the Netherlands).

The selection hypothesis offers another explanation for the empirical findings. This hypothesis is clearly explained in Manting (1992). About direct marriage she says:

> Couples who hold more traditional values and attitudes towards marriage and divorce, will marry without having cohabited before. They are strongly committed to the institution of marriage and attach a high value to it. Their acceptance of divorce is much lower than that of people who are less traditional in their values and attitudes.

In contrast, about cohabitation she argues:

> Couples who attach less importance to the institution of marriage, cohabit. Eventually, they marry out of reasons of security, children or pressure from others. Although they marry, they still have a lower attachment to marriage as a permanent institution than those who did not cohabit.

The outcomes of consensual unions have been studied in the literature on the basis of life-history surveys. Leridon (1990a and 1990b) analyzed the fate of consensual unions begun between 1968 and 1982 in France. He found that after a period of five years approximately three-fifths of all consensual unions were transformed into marriage, one-fifth were dissolved, and one-fifth remained consensual unions. Among the continued cohabitations 50 percent had a child; 80 percent of couples in the transformed unions had a child; and among the separated unions about 15 percent had a child. Changes over time were relatively small; transformation into marriage generally became less common.

Hoem and Rennermalm (1985) studied the fate of childless consensual unions in Sweden for the birth cohorts for 1936 to 1960. Their results are not directly comparable to the French results, since they studied only the first event after union formation. In the oldest cohort, born between 1936 and 1940, 3 percent were still cohabiting without children after a period of five years; 76 percent of the couples were married (transformation); 16 percent of the couples had a child; and only 4 percent of the couples experienced a dehabitation. The findings on the youngest cohort were remarkable; some 14 percent were still cohabiting without children five years later. Dehabitation was the first event in 36 percent of the couples, while 31 percent of the couples had a child. Transformation of the union into marriage was the first event in only 18 percent.

Blanc (1987) studied the fate of second consensual unions in Sweden begun in 1970 or later. After a period of four years approximately one-third of all couples were still cohabiting; one-third had transformed the union into marriage; and another third had separated.

In this study, again, we cannot follow single individuals in a life-history perspective. Instead, couple dissolution rates by union status derived from the 1980, 1985, and 1990 censuses are compared. Direct standardization is used to measure differentials. In this case, the total married population is taken as standard.[20] All age groups 20 and over are taken together. The resulting age-standardized comparative couple dissolution figures are given in *Table 4.15*. It should be emphasized that the figures are only standardized by age; union duration has not been controlled. Also, we cannot distinguish dissolution rates of married couples with and without cohabitation prior to marriage. Nevertheless, the stability of consensual unions can be compared with that of marital unions.

In 1980, the overall rate of dehabitation was four times larger than the rate of divorce. By 1990, the difference between the two rates had decreased to three to one. This decline is both a consequence of the increasing length of the average consensual union and of the continued acceptance of cohabitation as a social institution. *Table 4.15* shows a notable heterogeneity of the group of

Table 4.15. Age-standardized dissolution rates by union status in 1980, 1985, and 1990. Divorce rates of those married are set at 100.[a]

	Women			Men		
Type of couple dissolution	1980	1985	1990	1980	1985	1990
Divorce rates						
All married couples	100	100	100	100	100	100
Dehabitation rates						
Cohabiting, never married	259	233	216	267	244	228
Cohabiting, divorced	598	509	448	589	526	439
All cohabitants	400	334	293	392	334	299

[a]Direct standardization; total married population is taken as standard age distribution.

Table 4.16. Percentage changes in age-standardized comparative couple dissolution rates from 1980 to 1985 and 1985 to 1990.

	Women			Men		
Age group	Divorce	Dehabit. of never married	Dehabit. of divorced	Divorce	Dehabit. of never married	Dehabit. of divorced
1980–1985						
20–39	2	–3	–6	0	–3	2
40–79	11	–9	–18	9	–7	–15
1985–1990						
20–39	17	10	4	16	5	–9
40–79	11	1	–3	12	8	–1

cohabitants: dehabitation rates of legally divorced cohabitants are twice as high as those of their never-married counterparts. In 1990, therefore, dehabitation rates of never-married cohabitants were only twice as high as corresponding divorce rates. The heterogeneity could be even greater if we include the number of previous cohabitations. It should be noted that in this respect cohabitants are not different from married persons; divorce rates of remarried individuals exceed those of first married individuals by about 100 percent.

If we compare married and cohabiting couples with similar characteristics differentials in dissolution rates would certainly be much lower. Taking into consideration both age and duration of union, Nilsson (1992) found that in Sweden in 1985 the dissolution rate of consensual unions exceeded that of marriages by some 70 to 80 percent, with differentials increasing with union duration.[21] Considering age and the number of children up to age 17 present in the union, the difference was still about 2.7 to 1.

Changes in divorce and dehabitation rates are of particular interest. *Table 4.16* gives changes in age-standardized comparative couple dissolution rates between 1980–1985 and 1985–1990. Omitting union duration creates only a small bias. To give a more precise picture, age groups 20–39 and 40–79 are considered separately. The table shows that divorce rates increased among men and women at all ages. Between 1980 and 1985 divorce rates among the 40–79 age group increased by some 10 percent; the increase between 1985 and 1990 was in the same order of magnitude. The sudden rise in divorce rates among younger adults between 1985 and 1990 is to a large extent caused by the marriage peak in December 1989. Given the particularly large number of marriages in 1989, an increase in divorce rates in the coming years is quite likely. Indeed, aggregate divorce statistics show a remarkable increase in divorce among marriages of short duration during the years 1990 and 1991.

Trends in dehabitation are less consistent. Between 1980 and 1985, dehabitation rates fell significantly, in particular among the 40 to 79 age group, with declines between 7 and 18 percent. Between 1985 and 1990, however, dehabitation rates generally increased among never-married cohabitants, an increase that roughly compensated the decline in the preceding period. However, in relation to divorce rates, dehabitation rates still declined. This increase in dissolution rates of never-married cohabitants is again due to the 1989 marriage peak. During December 1989 more than 15 percent of all couples cohabiting decided to marry; the majority of these transformations involved never-married cohabitants. As a consequence, the composition of this group changed drastically between 1989 and 1990. Obviously, those never-married cohabitants with a higher commitment to their union were married; those who continued their cohabitation are those at a relatively higher dissolution risk. Therefore, the dehabitation rates of never-married cohabitants increased unexpectedly between 1985 and 1990. There is no reason to assume that this increase will continue far beyond 1990; rather, dehabitation rates should start to decline again when the composition of the group is balanced. This presumption is confirmed by the continuing decline in dehabitation rates among divorced cohabitants between 1985 and 1990. This group was only slightly affected by the 1989 marriage peak.

Given the trends in dissolution rates between 1980 and 1990, a continuing increase in divorce rates and a continuing decline in dehabitation rates seem likely. Marriages and consensual unions have become increasingly similar with regard to duration and also – to a lesser extent – to reproduction and mortality, just as the partnership transition postulates; hence their stability becomes more similar also. Consequences of alternative rates of couple dissolution are described in Section 4.5.

4.4   Modeling Union Status

The increase in the number of cohabiting couples makes the four-state marital-status model inadequate. This model is only of limited value for estimating the impact of people's living arrangements. For a country such as Sweden, where cohabitation increased rapidly during the 1960s and 1970s, knowledge on the future of cohabitation and its effects on marriage would have been valuable to administrative bodies, scientists, jurists, and others. Taking the point of view of a jurist, Agell (1981, p. 291) points out:

> The question is to what extent the increasing number of cohabiting couples also implies a tendency for these couples never to marry, so that in the long run it will become usual for cohabitation outside marriage to be dissolved only by death. It seems at present impossible to form any definite opinion on this question, which, however, is particularly interesting from the viewpoints of legal policy.

With the excellent data available from Sweden, it is possible to comment on likely future developments. In this section I use a multistate projection model to calculate future proportions of the Swedish population living in consensual unions, in marital unions, or as singles. A number of alternative scenarios are tested, generated on the basis of recent developments in rates of couple formation and couple dissolution. First, however, the exact formulation of the nine-state union-status projection model is given and its consistency requirements are described.

4.4.1   The union-status projection model

The union-status concept considers nine different states: living alone (single), by legal marital status (four states); marital union (one state); and consensual union, again by legal marital status (four states). Hence, a legally married person can be identified in the model as living with his or her spouse (married) or as living single, but legally married, or as living in a consensual union with somebody other than his or her spouse, but legally married. With these nine union statuses (and excluding external migration), the theoretical number of transitions is 81. Of these, nine are nonevents (e.g., from single, never married to single, never married). Another 14 transitions are not possible because one cannot return to the never-married state after having been in a married state. Another 36 transitions are a consequence of multiple events (two or more events), such as from cohabiting, never married to single, divorced. This transition involves a transformation of a consensual union into marriage

Table 4.17. Transition flows in the union-status model with nine states, no migration.

Status before the transition	Sin, nm	Sin, mar	Sin, div	Sin, wid	Mar	Coh, nm	Coh, mar	Coh, div	Coh, wid	Death
Single, nev.mar. (sn)	–	×	×	×	M	C	×	×	×	D
Single, married (sm)	*	–	Div^a	W^a	R^a	*	C	×	×	D
Single, divorced (sd)	*	×	–	×	M	*	×	C	×	D
Single, widowed (sw)	*	×	×	–	M	*	×	×	C	D
Married (m)	*	S	Div	W	–	*	×	×	×	D
Cohab., nev.mar. (cn)	Deh	×	×	×	T	–	×	×	×	D
Cohab., married (cm)	*	Deh	×	×	×	*	–	Div^a	W^a	D
Cohab., divorced (cd)	*	×	Deh	×	T	*	×	–	×	D
Cohab. widowed (cw)	*	×	×	Deh	T	*	×	×	–	D
Not yet born	B	*	*	*	*	*	*	*	*	*

^{a}Not available from the Swedish data set, but the number of cases is small.
B = birth, D = death, C = forming a new consensual union, M = marriage, T = transformation of a consensual union into marriage, Div = divorce, Deh = dehabitation of a consensual union, S = separation of a marriage, W = widowhood/widowerhood, R = reconciliation with married spouse, * = impossible event, × = multiple events, and – = no event.

followed by divorce. By assumption, transitions resulting from multiple events are excluded from the model; only the first event is included in the Swedish data set. The corresponding bias, however, is small since the transition flows refer to a one-year period.

Of the remaining 22 transitions, 5 are not given in the data set: divorce and widowhood/widowerhood of legally married singles and cohabitants, and reconciled married couples (from the single, married state to the married state). The number of reconciled couples, however, is extremely low. Omitting the other four flows does create a certain bias; however, only the legal marital-status distributions within union-status aggregates (single, married, cohabiting), and not those aggregates themselves, are affected. Seventeen transitions remain: three for marriage, three for transformation, four for cohabitation, four for dehabitation, and one each for separation, divorce, and widowhood/widowerhood. Another nine transitions result from the exit from the state space (through deaths by status). All newborns enter the model as single, never married, but they result from the addition of natality of women in all nine categories. The matrix of transition flows is given in *Table 4.17*.

For each sex we have the following component-of-growth equations over the time interval to $t + h$, h being the projection interval (one year in the case of the following union-status projections):

$$
\begin{aligned}
P_{sn}(t+h) &= P_{sn}(t) + B(t,t+h) + Deh_{cn}(t,t+h) - M_{sn}(t,t+h) \\
&\quad - C_{sn}(t,t+h) - D_{sn}(t,t+h) \\
P_{sm}(t+h) &= P_{sm}(t) + S(t,t+h) + Deh_{cm}(t,th) - C_{sm}(t,t+h) \\
&\quad - D_{sm}(t,t+h) \\
P_{sd}(t+h) &= P_{sd}(t) + Div_m(t,t+h) + Deh_{cd}(t,t+h) \\
&\quad - M_{sd}(t,t+h) - C_{sd}(t,t+h) - D_{sd}(t,t+h) \\
P_{sw}(t+h) &= P_{sw}(t) + W_m(t,t+h) + Deh_{cw}(t,t+h) \\
&\quad - M_{sw}(t,t+h) - C_{sw}(t,t+h) - D_{sw}(t,t+h) \\
P_m(t+h) &= P_m(t) + M_{sn}(t,t+h) + M_{sd}(t,t+h) + M_{sw}(t,t+h) \\
&\quad + T_{cn}(t,t+h) + T_{cd}(t,t+h) + T_{cw}(t,t+h) - S(t,t+h) \\
&\quad - Div_m(t,t+h) - W_m(t,t+h) - D_m(t,t+h) \\
P_{cn}(t+h) &= P_{cn}(t) + C_{sn}(t,t+h) - T_{cn}(t,t+h) - Deh_{cn}(t,t+h) \\
&\quad - D_{cn}(t,t+h) \\
P_{cm}(t+h) &= P_{cm}(t) + C_{sm}(t,th) - Deh_{cm}(t,t+h) - D_{cm}(t,t+h) \\
P_{cd}(t+h) &= P_{cd}(t) + C_{sd}(t,t+h) - T_{cd}(t,t+h) - Deh_{cd}(t,t+h) \\
&\quad - D_{cd}(t,t+h) \\
P_{cw}(t+h) &= P_{cw}(t) + C_{sw}(t,t+h) - T_{cw}(t,t+h) - Deh_{cw}(t,t+h) \\
&\quad - D_{cw}(t,t+h) \;,
\end{aligned}
$$

where P is population; B, D, M, T, C, Deh, Div, S, and W are given in *Table 4.17*. The index indicates union status (single, never married; single, married; single, divorced; single, widowed; married; cohabiting, never married; cohabiting, married; cohabiting, divorced; and cohabiting, widowed).

The union-status model requires a number of consistency constraints. The number of male cohabitations, marriages, transformations, divorces, dehabitations, and separations must equal the respective number of female transitions. In addition, the number of widows (widowers) must equal the number of deaths among married males (females).[22] Hence, the following consistency requirements must be fulfilled (all the transitions refer to the period to $t + h$, and the indices denote gender and union status):[23]

$$
\begin{aligned}
M_{sn,\sigma} + M_{sd,\sigma} + M_{sw,\sigma} &= M_{sn,\varphi} + M_{sd,\varphi} + M_{sw,\varphi} \\
T_{cn,\sigma} + T_{cd,\sigma} + T_{cw,\sigma} &= T_{cn,\varphi} + T_{cd,\varphi} + T_{cw,\varphi} \\
C_{sn,\sigma} + C_{sm,\sigma} + C_{sd,\sigma} + C_{sw,\sigma} &= C_{sn,\varphi} + C_{sm,\varphi} + C_{sd,\varphi} + C_{sw,\varphi} \\
Deh_{cn,\sigma} + Deh_{cm,\sigma} + Deh_{cd,\sigma} + Deh_{cw,\sigma} &= Deh_{cn,\varphi} + Deh_{cm,\varphi} + Deh_{cd,\varphi} + Deh_{cw,\varphi} \\
Div_{m,\sigma}\,[+Div_{sm,\sigma} + Div_{cm,\sigma}] &= Div_{m,\varphi}\,[+Div_{sm,\varphi} + Div_{cm,\varphi}] \\
S_{m,\sigma} &= S_{m,\varphi} \\
W_{m,\sigma} &= D_{m,\varphi} \\
D_{m,\sigma} &= W_{m,\varphi} \;.
\end{aligned}
$$

For the union-status projections, the *LIPRO* projection model is used. Although the model allows for various ways for treating consistency specifications, the harmonic mean method that is used in the *DIALOG* software has been chosen (see Section 1.6 for a description of the harmonic mean method). All data in the Swedish data set (and hence also in the projection model) are given in single-year age groups up to age group 95 and over. Single-year age groups are particularly useful in the context of status-specific population projections as many of the transitions are not uniformly distributed over larger (e.g., five-year) age groups. For example, among the 15- to 19-year-old population, a large part of couple formations is concentrated at ages 18 and 19. Changing age structures would generate a significant bias.

4.4.2 The extended union-status projection model

For the extended union-status concept, with its 26 different states, the projection model becomes much more complex. The number of possible transitions and of required consistency constraints increases significantly. For example, consistency would be required between some of the transitions and fertility, since the transition from the status "single, never married, with partner, without child" to "single, never married, with partner, and with a child" is not independent of fertility. In particular, scenario setting becomes burdensome.

As the Swedish data set does not allow for more detail than is necessary for the 9-state union-status concept, the exact formulation of the 26-state extended union-status model is not discussed further.

4.5 Population Projections by Union Status

In this section, the Swedish data are used in the union-status projection model. Alternative scenarios on the future developments of couple formation and dissolution in Sweden are specified and the results are discussed in detail.

For various reasons 1985 is taken as the starting year. The data for the year 1990 are biased due to both the significant increase in the nonresponse rate and, more importantly, the marriage peak that occurred in December 1989. The latter problem is that some of the rates estimated for 1990 are seriously distorted as a consequence of the marriage peak (for example, rates of direct marriage and of cohabitation), while others are not. The effect of the marriage peak on the population distribution certainly cannot be ignored, but it can be reconstructed in the model. The effects on some of the rates, however, must be considered irrelevant for the medium- and long-term future. Also, an interesting comparison of constant 1985 and constant 1990 rates is possible. In addition, by taking 1985 as the starting year the results from this model can be compared more thoroughly with the results from the marital-status projections given in Chapter 2.

The model projects the Swedish population some 30 years into the future (1990 to 2020); this time horizon corresponds approximately to one generation. Beyond 2020 it is very difficult to make any assumptions on the role of marriage and cohabitation in Swedish society. Even during this 30-year period, major breaking points could occur, for example, from changes in legislation or policy.

4.5.1   Scenario assumptions

Only rates of couple formation and dissolution have been varied, status-specific fertility and mortality rates are kept constant at their current level. Two major reasons can be given for this: changing too many parameters complicates the interpretation of results; and our goal is to determine the future union-status distribution of the Swedish population not the future number of births or the total population size.[24]

In addition, there are other significant reasons for maintaining current rates in the model. In the case of fertility, results from Section 4.3.1 show that there has been a small increase in consensual-union fertility relative to marital fertility between 1985 and 1990. While this trend may continue, the increasing average duration of consensual unions should reduce overall fertility levels of cohabiting women (as fertility generally decreases with union duration). Taking constant status-specific fertility rates seems a robust strategy.

For mortality, Section 4.3.2 shows that there has been a relative increase in mortality rates of singles between 1980 and 1990. Due to compositional changes there has been an overproportional decline in mortality among both the married and the cohabiting populations. This trend will probably continue, but it will not have a significant effect on the union-status distribution. Mortality rates are also kept constant for methodological reasons. Widowhood/widowerhood is a direct consequence of death rates of married partners and must be changed accordingly. In the model this does not create any serious problems when analyzing the married population, but it does create problems when analyzing the cohabiting population. Dehabitation rates in this data set are a combination of voluntary and involuntary couple dissolution; they are not independent of mortality. A straightforward solution is, therefore, to keep mortality rates as well as *quasi-widowhood* rates of cohabitants constant, and to

Table 4.18. Minimum, middle, and maximum levels of couple formation and couple dissolution rates by 2020 (1985 = 100).

Type of transition	Minimum	Middle	Maximum
Cohabitation	100	105	110
Marriage	60	80	100
Transformation	40	50	60
Divorce	120	140	160
Dehabitation	60	75	90

make the change in rates of dehabitation only dependent on trends in voluntary dissolution of cohabiting couples.

Regarding rates of couple formation and dissolution, clear trends can be derived from the analysis in Section 4.3; the reversal of some of the trends during the marriage peak period is of course not of great importance for the future. Marriage rates declined over recent decades until 1989, when the marriage peak occurred, and then declined again. They will probably continue to decline somewhat, and cohabitation rates will continue to increase correspondingly. Transformation rates declined rapidly between 1980 and 1990, and will most certainly continue to do so. Divorce rates still showed an increasing trend, a trend that started decades ago, and dehabitation rates fell significantly. Both trends are likely to continue. Other trends seem unlikely. On the basis of these forecasts, a plausible range of future change has been specified for each major transition. In *Table 4.18*, minimum, middle, and maximum levels assumed to be reached by 2020 are given; those levels are shown relative to the level observed in 1985.

At the maximum level, marriage rates can be expected to remain stable, while the minimum is set at 60 percent of the 1985 level. Cohabitation rates increase accordingly to keep the total number of couple formations unchanged.[25] Transformation rates will almost certainly continue to decline very rapidly. It is assumed that by 2020 they will reach a level of between 40 and 60 percent of their 1985 level. The increase in divorce is assumed to be in the order of 20 to 60 percent; and the decline in dehabitation, in the order of 10 to 40 percent. In the most extreme case, by 2020 the rates of dehabitation and divorce would be approximately equal.

On the basis of these ranges, a number of scenarios can be defined. The *baseline scenario* assumes that, by 2020, the middle levels specified are reached in all rates of couple formation and dissolution; that is, marriage, transformation, and dehabitation are assumed to decline and cohabitation and divorce are assumed to increase (see *Table 4.18*). The *marriage scenario* assumes that marriage is favored. Marriage and cohabitation rates remain constant. Transformation rates still decline rapidly but only to their maximum 60 percent level. Divorce increases to 120 percent, and dehabitation declines to 90 percent. The *cohabitation scenario* assumes exactly the opposite: cohabitation is favored. Marriage, transformation, and dehabitation decline to their minimum levels, while cohabitation and divorce increase to their maximum. These three scenarios form the core of the projection analysis; they define a plausible range of future union-status distributions.

In addition, a number of alternative scenarios are specified, mostly for comparative reasons. The *1990 rates scenario* assumes that all transition rates remain constant at their 1990 level. This is not a likely scenario since it ignores expected future changes, but it shows how much change is already embodied in the current structure of the Swedish population and current levels of transition rates. To investigate the effects of the 1989 marriage peak, the *1985 rates scenario* assumes constant 1985 rates of couple formation and dissolution, neglecting the developments between 1985 and 1990.

The effects of a number of transitions are also explored. The *low rates scenario* assumes that by 2020 the rates of all transitions reach their minimum level, that is, forming and dissolving unions are relatively rare. The *high rates scenario* assumes that they reach their maximum levels; hence, transitions are frequent. Finally, the *no marriage scenario* assumes that all unions are entered through cohabitation and that direct marriage rates of singles reach zero by the year 2000. The number of cohabitations is increased accordingly. Other assumptions in this last scenario are the same as those in the *baseline scenario*; hence, this scenario is a plausible extreme case scenario.

4.5.2 Scenario results

The union-status distribution of the Swedish population is likely to change substantially in the coming decades. The projected distribution of the population aged 15 to 64 is given by gender in *Table 4.19* for 1985, 2000, and 2020. The five most relevant scenarios are selected.

The proportion living single continues to increase somewhat – by some 2 to 4 percentage points; in other words, the proportion of the population living in unions continues to decline. This is mostly due to the high and, in the case of divorce, still increasing rates of couple dissolution that lead to longer periods of single life. The differences between scenarios are negligible. Scenarios, however, do differ with respect to the form couples choose for their union. Under the baseline scenario, for example, the proportion of married

Table 4.19. Union-status distribution of the population aged 15 to 64 by gender, in 1985, 2000, and 2020.

Scenario	Year	Swedish women (in %)			Swedish men (in %)		
		Cohabit.	Married	Single	Cohabit.	Married	Single
Observed	1985	14	50	36	14	45	41
Baseline	2000	21	43	36	20	39	41
scenario	2020	30	31	39	29	44	27
Marriage	2000	20	44	36	20	41	39
scenario	2020	27	34	39	25	45	30
Cohabitation	2000	21	43	36	41	21	38
scenario	2020	34	28	38	32	43	25
1990 rates	2000	20	44	36	19	41	40
scenario	2020	23	37	40	22	45	33
No marriage	2000	22	42	36	21	41	38
scenario	2020	33	27	40	32	45	23

women between ages 15 and 64 declines from 50 percent in 1985 to only 31 percent by 2020. At that time, every second couple in this age group would live in a consensual union. This development is not surprising, since all the trends described above and assumed under the baseline scenario point in this direction: marriage declines and divorce increases, and, at the same time, transformation and dehabitation of consensual unions become less frequent. If all transition rates stay at their 1990 level (1990 rates scenario), the proportion of married women in this age group would still decline to 37 percent by 2020. Under the scenario that favors marriage, this proportion declines to only 34 percent, mostly as a consequence of the increased likelihood of a continuation of a consensual union. This is even more likely the case under the cohabitation scenario; in this scenario the proportion of married women decreases to some 28 percent by 2020. Interestingly, the proportion of singles is lower in this scenario as compared with the marriage scenario. The no marriage scenario results in a trend similar to that in the cohabitation scenario; in the former scenario the higher rates of transformation and dehabitation are compensated by the higher cohabitation rates and the absence of direct marriages.

Other possible (and plausible) developments of consensual unions are shown in more detail in *Table 4.20*. The table distinguishes between the population aged 15–64 and the elderly population aged 65 and over; the total number of consensual unions and their proportion among all unions are given.

Under all scenarios, the number of consensual unions increases remarkably. Under the baseline scenario, it more than doubles in the 15–64 age group (from

Table 4.20. Total number of cohabiting couples and proportions of consensual unions among all unions, by large age groups in 1985, 2000, and 2020.

Scenario	Year	Number of cohabiting couples (in 1,000)		Proportion of consensual unions (in %)	
		Ages 15–64	Ages 65+	Ages 15–64	Ages 65+
Observed	1985	378	12	22.2	3.7
Baseline	2000	554	22	32.5	6.5
scenario	2020	761	64	48.9	16.1
Marriage	2000	542	21	31.8	6.4
scenario	2020	680	57	44.2	14.4
Cohabitation	2000	565	22	33.1	6.6
scenario	2020	852	72	54.1	18.1
1990 rates	2000	529	21	31.1	6.3
scenario	2020	597	52	39.0	13.1
1985 rates	2000	521	21	30.5	6.4
scenario	2020	550	50	35.3	12.5
No marriage	2000	585	22	34.4	6.6
scenario	2020	850	70	55.6	17.7

378,000 in 1985 to 761,000 by 2020) and increases more than fivefold among the elderly (from 12,000 to 64,000). These figures correspond to 48.9 and 16.1 percent of the total number of unions, respectively, compared with 22.2 and 3.7 percent in 1985. Even under the unrealistic 1990 rates scenario the number of consensual unions would increase by 60 percent among the 15–64 age group and even fourfold among the elderly group.

Interestingly, notwithstanding the enormous marriage peak in 1989, for 2000 the difference between the 1990 rates scenario and the 1985 rates scenario is very small. The projected number of consensual unions is even slightly higher under the 1990 rates scenario. This is due to the continued decline in transformation rates and the continued increase in divorce rates between 1985 and 1990, which – already by the turn of the century – has more than compensated the effects of the 1989 marriage peak. Trends in the elderly population are only slightly influenced by changes in rates but are largely determined by the current population structure.

Among the population aged 15 to 64, the number of consensual unions is projected to vary from 680,000 (or 44.2 percent of all unions) under the marriage scenario to 852,000 (or 54.1 percent) under the cohabitation scenario in 2020. The difference between these two extremes, the marriage and the co-habitation scenarios, is explained by a combination of contrasting assumptions in all major transition rates. Varying transformation rates have the strongest

Table 4.21. Annual number of couple formations and couple dissolutions, in 1,000 in 1985, 2000 and 2020.

Scenario	Year	Marriage	Cohabit.	Transform.	Divorce	Dehabit.
Observed	1985	11	77	28	20	32
Baseline	2000	10	74	26	18	34
scenario	2020	9	74	22	15	37
Marriage	2000	11	73	26	18	35
scenario	2020	11	73	23	14	40
Cohabitation	2000	10	75	25	20	33
scenario	2020	6	75	19	15	33
1990 rates	2000	11	73	29	18	36
scenario	2020	11	74	30	15	40
No marriage	2000	0	84	28	17	36
scenario	2020	0	83	24	12	41
Low rates	2000	10	73	25	18	33
scenario	2020	6	70	18	12	31
High rates	2000	11	75	27	20	35
scenario	2020	11	79	25	18	43

impact; they account for 39 percent of the difference between the two scenarios. Dehabitation rates and marriage/cohabitation rates have approximately the same impact, or 22 percent each, while 17 percent of the difference is due to different divorce assumptions.

Another interesting result of the scenario analysis is the projected annual number of couple formations and dissolutions; these findings are given in *Table 4.21*, again for the years 1985, 2000, and 2020. These numbers depend on the level of the rates assumed in the scenario as well as on the respective population distribution across union status. For example, transformation, dehabitation, and divorce rates are identical under the baseline and the no marriage scenarios, but – due to the larger number of consensual unions and the lower number of marital unions – in the latter scenario we find a larger number of transformations and dehabitations and a lower number of divorces.

With a few exceptions, the total number of couple formations and dissolutions declines. The number of transformations declines under all scenarios – except in the 1990 rates scenario – albeit there are significant increases in the total number of cohabiting couples; this is a consequence of the assumed rapid decline in transformation rates. The number of dehabitations, however, increases under all scenarios; the decline assumed in dehabitation rates is not strong enough to compensate the increase in the projected number of consensual unions.

The number of newly formed cohabitations declines slightly in all scenarios, except in the no marriage scenario, where all direct marriages are replaced by cohabitations. The number of marriages declines or remains unchanged under the marriage and the 1990 rates scenarios, and the number of divorces declines significantly under all scenarios.

The assumptions in the low and high rates scenarios are not necessarily realistic, but it is interesting to discuss the effects of relatively frequent and infrequent couple formations and dissolutions. First, the large number of couple dissolutions in the high rates scenario surpasses the large number of couple formations; the projected proportion of singles in the high rates scenario exceeds the respective proportion obtained under the baseline scenario. Second, the results from the low rates scenario show not only larger proportions living in unions, but – among those living in unions – a significantly higher proportion of cohabitants (between the levels obtained in the baseline and the cohabitation scenarios). The low number of transformations and dehabitations has a significantly stronger effect on the stability of consensual unions than the low number of divorces on the stability of marital unions.

A major finding of this projection exercise is the robustness of results over these scenarios with quite different assumptions on the future development of couple formation and dissolution rates. But do these scenario assumptions indeed cover the possible range of future trends? Are other developments equally likely? And, would alternative trends alter the projection results significantly?

It seems that the scenario assumptions cover, at least, the most plausible future range. Other developments, which also seem possible, would be sudden increases in marriage and especially transformation rates due to political intervention, similar to the events in December 1989. However, the calculations show that such an unexpected short-term revival of marriage would not significantly alter the long-term trends in marriage and cohabitation. At most, it would delay the trends. Differences between the 1985 rates and the 1990 rates scenarios are evident until 1995, but diminish as early as the turn of the century.

A totally different development, contrary to what has been observed in Sweden during the past three decades, would be a revival of marriage over the long term. However, given the postulated irreversibility of the partnership transition, such a revival could only result from a major societal, political, or legal adjustment. Under such circumstances the partnership transition would increasingly take place within marriage because the society and the legislature had already reacted. In this case, the projections in *Tables 4.20* and *4.21* are still relevant since they tell us when the partnership transition – be it within marriage or through increased cohabitation – would be completed. The projected proportion of consensual unions would then mainly indicate future, general developments in partnerships.

At this time, a major change in society is not evident, and the trends suggested by the model results are likely to continue. In Sweden, and elsewhere, the legal treatment of cohabitation is still extremely unsatisfactory. The calculations, therefore, indicate that there is a real need for society and for the legislature to react; this need exists today but increases substantially in the future. The nuclear family is likely to continue to be popular in the twenty-first century, but changes in the needs and demands of couples in a rapidly changing society mean that an ever-increasing proportion of the population would live outside a reasonable and often necessary legal frame. Sensible political reactions to these future trends are discussed in Chapter 5, in particular in Section 5.2.2.

4.5.3   Period versus cohort perspective

Thus far only results for large age groups for the period from 1990 to 2020 have been described. For the baseline scenario, *Figure 4.4* presents the percentage of women living in consensual unions as a proportion of women living in all unions, by five-year age group. Projected proportions for the years 2010, 2030, and 2050 are compared with observed values for the years 1975 and 1985. The figures for the years 2030 and 2050 are given to show the long-term impact of the scenario.[26] In 1975, cohabitation was frequent at young ages, but almost nonexistent among women aged 30 and over. By 1985 cohabitation had become more widespread at all ages, but with very little increases beyond age 60. Over all age groups, the proportion of consensual unions increased from 11 percent in 1975 to 19 percent in 1985.

If trends continue as assumed under the baseline scenario, consensual unions will become even more popular in the future: 35 percent by 2010, 48 percent by 2030, and 54 percent by 2050 of all couples will live together without being legally married. Between 1985 and 2010, the largest increase is projected to be among 30- to 50-year-old women. By 2030 the largest increases are found among women beyond childbearing age. Among 15- to 35-year-old women, a stable level is reached by 2030; ultimate stable levels for all age groups – under the assumption of no further changes in transition rates after 2020 – are reached between 2050 and 2060. At that time, the proportion living in consensual unions is estimated to be at 40 percent even among women in their 60s and 70s.

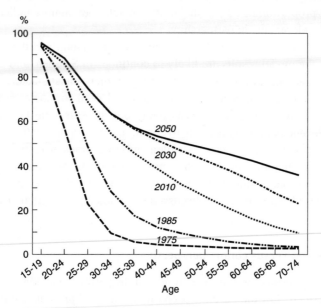

Figure 4.4. Proportion of women in consensual unions among all women living in unions, by age, from 1975 to 2050.

Table 4.22. Age-specific cohabitation sequence ratios and respective Gini coefficients, period data from 1975 to 2050.

Age group	1975	1980	1985	1990	1995	2000	2005	2010	2030	2050
Cohabitation sequence ratio from one age group to the subsequent age group										
15–19	0.64	0.76	0.84	0.82	0.84	0.86	0.89	0.91	0.93	0.93
20–24	0.40	0.54	0.62	0.62	0.67	0.72	0.76	0.80	0.85	0.85
25–29	0.42	0.49	0.58	0.56	0.63	0.70	0.75	0.79	0.85	0.85
30–34	0.59	0.57	0.62	0.66	0.73	0.78	0.81	0.84	0.89	0.90
35–39	0.79	0.72	0.69	0.76	0.80	0.82	0.83	0.84	0.91	0.93
40–44	0.89	0.81	0.79	0.80	0.81	0.82	0.82	0.82	0.91	0.95
45–49	0.90	0.82	0.79	0.82	0.83	0.83	0.83	0.83	0.91	0.95
50–54	0.86	0.83	0.77	0.79	0.80	0.80	0.80	0.80	0.90	0.95
55–59	0.93	0.81	0.82	0.77	0.77	0.77	0.77	0.77	0.87	0.94
60–64	1.00	0.90	0.83	0.84	0.81	0.79	0.78	0.78	0.83	0.92
65–69	1.00	0.91	0.90	0.86	0.82	0.80	0.79	0.78	0.83	0.92
Gini coefficient of sequence ratios										
Gini	0.132	0.096	0.068	0.061	0.038	0.023	0.017	0.015	0.018	0.018

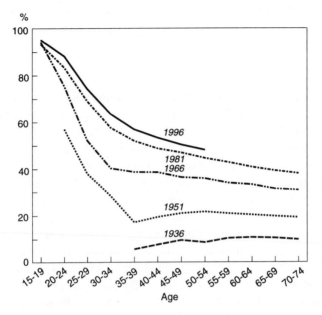

Figure 4.5. Proportion of women in consensual unions among all women living in unions, by age. Data have been arranged according to birth cohort.

Table 4.23. Age-specific cohabitation sequence ratios and respective Gini coefficients, cohort-arranged data for birth cohorts from 1931 to 1996.

Age group	1931– 1935	1941– 1945	1951– 1955	1956– 1960	1961– 1965	1966– 1970	1971– 1975	1976– 1980	1986– 1990	1996– 2000
Cohabitation sequence ratio from one age group to the subsequent age group										
15–19	–	–	–	0.80	0.85	0.80	0.85	0.87	0.91	0.93
20–24	–	–	0.67	0.69	0.59	0.69	0.74	0.79	0.83	0.84
25–29	–	–	0.75	0.53	0.71	0.77	0.82	0.86	0.85	0.85
30–34	–	1.12	0.61	0.94	0.95	0.96	0.96	0.89	0.90	0.90
35–39	–	1.13	1.13	1.06	1.02	1.00	0.93	0.94	0.95	0.94
40–44	1.40	0.87	1.08	1.02	0.98	0.94	0.97	0.96	0.94	0.94
45–49	1.21	1.24	1.03	0.99	0.98	0.98	0.95	0.97	0.96	0.95
50–54	0.91	1.07	0.96	0.97	0.96	0.95	0.97	0.95	0.95	–
55–59	1.17	0.97	0.97	0.97	0.97	0.98	0.95	0.96	0.96	–
60–64	1.06	0.94	0.97	0.97	0.96	0.94	0.97	0.95	–	–
65–69	0.98	1.00	0.97	0.97	0.97	0.98	0.95	0.97	–	–
Gini coefficient of sequence ratios										
Gini	–	–	0.088	0.073	0.063	0.046	0.034	0.028	–	–

A particularly useful supplement to the analysis is the study of the behavior of Swedish birth cohorts. Data for the period from 1975 to 1990 give only limited cohort information; however, age-specific projections can be estimated for a number of cohorts if we consider long-term future trends. *Figure 4.5* also gives the percentage of women in consensual unions as a proportion of all unions, but this time rearranged by birth cohort. Three conclusions can be drawn. First, the age relationship found with period data is strongly confirmed from the cohort perspective; the pattern looks very much the same in both figures. Second, among the oldest birth cohorts the proportion of consensual unions even increases with age; a fact that strongly supports the notion of cohabitation as a period phenomenon. Third, cohort trends follow the same pattern as period trends; changes in the function of cohabitation suggested by the partnership transition seem to hold under the cohort perspective.

From the age-specific proportions living in consensual unions we can determine cohabitation sequence ratios and their equality, which can be used as a single summary indicator in the course of the proposed partnership transition. These calculations were performed using period data (*Table 4.22*) and using cohort-arranged data (*Table 4.23*). By 2030, every second union is a consensual and dehabitation rates are almost as low as divorce rates; thus, cohabitation will certainly have become a type of marriage.[27] A major question arises: What will be the difference between marriage and cohabitation by that time? This question is taken up in Chapter 5. In this chapter we investigate whether inequality between cohabitation sequence ratios continues to decline, as hypothesized in Chapter 3.

The trend toward equal cohabitation sequence ratios, clearly evident between 1975 and 1985, continues until 2010, when all sequence ratios – except for the first – are in the narrow range between 0.77 and 0.84 (see *Table 4.22*). The Gini coefficient, which is used to measure equality/inequality of sequence ratios, declined from 0.132 in 1975 to 0.068 in 1985; it declines further to only 0.015 by the year 2010 if the assumptions of the baseline scenario materialize. After 2010 projected sequence ratios continue to increase beyond 0.92 and become nearly the same at almost all ages; this theory was put forward in Chapter 3. On the other hand, the sequence ratios remain significantly lower at ages 25 to 30, the main childbearing ages (where the sequence ratio stabilizes at a level around 0.85). Under this scenario, even by the year 2050 transforming a consensual union into marriage would be more likely at age 30 than at any other age. Therefore, the Gini coefficient does not decline further after the year 2010.

The data in *Table 4.23* support the conclusions found on the basis of period data: Gini coefficients gradually decline from 0.088 for the birth cohort of 1951–1955 to 0.028 for the birth cohort of 1976–1980. Cohort data show the same drop in sequence ratios at age 30, and they show that beyond age 40 very few consensual unions are transformed into marriage.

It seems that the level of equality of the sequence ratios reached between 2030 and 2050 is so high, or Gini coefficients so low, that – purely judged from the analysis of proportions living in consensual unions – the partnership transition might be considered completed.

Notes

[1] These data sets, available for the years 1980, 1985, and 1990, were generated and kindly provided by Åke Nilsson and Håkån Sellerfors from the Population Unit of Statistics Sweden, S-70189 Örebro, Sweden.

[2] These are just some of the problems that arise from the use of surveys or from the combination of census and vital statistics information, see Prinz *et al.* (1995).

[3] To be more explicit: if a man and a woman declare on the census form that they live in a consensual union at the time of the census and if they have moved from different addresses to a joint address during the year before the census, this move is registered as a formation of a consensual union. Dissolutions of consensual unions are obtained analogously.

[4] Nilsson (1992) reports that propaganda for marriage came from various sides: from trade unions, from the church (which organized mass weddings), and, in particular, from local newspapers.

[5] Both cohabitants must specify on the census form that they live in the same flat and that they live in a consensual union.

[6] Throughout this study, only the census estimates are analyzed.

[7] For the projection period 1985 to 1990, constant 1985 fertility, mortality, couple formation, and couple dissolution rates were applied to the population structure. Additional projection results for longer time horizons and with alternative assumptions are undertaken and discussed in Section 4.5.

[8] These calculations confirm the observation that almost all additional marriages registered in December 1989 were contracted by cohabiting couples.

[9] Due to limited data in many European countries, the sequence ratios in Chapter 3 are only calculated over broad age groups (from ages 15–24 to ages 55–64). In this section, however, five-year age group data from ages 15–19 up to ages 70–74 are used. Hence, Gini coefficients measure the equality over 11 sequence ratios. As a consequence, the results in this section are somewhat more elaborate, and they cannot directly be compared with those given in Chapter 3.

[10] See Section 4.3.1. for more details on fertility among married, cohabiting, and single women.

[11] These results were derived from interviews with a subsample of the 1985 Employment Survey.

[12] These results were derived from the 1977 Norwegian fertility survey.

[13] These results were derived from the 1981 Swedish fertility survey.

[14] In this case, the sum of the married and the cohabiting populations – which are very different in age structures – is taken as the standard age distribution.

[15] Remember that only ages 25 to 40 are included here; over this age spectrum consensual union fertility is slightly higher than marital fertility when measured in comparative fertility figures.

[16] The corresponding total fertility rate for the year 1990 is slightly higher, 2.14 children, because the fertility table underestimates the number of children among women with more than four children.

[17] As in Chapter 2, direct standardization with the total population as standard is used.

[18] Since this study focuses on Europe, the American literature is not considered.

[19] Standardization is carried out separately for each year and gender.

[20] Standardization is again carried out separately for each year and gender.

[21] In this data set, duration of consensual unions is only known for the past five years.

[22] It should be noted that in this model no difference is made between voluntary dissolutions of cohabiting couples and involuntary dissolutions caused by the death of the cohabiting partner; the number of dehabitations is an aggregate measure of both. This model simplification was necessary since the Swedish data are not further disaggregated. Also, due to the age structure of cohabitants the number of involuntary dissolutions of consensual unions is extremely low.

[23] Brackets in the fifth consistency requirement mean that all three states of divorces should be added but in the Swedish data set only the first type (Div_m) exists.

[24] As a matter of fact, since current fertility levels are very high (around replacement level) and since external migration is ignored, future total population size is projected to remain virtually constant.

[25] Keeping the sum of the annual number of all marriages and cohabitations constant is a reasonable assumption. As already today most new unions are entered through cohabitation, a 40 percent decline in marriage rates corresponds to a 10 percent increase in cohabitation rates.

[26] To obtain results beyond 2020, all transitions rates (marriage, cohabitation, transformation, divorce, and dehabitation) are kept constant at the level specified in the baseline scenario for the year 2020.

[27] I have not compared the long-term changes in fertility and mortality of cohabiting couples and married couples, but it seems likely that differences will continue to diminish in these indicators.

Chapter 5

The Future of Marital Status and Union Status

This final chapter is a comprehensive synthesis and conclusion of the findings presented in the previous chapters. It has two main parts. The first part compares the results obtained in Chapters 2 and 4. On the basis of Swedish data and calculations, it illustrates to what extent marital-status analyses and projections lead to biased or even wrong conclusions, and the reasons why union-status analyses and projections are more appropriate.

The second part deals with future challenges. To make union-status analyses of countries other than Sweden, the quality of data on cohabitation must be improved. This can be done either through the development of new estimation techniques or, more comprehensively, through a principal change in the registration of couples. Both solutions are discussed.

5.1 Marital Status Versus Union Status

Chapters 2 and 4 give a detailed description both of demographic differentials and of population projections by marital status and union status, respectively. While it is obvious that the inclusion of consensual unions alters the conclusions from Chapter 2 significantly, it is not yet clear which conclusions still hold and which are wrong or at least misleading. Findings regarding demographic differentials, as well as population projections, obtained in Chapters 2 and 4 are discussed and compared in this section. All results refer to Sweden.

5.1.1 Status-specific analysis

The analysis of marital-status differentials in fertility and mortality and of marriage and divorce trends in Chapter 2 gives an incomplete and extremely distorted picture of society and its underlying processes. The union-status-specific analysis for Sweden in Chapter 4 further investigates many of the surprising findings in Chapter 2 and indeed draws a very different conclusion from the current developments in Europe.

Fertility

According to Chapter 2, marital fertility declined between 1963 and 1985 by some 28 percent, on average, for the 10 countries included in this study, while fertility among unmarried women increased by some 50 percent, on average. Hence, nonmarital fertility increased remarkably in relation to marital fertility. We can assume that these trends are a consequence of changes in fertility rates among cohabiting women. From this development it is difficult to envision the impacts on future overall fertility levels in the countries of Europe. During the 1980s changes in overall fertility were, to a large extent, caused by changes in the populations' marital-status composition. In this period, marital fertility did not decline any further in many countries, but, because the proportion of unmarried women in childbearing ages increased rapidly, overall fertility continued to decline. Population projections by marital status forecast a strong decline in the proportion of married women in the future. But will fertility continue its rapid decline?

The fertility analysis in Chapter 4 shows that in a country such as Sweden, where the proposed partnership transition is well advanced and cohabitation is accepted as a permanent alternative to marriage, fertility outside marriage may become the norm. At a certain stage of transition the level of consensual-union fertility is expected to be equal to the level of marital fertility. The fertility cycle of the partnership transition has several phases. In the first phase, consensual unions become accepted as a prelude to marriage; fertility among cohabiting women is very low. Overall fertility decreases; the extent of this decrease depends on the popularity of consensual unions during this phase. In the second phase, consensual unions become accepted as an alternative to marriage; now fertility among cohabiting women increases, both in absolute terms and, more importantly, relative to marital fertility. Part of this phase was observed in Sweden between 1985 and 1990. During this second phase the impact on overall fertility largely depends on the speed of increase in consensual-union fertility in relation to the speed of the continuing increase in the popularity of consensual unions. Eventually, overall fertility should increase again, but it could continue to decline – although this decline should slow down – before the changes in population composition allow fertility to increase.

For a number of reasons the extent of decline and subsequent increase in overall fertility can strongly differ from country to country. A decisive factor in this context is the rate of changes in society, in particular regarding the changing roles of women and men, changes in norms and attitudes, and changes in legislation. For example, the faster cohabitation and, in particular, out-of-marital-union births are accepted by the society and taken into account by legislation, the slower the decline will be in overall fertility during the first phase. The example of Sweden shows that there are several other reasons for overall fertility to decline or to increase. In the context of period fertility, the timing of birth has the greatest influence; innumerable social and economic reasons can influence fertility behavior – for example, the availability of child-care facilities or expected child-care costs. In many cases these factors are stronger than the fertility cycle resulting from the partnership-transition hypothesis. The overall fertility increase in Sweden between 1985 and 1990 was caused largely by an unexpected increase in fertility rates among all groups of women, and only to a small extent by the overproportional increase in fertility among cohabiting women.

Eventually, the fertility level of cohabiting women may be as high as that of married women. There could, however, be quite significant differences and therefore changes in fertility distribution or concentration. From the 1990 parity-specific fertility data for Sweden it has been predicted that a significantly large proportion of cohabiting women may remain childless and, among cohabiting women with children, a large proportion may have three or more children. These projections indicate a development toward a heterogeneous society in which some women specialize in childbearing and others in working outside the home.

One very important aspect must be added to the analysis, namely, the increase in the number and proportion of single women in childbearing ages projected with the Swedish data. This increase, which started in Sweden during the 1970s, is likely to take place in all of Europe. Since, throughout Europe fertility among single women is very low, this shift in the union-status distribution could cause a further decline in overall fertility levels. Childlessness among single women in Sweden in 1990 was at least 60 percent.

In conclusion, union-status-specific fertility analysis is important in order to understand ongoing changes in fertility behavior in the societies of Europe and to project possible changes in fertility. Marital-status-specific fertility analysis gives an incomplete picture of the situation in most European countries. Also in countries with still lower levels of cohabitation the composition of the unmarried states is changing rapidly, making union-status-specific analysis indispensable.

Mortality

With regard to mortality the most striking findings in Chapter 2 are that excess mortality of the unmarried population has increased at all ages during the past two decades, more pronounced among women, and that there are amazing similarities in both the levels of and the changes in excess mortality among the countries. Mortality of unmarried men and women is, respectively, 50 percent and 30 percent higher than among their married counterparts.

In most countries the proportion married has declined; hence, the unmarried population should have become a less selective group. Among those unmarried the proportion living in a consensual union has increased. Why then has excess mortality of unmarried people increased? Shouldn't we rather see a decline in excess mortality of these groups? Neither the selection nor the protection theory seems to provide an explanation. Marital-status differentials in mortality have gained in significance, but at the same time marital-status-specific mortality analysis fails to explain why.

Union-status-specific mortality analysis succeeds in resolving these contradictory findings. In Sweden, during the 1980s mortality declined in all groups of the population. In relation to overall mortality improvements, however, quite significant conclusions can be drawn. Mortality rates among singles declined only very modestly, while these rates declined significantly among both married and cohabiting couples. In all cases these developments over time are a consequence of changes in the composition of the union-status subgroups or, to put it differently, due to shifts in boundaries between the three groups.

The group of cohabitants grew and became a less select group of the population than it was before. The share of permanent consensual unions increased and therefore the share of the deviant group declined. As a consequence, the decline of mortality rates of cohabiting couples was steeper than average. Similarly, the group of married couples became smaller and more homogeneous than it was before. Those couples with relatively high death risks chose cohabitation; hence, the decline of mortality rates among married couples was also steeper than average. Relative to each other, however, mortality rates among married and cohabiting couples did not change significantly. The group of singles also became markedly larger during the 1980s. This increase signified that in 1990 a large proportion of this group was made up of individuals who chose to remain single to keep their established lifestyle. Therefore, excess mortality of singles in relation to that of married individuals increased from 18 percent in 1980 to 35 percent in 1990 among women and from 53 percent to 68 percent among men over the same time period.

How do these changes in union-status mortality differentials explain the increase in excess mortality of the unmarried group obtained from marital-status-specific analysis? In Sweden, cohabitants are still a minority among the group of all unmarried individuals, in particular among the elderly who account for most of the difference in mortality differentials when measured by age-standardized comparative mortality figures. For all unmarried groups taken together, the increase in excess mortality of singles more than compensated the changes in excess mortality of cohabitants; relative to the mortality of married persons, the mortality rates of cohabitants have almost remained unchanged. Excess mortality of the unmarried population can be expected to continue its increase in all countries providing that the proportion of singles increases. However, even if the proportion of couples remains unchanged, the increase in cohabitation would not lead to a decline in excess mortality of the unmarried group simply because of increasing homogeneity of the group of married couples. Only if the proportion of cohabiting couples increases at the expense of singles rather than at the expense of married couples, could the excess mortality of the unmarried group decline.

The theories that healthy individuals are selected to marry and that married couples are better protected than singles have to be reconsidered. Selection of healthier persons into marriage is no longer an appropriate explanation, particularly considering the changes in mortality differentials over recent decades. We can, however, discuss the selection of one or the other type of union. Those who remain relatively independent when forming a union select cohabitation, while others select marriage. There is, of course, a certain overlap between the two groups, mostly because the meaning of marriage itself is also changing. Marriage seems to offer better protection to couples than cohabitation. All couples are protected by having a partner, but more so if they choose legal marriage. In this context it would be interesting to compare mortality rates of couples by union duration, in particular to see whether a significant difference in mortality rates exists between couples cohabiting for two years and couples cohabiting for ten years (temporary versus permanent cohabitation).

In contrast to fertility, overall mortality is only slightly influenced by a population's marital- and union-status compositions. If the single proportion, in particular among the elderly, continues to increase, as has been projected for Sweden, this increase will certainly have an effect on overall mortality levels, but this effect is negligible in relation to all other effects resulting from medical improvements or changes in health systems. The analysis of union-status-specific mortality, however, is very important for the exploration of the partnership transition and of changes in the formation and living arrangements of couples. The point at which people balance their need for "individuation" or personal separateness with their need for identification as a couple has a distinct impact on the type of union chosen, on the union's stability, and ultimately on the mortality of the partners in the union.

Formation and Dissolution of Unions

Chapter 2 points out that large shifts in marital-status dynamics have been observed in recent decades in all countries of Europe: marriage intensities declined by some 30 percent, on average, between 1960 and 1985 and divorce intensities increased by some 250 percent, on average, during the same period. Again taking the average of the 10 countries in this study, by the mid-1980s the proportion ever marrying had declined to 77 percent among men and 83 percent among women, with one out of four marriages ending in divorce. In Sweden, the most extreme case, the proportion ever marrying was even 15 percentage points lower and the proportion of marriages ending in divorce 10 percentage points higher. But what do these levels and changes tell us about actual rates of couple formation and dissolution? Has the propensity to form a family declined? Do the observed levels in divorce reflect the instability of today's relationships?

The Swedish data show that there is little similarity between trends in marriage and divorce, on the one hand, and trends in couple formation and dissolution, on the other hand. Traditional marriage and divorce statistics give no information about the length of single life (living alone) or about actual union stability. The number of couple formations changed relatively little between 1960 and 1990. In Sweden it even increased among those aged 35 years and over, while there was practically no change among young adults. The increase in couple formation rates above age 35 was largely caused by the increasing number of higher-order unions, which in turn is a result of the declining stability of unions in general. The low estimate of the proportion ever marrying is hardly of any relevance, since the proportion ever cohabiting exceeds 80 percent. The data for 1985 show that the proportion ever cohabiting or marrying in Sweden is more than 90 percent. First marriages and, in particular, remarriages have often been replaced by permanent cohabitation. In 1985, more than 85 percent of Swedes forming a second- or higher-order union preferred cohabitation to marriage.

While marriage data strongly underestimate the propensity to form a union, divorce data – which already give very high rates – overestimate actual union stability. Consensual unions, rapidly increasing in number, are clearly less stable than marital unions. According to life-table calculations based on 1985 rates, about every third marriage in Sweden ends in divorce, but every second consensual union ends in dehabitation. Among those cohabitations that are not dissolved, most are transformed into marriages with relatively high levels of dissolution risks. If couple formation and dissolution rates remain constant, only 10 percent of all consensual unions but almost 70 percent of all marital unions would continue until the death of one of the partners. Sweden has the highest divorce rate among all European countries, and its couple dissolution rate is even higher. In 1990, 80 percent of all couples lived in a marital union; however, less than half of all couple dissolutions were covered in legal divorce statistics, simply because dehabitation rates are so much higher. Commitment to the union has obviously declined, at least in the sense that it is no longer regarded as necessary to remain in a troubled union. This development means that a rapidly increasing number of children experience a family dissolution. The Swedish data set used in this study does not distinguish between consensual unions with children and those without; however, according to Nilsson (1992) dissolution rates of couples without children are only some 15 to 20 percent higher than those of couples with one child. Considering marriages and consensual unions by number of children between ages 0 and 17, dehabitation rates are still 2.5 to 3 times higher than divorce rates.

It is difficult to speculate on future rates of couple formation and dissolution in the context of the proposed partnership transition. Obviously one hypothesis is that the nuclear family is not threatened; hence, rates of couple formation are likely to change very little. However, these rates are also strongly influenced by the prevalence of divorce and dehabitation. Further increases in the rates of couple dissolution are probable since freedom and independence within partnership will certainly continue to grow.

People will continue to need a sense of togetherness to be able to express their sense of individuality, but this function can probably be fulfilled by successive partners. In the course of the partnership transition, major shifts in the size of dissolution rates will be relative to each other. If the group of cohabitants continues to grow rapidly, dehabitation risks will continue to decline relative to the rates of divorce. Nevertheless, overall couple instability is likely to increase. If the number of couple dissolutions increases, the number of couple formations is likely to increase also, because the propensity to form a union, either marital or consensual, is much higher among those who have dissolved an earlier union.

Heterogeneity in society, with some groups of the population forming and dissolving unions easily and frequently and other groups trying to keep a permanent union, will probably increase.

5.1.2 Status-specific models and projections

According to the four-state marital-status model the distribution of the Swedish population is expected to change markedly. The proportion of married people will decline, corresponding to the increases in the proportion of never-married young adults and the proportion of divorced among the elderly. This development, however, does not tell us anything about the number and proportion of people living as a single or in a union. In addition, in a number of circumstances this marital-status model fails to project the future marital-status distribution and the number of births.

Tables 5.1 and *5.2* show that there are several limitations in the marital-status model. They give projected proportions of Swedish women aged 15 to 64 by marital and union status and the estimated number of births obtained from the marital-status model (*Table 5.1*) and from the union-status model (*Table 5.2*) for the year 2020. Four very simple alternative scenarios are used: the first scenario (constant rates) assumes constant 1985 rates in all couple formation and dissolution rates; the second scenario (marriage decline) assumes that marriage rates of singles and cohabitants decline by 50 percent until 2020; the third scenario (transformation decline) assumes that only the marriage rates of cohabitants (that is, transformation rates) decline by 50 percent until 2020; and the fourth scenario (dehabitation decline) assumes that the rates of dehabitation of consensual unions decline by 50 percent. Fertility and mortality rates are again kept constant throughout the period.

The marital-status model produces a tremendous decline in the married proportion but does not hint at the development of the proportion of singles or couples. It can only project the future legal marital-status distribution if parallel changes in couple formation intensities in all marital-status subgroups are assumed, such as under the constant rates scenario (with no changes) or the marriage decline scenario. These assumptions are restrictive and do not mirror recent developments in Sweden, with very high and rapidly declining

Table 5.1. Selected results from the marital-status model in 1985 and 2020.

	Proportion of women aged 15 to 64 by status					Total number
Scenario	Never married	Divorced	Married	Single	Cohab-iting	of births (1985 = 100)
Distribution in 1985	36	11	50	36	14	100
Distribution in 2020						
Constant rates	50	10	39	–	–	90
Marriage decline	65	8	26	–	–	80
		100		100		

Table 5.2. Selected results from the union-status model, 1985 and 2020.

	Proportion of women aged 15 to 64 by status					Total number
Scenario	Never married	Divorced	Married	Single	Cohab-iting	of births (1985 = 100)
Distribution in 1985	36	11	50	36	14	100
Distribution in 2020						
Constant rates	50	10	40	38	22	90
Marriage decline	64	9	27	42	31	84
Transformation decline	60	9	30	41	29	87
Dehabitation decline	48	10	41	34	25	97
		100		100		

marriage rates among cohabitants (transformation rates) and low and slowly changing marriage rates among singles.

Even if the legal marital-status distribution is projected correctly under the marriage decline scenario, the number of births is significantly underestimated (compare *Tables 5.1* and *5.2*). The reason for this is that with the marital-status model the strong marriage decline leads to an increase in the proportion of unmarried women who have notably lower fertility rates than married women. With the union-status model, however, the decline in marriage leads to a large proportion of cohabiting women who already have relatively high fertility. Hence, the estimated number of births and, consequently, the estimated population size are significantly biased with the marital-status model, even under the simple marriage decline scenario.

More importantly, many of the relevant changes in couple formation and dissolution rates cannot be incorporated into the marital-status model. *Table 5.2* shows that changes in transformation and dehabitation rates – which are not an element of the marital-status model – have a strong effect on the legal marital-status distribution and, hence, on the number of births and on population size. The data analysis in Chapter 4 shows that these transformation and dehabitation rates are declining rapidly in Sweden today. Furthermore, the dehabitation decline scenario, which assumes a change within legal marital-status subgroups, projects that the proportion of single women could decline even as the unmarried proportion increases significantly. This result can only be obtained from a union-status model.

The conclusion is that, at least for a country such as Sweden, a union-status model is essential, not only to estimate the future union-status distribution but also to estimate the future marital-status distribution and future population size. For what purpose, then, is a legal marital-status model still useful? Is such a model, for example, still appropriate for a country where cohabitation is much less frequent than it is in Sweden?

The answer to the last question is no. Differences in marriage rates between singles and cohabitants are certainly as pronounced in other countries as in Sweden or – as is shown by declining differentials in Sweden during the 1980s – perhaps even more pronounced as long as cohabitation is the behavior of a minority. Also one can expect changes to be particularly strong when cohabitation changes from being a deviant phenomenon to being accepted as a prelude to marriage and further as an alternative to marriage. A major difference between Sweden and Italy, a country that is still in an early stage of transition, is the following. In Sweden cohabitation and marriage rates stabilize while the continuing increase in the proportion cohabiting results from an increasing durability of consensual unions in the form of declining dehabitation and transformation rates. Increases in the number of consensual unions in Italy are mostly a consequence of declining direct marriage and increasing cohabitation rates. In both cases a union-status model is needed to project the correct marital-status distribution.

A reliable estimate of the future marital-status distribution using the marital-status model is only obtained under constant rates assumptions, a situation that does not exist anywhere in Europe. Today couple formation and dissolution rates are changing more rapidly than fertility and mortality rates. Furthermore, even if the legal marital-status distribution can be projected correctly, it does not provide an accurate estimate about actual living arrangements in Europe.

There are only three situations under which the use of marital-status modeling is rational. First, it may be used as a preliminary step in a more complex analysis on union status. Second, it is helpful in international comparative studies where data limitations make using traditional concepts unavoidable; even in this situation, however, information on the legal marital-status distribution without additional data on the spread of consensual unions is not sufficient. The most relevant situation under which marital-status modeling is appropriate is in the context of problems related to the elderly. In many countries the proportion of cohabitants at ages 50 and over is small and will remain small in the near future; even in Sweden 95 percent of all couples in this age group are legally married. Also many legal regulations, such as the so-called survivor's pension benefits, are still based only on legal marital status; therefore, the use of marital-status projections are justified. However, it must be repeated that – due to the growing heterogeneity within groups of legal marital status – a reasonable marital-status projection requires a union-status model in most cases.

It is to be expected that in areas of policy concern, union status will increasingly replace the traditional *de jure* marital-status criterion. There are many reasons for analyses and projections of union status. Haskey and Kiernan (1989), for example, mention four major areas of interest: legal implications that concern the rights and responsibilities of cohabitants and of their children; state financial implications that include decisions about the payment of social security benefits; social policy implications that include the effects of national policies on families and households; and last, but not least, purely demographic implications.

5.2   Challenges for the Future

Much has been said about the limitations of marital-status analysis and modeling and the need to apply the proposed union-status concept. But, how should one use the union-status approach if the data do not allow even the simplest analysis or if information on consensual unions just does not exist? Researchers are frequently confronted with data that are unsuitable for use in models. Sometimes a simple approach must be taken to match data and models. In the present context, however, arguments for union-status modeling are overwhelming, and we therefore have to think of another solution: to adapt data to make union-status analysis and projections possible.

But how can the data be improved? In this section two totally different approaches are discussed: a technical and mathematical approach and a political and social approach. Given that the amount of data cannot be increased, data can only be improved by refining the estimation procedures. The second solution, straightforward in its objective, is to improve data collection itself; this, however, involves a number of political and legal issues.

5.2.1   Refined data estimation

Sweden is the only European country with adequate data on the formation and dissolution of consensual unions. To improve existing data sets in other European countries, two solutions seem viable: to develop techniques for estimating parameters of the union-status model from incomplete or missing data or to borrow information on union-status dynamics from other sources or countries.

Techniques to derive indirect data estimations for living-arrangement models from scarce data are comparable with indirect estimation techniques that attempt to measure values of basic demographic parameters in statistically underdeveloped countries or regions. In the field of mortality, for example, this problem was solved either by using model life tables (Coale and Demeny, 1983) or by developing other procedures based on data from censuses, surveys, or sample registration areas (Shryock *et al.*, 1976). Recently, methods have been developed to estimate events in family demography (Preston, 1987), but they have not been developed far enough to be used in this study.

In many cases this study has used only one cross-sectional observation on the current population structure, with no data on events or transitions. Under such circumstances, the only solution is to borrow information on transition probabilities from other sources. This does not necessarily mean that the model's behavior would be completely arbitrary. For a certain period the behavior of the system is more sensitive to the initial population structure than to the inputs describing the dynamics of the system. An important condition is that accurate information regarding the breakdown by union status of the population stock in the starting year is available. By experimenting with borrowed information (namely, assuming alternative scenarios) one may obtain a good estimate of possible future trends in union-status distribution.

The idea of borrowing information on dynamics from other sources, in this case from the Swedish data set, is applied in the following analysis. Substituting some of the existing Swedish flow estimates for missing flows in another country is particularly promising for countries that are similar to Sweden with regard to trends in cohabitation. Of the 10 countries in this study, the demographic indicators of Norway are closest to those of Sweden. In 1985 Norway ranked second after Sweden in level of cohabitation, and it has since experienced an enormous boom in consensual unions.

Several assumptions must be made to apply the Swedish data to the case of Norway. The calculation begins with the year 1985 for which a reliable estimate on the number of consensual unions in Norway is available from the

Table 5.3. Union-status distribution of Norwegian women and distribution of births in 1985, 2000, 2020, and 2050.

Scenario	Year	Proportion of single women		Consensual unions in % of all unions		Proportion of births	
		Ages 15–64	Ages 65+	Ages 15–64	Ages 65+	Mar.	Coh.
Observed	1985	31	61	10.9	0.7	73	14
Divorce and	2000	33	61	17.6	4.6	60	23
marriage rates	2020	34	58	19.7	9.1	59	23
remain constant	2050	34	65	20.0	13.1	59	23
Divorce and	2000	36	61	23.9	4.7	47	30
marriage rates	2020	38	61	28.4	11.3	46	33
at Swedish level	2050	39	68	29.1	18.5	46	33

Health Survey. The union-status structure of Norway in 1985 is estimated from the union-status distribution in 1980 (which is given in the 1980 census), the changes in marital status between 1980 and 1985, and the proportion of consensual unions in 1985. Norway's fertility and mortality rates are taken from the population register and adjusted to union-status differentials in fertility and mortality in Sweden. The specification of transition probabilities is extremely important. Direct marriage and transformation rates are estimated using Norway's marriage rates in 1985. Divorce and widowhood/widowerhood rates are taken directly from Norway's population register. Rates of cohabitation and dehabitation are not available for Norway; they must be borrowed from Sweden.

Two scenarios are specified; one assumes that all rates remain constant at the levels specified for the starting year; the other assumes that by 1990 the marriage and divorce rates in Norway reached the respective levels observed in Sweden in 1985. All other rates are kept constant. The latter scenario is particularly interesting because the period 1985 to 1990 was a period of rapid change in Norway; marriage rates rapidly declined and were close to Swedish levels, and divorce rates continued to increase.

Table 5.3 summarizes the most interesting findings. Since a continuation of observed trends – for example, increasing stability of consensual unions through declining transformation and dehabitation rates – is not considered, changes in the union-status structure are relatively moderate. If legal conditions remain unchanged, the model shows that the proportion of consensual unions is likely to increase rapidly.

Two results are particularly noteworthy: the proportion of couples will decline, and among these couples the proportion of cohabitants will increase.

These findings are similar to the events that took place in Sweden. Among elderly women, the increase in the proportion of singles is most pronounced after the year 2020, and in the group of women aged 15 to 64 the increase is greatest between today and the turn of the century. Among elderly men, increases in the proportion of singles are even larger than they are for women. By 2020, between one-fifth and one-third of all women between ages 15 and 64 who live in a union will live in a consensual union; by that time consensual unions will also be an accepted living arrangement among the elderly. As a consequence of shifts in the union-status distribution, the proportion of out-of-marital-union births could soon exceed 50 percent, with every third child born in a consensual union.

Notwithstanding the lack of some basic data on union-status dynamics in Norway, these results are not at all unreasonable. Borrowing Swedish data on transition probabilities gives highly rational future union-status distributions for Norway. This country seems to be close behind Sweden, with an approximate time lag of 10–15 years. It is tempting to conclude that other European countries will also follow, which is indeed suggested by the proposed partnership transition; however, due to the low quality of data sets in other countries, further projections are not investigated. For many other European countries borrowing some of the missing data from Sweden is infeasible. Thus, it is important to improve data collection on all unions.

5.2.2   A new registration system

To avoid technical and mathematical problems of missing union-status data, the registration of couples must be modified. The number of couples has changed very little; nevertheless, an increasing number of couples are not officially registered. In many cases people escape registration because legal marriage has become inconvenient. For an increasing number of people duties and responsibilities associated with marriage are no longer compatible with their actual needs. It is incorrect to conclude that no demand for legislation exists for this group of the population. More options are needed than ever before to meet the many requirements of today's partnerships. It is wrong to equate consensual unions with marriages in all legal aspects, and it is equally wrong not to offer a legal system to those who reject marriage. Registration of a partnership must be made a requirement, but it must also be convenient, advantageous, and easy to fulfill. Since demands are highly heterogeneous, a reasonable choice must be offered. Whether changes in the registration system would reform marriage or simply replace it by offering a new system is of minor importance.

Expanding the proposal introduced by Straver *et al.* (1980), I suggest using a functional approach to partnership. Relationships should be distinguished according to basic functions or areas of responsibility. Each couple chooses a combination of functions. The basic idea would be that each function is associated with a set of rules that specify the respective legal status, its obligations, responsibilities, and benefits. If the partners want to enter into such legal relationships, they would have to define which functions they wish to fulfill and to have protected by legislation. Traditional marriage law would no longer be applicable, but choosing all possible functions would come close to it.

This approach allows flexibility and is in line with recent developments toward a pluralistic society. All couples that want legal security, at least for certain areas of responsibility, are registered. Since the couple itself, and not the authorities, determines the definition of the relationship, some form of registration would be beneficial for most couples. If nonregistration is preferred, partners would be treated as singles in all respects.

The first task would be to specify relevant areas of responsibility; legislators would then have to define the associated regulations in detail.[1] Some important areas are obvious:

- Accommodation: A couple could live in a joint household or in two separate households. Only a joint household involves rules regarding tenancy or mutual accountability of household debts.
- Roles: If a traditional form of living arrangement is preferred, presumably with one partner working outside the home and the other being responsible for the household (and the children), then in case of union dissolution payment of alimony to the partner responsible for the household must be ensured.
- Finances (during union): If each partner has a job and income, a common purse or separate purses must be determined. This question is closely related to issues regarding (common) property purchased during the relationship.
- Sustenance (after union): A couple could determine that one partner should contribute to the other's income. Mutual sustenance could include pension benefits after the partner's death and low inheritance tax.
- Children: A particularly important area of responsibility is the care of children. To a certain extent this function must be regulated independently since it is the state's obligation to protect the interests of children; in

all other respects much less intervention by the state is necessary. In this area we must make a distinction between children from a previous relationship and children from the current union. With regard to the former issues such as inheritance, parental authority, and perhaps adoption must be considered as far as this is in the child's interest. Equal protection for and support to all children is required; this is not necessarily related to the type of partnership the parents have chosen. Laws concerning alimony, inheritance, and maternity and paternity benefits must be mandatory.

Providing that each function is unequivocally associated with a set of rules, no problems should arise from the very different combinations that are feasible. Some issues, however, might need to be defined differently for different combinations of functions of a partnership. In practice, therefore, we may see a limited number of alternative partnership types – maybe four, possibly six – develop. Hence, a couple would not only have the choice of marrying or cohabiting, but have a choice between several options of partnership. Some issues, such as taxation law, would be applied to the individual and would not be affected by the choice of partnership.

In the context of this functional approach to partnership, a number of additional issues must be clarified. First, changes in functions of the union must be possible; partners should be allowed to jointly change their *personal marriage* whenever they like. Unilateral adjustments or changes within the partnership would not be possible. It should, however, be possible to dissolve a union without agreement from the partner. In this case one must fulfill the legal obligations and responsibilities specified for the respective type of partnership at the time of dissolution. From a legal point of view several successive relationships would not cause severe problems. A new relationship could only be officially registered after dissolution of the previous union. Legal obligations can, of course, exist for more than one (previous) union.

A number of currently unclear situations could be avoided. So far, most countries have slowly extended some of the obligations and benefits of married couples to cohabiting couples. Upon the death of a cohabiting man or woman who is legally married to someone else, an unusual situation arises for which no laws exist. Should pension benefits go to the current cohabitant or the former spouse or both? Such a question would not arise if a functional approach were adopted, and marriage and cohabitation were part of the same legal system. An additional advantage of the functional approach is that people who have been forbidden by law to marry could legally form unions. For example, homosexual and lesbian couples would not be discriminated against; they would be legally recognized and protected.

It must be emphasized that the functional approach covers more than the group of currently married and cohabiting couples. Relationships with even weaker ties, for example, living apart together (LAT) relationships, would also be included in this system.

Transitional rules could be enacted until the new system matures. For example, married couples could choose either to accept the new rules or to continue to live according to current marriage law. Cohabiting couples, on the other hand, must register to be legally protected. Since this would improve their status, most cohabitants would probably do so.

This system would ensure complete information about stocks and flows of the total population. Those couples that choose to remain unregistered will not be treated legally as a couple. It can be assumed that the behavior of the partners in those couples will be similar to the behavior of individuals living alone. All couples with children are forced to register, and all children are treated equally.

This new system may contribute to a reduction in rates of couple dissolution. Through the new regulation, couples must explicitly make a choice and, hence, would be forced to think about and openly discuss the functions, expectations, and responsibilities of their relationship. In this context it should be emphasized that this system presupposes a certain degree of gender equality; only full gender equality would guarantee a perfect functioning of the system. It is important that the new rules apply to all (new) couples. Today, some consider signing a marriage contract a sign of mistrust and misgivings; in the future this contract would simply become part of the functional system. If communication is stimulated from the very beginning, then misunderstandings would be avoided and union stability would increase. This functional approach would not only help to ensure nondiscrimination, but also provide better protection for children.

5.3 Concluding Remarks

The transition from a traditional, patriarchal relationship to a modern, gender-balanced partnership has been identified as the driving force behind increases in the number and proportion of consensual unions. This transition is a logical consequence of the secular development of the family and household, a development that has accompanied the change from household-based production to production in the market. In this evolution, three phases have been distinguished (see also Andrup *et al.*, 1980; Sogner, 1986). The agricultural phase is characterized by economic interdependence; husband and wife working together in their common household, but performing separate tasks according to traditional sex-differentiated work patterns. The industrial phase is characterized by economic dependence of women; the husband working outside the household for wages in the market, the wife working at home; and both co-operating to support the family according to sex-differentiated work patterns. The post-industrial phase is characterized by economic independence; husband and wife both working for wages in the market and the separate gender roles blurring and merging. Chances are good that most countries will soon enter the last phase.

It is crucial to acknowledge this development and to adapt social expectations and legal regulations accordingly. As rightly emphasized by Furstenberg (1992), family policies directed toward a re-establishment of the traditional family would only encourage a more rapid movement away from the conjugal family.[2] Adapting marriage and the family is unavoidable. Sogner (1986, p. 33), talking about traditional marriage, points out: "History is full of demolishing of old institutions that have come into bad repute; sometimes they are reformed from within, other times they may be discontinued and other institutions appear to meet the needs the old institutions used to meet." The functional approach proposed is one way to bring about this adaptation.

The family is one of the pillars of today's, as well as tomorrow's, society; family life will continue to play a central role in society. Precisely because of increasing individuality and mobility, people will need a shelter of trust and faith. The growing inability to maintain a long-term partnership does not threaten the importance of the family. The high and probably further increasing rates of couple dissolution are an expression of the search for the ideal family. But the meaning of the term *family* has changed. Family is no longer equivalent to marriage. Various types of family life exist; today, much more emphasis is put on the independence of men and women. For an increasing number of people, having several subsequent relationships will become the norm. Even this development will not necessarily threaten the family as such, although it could have severe effects on the well-being of the children involved if their needs are not seriously considered and satisfied by society. In a pluralistic society there are perhaps as many interpretations of the family as there are couples. And this pluralism must be taken into account by legislators and by demographers. An important question in today's liberal, democratic society is not whether we want pluralism, but rather how we deal with it.

A few decades ago marital status was of central importance in determining an individual's role and behavior. Today's society is changing rapidly, and the many different types of family status are as important today as marital status was during the 1950s. We must extend our definition of status to include all dimensions that are relevant. In other words, we must adjust to today's problems, and we must modify the current system for couple registration accordingly. Even the union-status concept suggested in this study, which considers a couple's legal and residential status, will not be sufficient in the future, but with the new registration system that would result from the application of the functional approach recognition and consideration of different groups of people seem to be guaranteed.

Demographic analysis is helpful in describing phenomena and trends and in making society aware of certain developments. Advancing hypotheses and strategies to deal with new occurrences goes beyond pure scientific analysis, and broadens our thinking about sociological phenomena. If this study contributes to the understanding of cohabitation and its role in the partnership process and if it helps to convince some demographers, bureaucrats, and legislators to give more attention to the phenomenon and its motivation, then it may be considered a worthwhile effort.

Notes

[1] Straver *et al.* identified five functions: affection, accommodation (housing), daily tasks (householding), care of each other's income (maintenance duties), and care of children (children from earlier relationships as well as from the present relationship).

[2] The increase in cohabitation is not necessarily a movement away from the conjugal family.

Appendix 1: The Gini Coefficient as a Measure of Equality

As stated by Hansluwka (1986, p. 137) when analyzing the measurement of social inequality of death, "there is now a growing tendency towards applying measures of inequality derived from the Lorenz curve, such as the Gini or the Atkinson coefficient." In general, Gini coefficients are calculated in the following manner:

$$G(x) = \frac{1}{2n^2\bar{x}} \sum_i \sum_j |x_i - x_j| \quad \longrightarrow \quad 0 \le G(x) \le \frac{n-1}{n} \ .$$

These coefficients can be interpreted as twice the area between the concentration (or the Lorenz) curve and the diagonal. In this application, however, we are not measuring the concentration of cohabitation sequence ratios, but rather their relative differences. Therefore, an alternative interpretation of the Gini coefficient seems more appropriate (see Foster, 1985, for further details and derivations). Assume that X_1 and X_2 are two randomly drawn (with replacement) variables, sequence ratios; the Gini coefficient, $G(x)$, is then equal to $E|X_1 - X_2|/(E|X_1| + E|X_2|)$ or to the expected (absolute) difference between randomly drawn samples, divided by the sum of their expected values.

This interpretation gives rise to an adjusted Gini coefficient that is a more accurate measure of inequality. Let X_1 and X_2 remain as random variables but this time drawn without replacement. This removes the possibility of being chosen twice and changes the probability of each pair to $1/[n(n-1)]$; hence the equation yields an adjusted Gini coefficient $G'(x)$ defined by:

$$G'(x) = \frac{1}{2n(n-1)\bar{x}} \sum_i \sum_j |x_i - x_j| \quad \Longrightarrow \quad 0 \le G(x) \le 1 \ .$$

Since $G'(x)$ is equal to $n/(n-1) * G(x)$, the two measures have rather different rankings. For instance, $G(x)$ gives (0,1) and (0,0,1,1) identical levels of inequality, while $G'(x)$ gives (0,0,1,1), a strictly lower level of inequality, and equates (0,1) with (0,0,0,1). These properties make $G'(x)$ the more appropriate measure for the purpose of comparing the inequality of sequence ratios. An additional advantage is that $G'(x)$ has a highest value of 1 in all population sizes, while the highest value of $G(x)$ is $(n-1)/n$, and hence depends on population size (n). This property of $G'(x)$ makes the comparison between countries easier.

Appendix 2: The Parity-specific Period Fertility Table

The period fertility table is created using two empirical variables: the parity-specific mean ages at childbearing, $x(i)$, i being birth order; and the parity-specific fertility rates, $r(i)$. In the life table, $r(i)$ is defined by

$$r(i) = l(i+1)/L(i) \ ,$$

where $l(i)$ is the number of persons still in the process of reproduction at parity i and $L(i)$ is the number of person-years lived at parity i.

The crucial step in the calculation of a period fertility table is the estimation of parity-progression ratios, $p(i)$, a pure measure of the quantum aspect, from the parity-specific fertility rates that contain both quantum and timing aspects. The parity progression ratio at parity i is defined as the parity-specific fertility rate times the exposure, conditioned by the probability of having reached parity i:

$$p(i) = l(i+1)/l(i) \qquad \text{or} \qquad [L(i)r(i)]/l(i) \ .$$

After a number of algebraic transformations (see Lutz, 1989, for an exact derivation), it is possible to express $p(i)$ in terms of $x(i)$ and $r(i)$:

$$p(i) = \{ [x(w) - x(i)] \, r(i) \} / \{ 1 + [x(w) - x(i+1)] \, r(i) \} \ ,$$

where $x(w)$ is the maximum childbearing age.

The parity progression ratios correspond to the survival probabilities in an ordinary life table. For example, $p(1)$, gives the probability that a woman of parity 1 *survives* to parity 2 (that is, gives birth to a second child). Now we calculate $l(i)$, the survivors or rather the number of women with parity i or more, and $L(i)$, the number of person-years lived at each parity (by all survivors) or the exposure time. The radix $l(0)$ is usually given with 100,000:

$$l(i+1) = l(i)p(i) \qquad \text{and} \qquad L(i) = l(i+1)/r(i) \ .$$

From the survivors, $l(i)$, we can directly derive the *deaths*, $d(i)$ – namely, those women who do not proceed to higher birth orders and remain at parity i until the end of the process, $x(w)$. From $d(i)$ we get the completed parity distribution, $c(i)$, which is implied by the period pattern of parity-specific fertility:

$$d(i) = l(i) - l(i+1) \qquad \text{and} \qquad c(i) = d(i)/l(0) \ .$$

This completed parity distribution must be interpreted with some caution since it is derived from a period approach, and not from a cohort approach. The synthetic cohort used here consists of several birth cohorts with different timing and intensity of childbearing. Hence, this is not necessarily the real eventual birth-order distribution of any real cohort.

The ordinary life table has the same problems and drawbacks. However, the advantage of using very recent data makes period (life) tables a valuable tool.

From the completed parity distribution we also obtain a useful summary indicator, the mean completed parity (MCP). It summarizes the quantum information provided by the fertility table and may be interpreted as the mean completed parity or the mean family size for women implied by recent period fertility behavior (sum over all parities i):

$$MCP = \Sigma\, ic(i)/100 \ .$$

The value of MCP should be comparable with the value of the total fertility rate, which is calculated from age-specific rates. Both indicators give the mean family size for a synthetic cohort based on observed period rates. The main difference between the two is that the MCP considers parity-specific behavior while the TFR considers age-specific behavior. Lutz (1989) has shown that the fact that the fertility table based on parity disregards the age structure is reason for some caution but is not cause to reject the application of the model.

References

Agell, A., 1980, Cohabitation without marriage in Swedish law, in J. Eekelaar and S. Katz, eds., *Marriage and Cohabitation in Contemporary Societies: Areas of Legal, Social and Ethical Change*, Butterworth, Toronto, Canada.

Agell, A., 1981, The Swedish legislation on marriage and cohabitation: A journey without a destination, *American Journal of Comparative Law*, 29(2):285–314.

Ahlburg, D., and Vaupel, J., 1990, Alternative projections of the US population, *Demography*, 27:639–652.

Andrup, H., Buchhofer, N., and Ziegert, K., 1980, Formal marriage under the crossfire of social change, in J. Eekelaar and S. Katz, eds., *Marriage and Cohabitation in Contemporary Societies: Areas of Legal, Social and Ethical Change*, Butterworth, Toronto, Canada.

Berent, J., and Festy, P., 1973, *Measuring the Impact of Some Demographic Factors on Post-War Trends in Crude Birth Rates in Europe*, Vol. 2, IUSSP International Population Conference, Liege, Belgium.

Blanc, A.K., 1984, Nonmarital cohabitation and fertility in the United States and Western Europe, *Population Research and Policy Review*, 3:181–193.

Blanc, A.K., 1987, The formation and dissolution of second unions: Marriage and cohabitation in Sweden and Norway, *Journal of Marriage and the Family*, 49:391–400.

Blom, S., 1992, Entry into First Marriage or Cohabitation by Norwegian Men and Women Born 1945 and 1960, Paper presented at the 10th Scandinavian Demographic Symposium, August, Lund, Sweden.

Brown, A., and Kiernan, K., 1981, Cohabitation in Great Britain: Evidence from the General Household Survey, *Population Trends*, 25:4–10.

Brunborg, H., 1979, *Cohabitation Without Marriage in Norway*, Article 116, Central Bureau of Statistics, Oslo, Norway.

Bumpass, L.L., 1990, What's happening to the family?, *Demography*, 27(4):483–498.

Carlson, E., and Klinger, A., 1987, Partners in life: Unmarried couples in Hungary, *European Journal of Population*, 3:85–99.

Castiglioni, M., and Zuanna, G.D., 1992, Nuptiality and Fertility in Italy During the Seventies and the Eighties, Paper presented at the EAPS/BIB seminar on Demographic Implications of Marital Status, 27–31 October, Bonn, Germany.

CBS (Central Bureau of Statistics), 1991, Netherlands Fertility Survey 1988, Demographic Working Papers, Department of Population Statistics, The Hague, The Netherlands.

Chafetz, J.S., 1992, *Chicken or Egg? A Theory of the Relationship between Feminist Movements and Family Change in Industrialized Societies*, Paper presented at the IUSSP/IRP seminar on Gender and Family Change in Industrialized Countries, 26–30 January, Rome, Italy.

Chiang, C.L., and van den Berg, B.J., 1982, A fertility table for the analysis of human reproduction, *Mathematical Biosciences*, **62**:237–251.

Cliquet, R., 1991, The second demographic transition: Fact or fiction?, *Population Studies*, **23**, Council of Europe Press, Strasbourg, France.

Cliquet, R., ed., 1993, The future of Europe's population, *Population Studies*, **26**, Council of Europe Press, Strasbourg, France.

Clive, E.M., 1980, Marriage: An unnecessary legal concept?, in J. Eekelaar and S. Katz, eds., *Marriage and Cohabitation in Contemporary Societies: Areas of Legal, Social and Ethical Change*, Butterworth, Toronto, Canada.

Coale, A., and Demeny, P., 1983, *Regional Model Life Tables and Stable Populations*, 2nd Edition, Academic Press, New York, NY, USA.

Council of Europe, 1991, *Recent Demographic Developments in Europe*, Council of Europe Press, Strasbourg, France.

Deech, R., 1980, The case against legal recognition of cohabitation, in J. Eekelaar and S. Katz, eds., *Marriage and Cohabitation in Contemporary Societies: Areas of Legal, Social and Ethical Change*, Butterworth, Toronto, Canada.

Duncan, W., 1980, Supporting the institution of marriage in the Republic of Ireland, in J. Eekelaar and S. Katz, eds., *Marriage and Cohabitation in Contemporary Societies: Areas of Legal, Social and Ethical Change*, Butterworth, Toronto, Canada.

Eekelaar, J., 1980, Crisis in the institution of marriage: An overview, in J. Eekelaar and S. Katz, eds., *Marriage and Cohabitation in Contemporary Societies: Areas of Legal, Social and Ethical Change*, Butterworth, Toronto, Canada.

Eichwalder, R., 1992, Lebensgemeinschaften (Consensual unions in Austria, 1986 and 1992), *Statistische Nachrichten*, **47**(12):931–934.

Espenshade, T., and Eisenberg Braun, R., 1982, Life course analysis and multistate demography: An application to marriage, divorce and remarriage, *Journal of Marriage and the Family*, **44**:1025–1036.

EUROSTAT, 1991, Two Long-Term Population Scenarios for the European Community, Scenarios prepared for the International Conference on Human Resources in Europe at the Dawn of the 21st Century, 27–29 November, Luxembourg.

Feichtinger, G., and Lutz, W., 1983, Eine Fruchtbarkeitstafel auf Paritûätsbasis (A fertility table based on parity), *Zeitschrift für Bevölkerungswissenschaften*, **9**(3):363–376.

Festy, P., 1985, Divorce, judicial separation and remarriage: Recent trends in the member states of the Council of Europe, *Population Studies*, **17**, Council of Europe Press, Strasbourg, France.

Fleiss, J., 1981, *Statistical Methods for Rates and Proportions*, 2nd Edition, John Wiley and Sons, New York, NY, USA.

Foster, J., 1985, Inequality measurement, in P. Young, ed., *Fair Allocation*, Proceedings of Symposia in Applied Mathematics, Vol. 33, American Mathematical Society, Providence, RI, USA.

Fresel-Lozey, M., 1992, Les nouvelles formes de conjugalité: Problèmes méthodologiques (New forms of living together: Methodological problem), *Population*, **3**:737–744.

Frinking, G., 1988, Childlessness in Europe: Trends and implications, in H. Moors and J. Schoorl, eds., *Lifestyles, Contraception and Parenthood*, Vol. 17, NIDI CBGS Publications, The Hague, The Netherlands.

Furstenberg, F., 1992, Family Change and the Welfare of Children: What Do We Know and What Can We Do About It?, Paper presented at the IUSSP/IRP seminar on Gender and Family Change in Industrialized Countries, 26–30 January, Rome, Italy.

Goldman, N., 1993, Marriage selection and mortality patterns: Inferences and fallacies, *Demography*, **30**(2):189–208.

Gonnot, J.-P., 1995, Demographic changes and the pension problem: Evidence from twelve countries, in J.P. Gonnot, N. Keilman, and Ch. Prinz, eds., *Social Security, Household and Family Dynamics in Aging Societies*, Kluwer, Dordrecht, The Netherlands.

Gonnot, J.-P., and Vukovich, G., 1989, Recent Trends in Living Arrangements in Fourteen Industrialized Countries, WP-89-34, International Institute for Applied Systems Analysis, Laxenburg, Austria.

Gonnot, J.-P., Keilman, N., and Prinz, Ch., eds., 1995, *Social Security, Household and Family Dynamics in Aging Societies*, Kluwer, Drodrecht, The Netherlands.

Graue, E.D., 1980, Cohabitation outside marriage as a problem of law and legislative policy in West Germany and other codified systems, in J. Eekelaar and S. Katz, eds., *Marriage and Cohabitation in Contemporary Societies: Areas of Legal, Social and Ethical Change*, Butterworth, Toronto, Canada.

Hansluwka, H., 1986, Reflections of the Measurement of Social Inequality of Death, Unpublished document, World Health Organization, Geneva, Switzerland.

Haskey, J., 1991, Formation and Dissolution of Unions in the Different Countries of Europe, Paper presented at the European Population Conference, 21–25 October, Paris, France.

Haskey, J., and Kiernan, K., 1989, Cohabitation in Great Britain: Characteristics and estimated numbers of cohabiting partners, *Population Trends*, **58**:23–32.

Haug, W., and Priester, T., 1992, Migration and Marital Status: The Case of Switzerland, Paper presented at the EAPS/BIB seminar on Demographic Implications of Marital Status, 27–31 October, Bonn, Germany.

Henslin, J., 1980, Cohabitation: Its context and meaning, in J. Henslin, ed., *Marriage and Family in a Changing Society*, The Free Press, New York, NY, USA.

Hoem, B., 1992, The Way to the Gender-Segregated Swedish Labour Market, Paper presented at the IUSSP/IRP seminar on Gender and Family Change in Industrialized Countries, 26–30 January, Rome, Italy.

Hoem, B., and Hoem, J., 1988, The Swedish family: Aspects of contemporary developments, *Journal of Family Issues*, **9**(3):397–424.

Hoem, J., 1986, The impact of education on modern union initiation, *European Journal of Population*, **2**:113–133.

Hoem, J., 1991, To marry, just in case ...: The Swedish widow's-pension reform and the peak in marriages in December 1989, *Acta Sociologica*, **34**:127–135.

Hoem, J., and Rennermalm, B., 1985, Modern family initiation in Sweden: Experience of women born between 1936 and 1960, *European Journal of Population*, **1**:81–112.

Hu, Y., and Goldman, N., 1990, Mortality differentials by marital status: An international comparison, *Demography*, **27**(2):233–249.

Joung, I., van de Mheen, H., Stronks, K., van Poppel, F., and Mackenbach, J., 1992, Differences in Self-Reported Morbidity by Marital Status and by Living Arrangement, Paper presented at the EAPS/BIB seminar on Demographic Implications of Marital Status, 27–31 October, Bonn, Germany.

Katus, K., 1992, Trends in Non-Marital Fertility in the Baltic Region, Paper presented at the EAPS/BIB seminar on Demographic Implications of Marital Status, 27–31 October, Bonn, Germany.

Keilman, N., 1992, Household Statistics in Europe: Consequences of Different Definitions, Paper prepared for the 1991 Quetelet Seminar on the Collection and Comparability of Demographic and Social Data in Europe, 17–20 September, Gembloux, Belgium.

Keilman, N., and Prinz, Ch., 1995a, Introduction, in J.P. Gonnot, N. Keilman, and Ch. Prinz. eds., *Social Security, Household and Family Dynamics in Aging Societies*, Kluwer, Dordrecht, The Netherlands.

Keilman, N., and Prinz, Ch., 1995b, Modelling the dynamics of living arrangements, in J.P. Gonnot, N. Keilman, and Ch. Prinz, eds., *Social Security, Household and Family Dynamics in Aging Societies*, Kluwer, Dordrecht, The Netherlands.

Keilman, N., Kuijsten, A., and Vossen, A., eds., 1988, *Modelling Household Formation and Dissolution*, Clarendon Press, Oxford, UK.

Keyfitz, N., 1985, *Applied Mathematical Demography*, 2nd Edition, Springer-Verlag, New York, NY, USA.

Kiernan, K., 1993, The future of partnership and fertility, *Population Studies*, **26**, Council of Europe Press, Strasbourg, France.

Kiernan, K., and Estaugh, V., 1993, *Cohabitation: Extra-marital Childrearing and Social Policy*, Occasional Paper 17, Family Policy Studies Centre, London, UK.

Kono, S., 1987, The headship rate method for projecting households, in J. Bongaarts, Th. Burch, and K. Wachter, eds., *Family Demography: Methods and Their Applications*, Clarendon Press, Oxford, UK.

Latten, J.J., 1992, The impact of aging, nuptial and social change on household positions in 2010, in United Nations, *Changing Population Age Structures Demographic and Economic Consequences and Implications*, United Nations, Geneva, Switzerland.

Leridon, H., 1990a, Cohabitation, marriage, separation: An analysis of life histories of French cohorts from 1968 to 1985, *Population Studies*, **44**:127–144.

Leridon, H., 1990b, Extra-marital cohabitation and fertility, *Population Studies*, **44**:469–487.

Leridon, H., and Villeneuve-Gokalp, C., 1989, The new couples: Number, characteristics and attitudes, *Population*, **44** (English Selection No. 1):203–235.

Lesthaege, R., 1992, The Second Demographic Transition in Western Countries: An Interpretation, IPD-Working Paper, Brussels, Belgium.

Lesthaege, R., and van de Kaa, D.J., 1986, Twee demografische transities (Two demographic transitions), in R. Lesthaege and D.J. van de Kaa, eds., *Groei of Krimp?*, beokuitgave Mens en Maatschappij, Van Loghum Slaterus, Deventer, The Netherlands.

Lewin, B., 1982, Unmarried cohabitation: A marriage form in a changing society, *Journal of Marriage and the Family*, **44**:763–773.

Linke, W., 1991, Statistics on households and families in the member countries of the Council of Europe: Definitions, methods, and sources, *INSEE Methodes*, **8**:117–124.

Livi-Bacci, M., 1985, Selectivity of marriage and mortality: Notes for future research, in N. Keyfitz, ed., *Population and Biology*, Ordina Editions, Liège, Belgium.

Lodrup, P., 1980, The position of children of unmarried but cohabiting parents, in J. Eekelaar and S. Katz, eds., *Marriage and Cohabitation in Contemporary Societies: Areas of Legal, Social and Ethical Change*, Butterworth, Toronto, Canada.

Long, L., 1992, Changing residence: Comparative perspectives on its relationship to age, sex, and marital status, *Population Studies*, **46**:141–158.

Lutz, W., 1989, *Distributional Aspects of Human Fertility: A Global Comparative Study*, Academic Press, London, UK.

Lutz, W., ed., 1991, *Future Demographic Trends in Europe and North America: What Can We Assume Today?*, Academic Press, London, UK.

Lutz, W., 1993, Nuptiality rates, in D. Bogue, E. Arriaga, and D. Anderton, eds., *Readings in Population Research Methodology, Nuptiality Analysis: Marriage, Dissolution, Remarriage*, Vol. 4, UNFPA, New York, NY, USA.

Lutz, W., and Feichtinger, G., 1985, A Life Table Approach to Parity Progression and Marital Status Transitions, Paper contributed to the IUSSP General Conference (Session F.13), Florence, Italy.

Lutz, W., and Prinz, Ch., 1991, Scenarios for the World Population in the Next Century: Excessive Growth or Extreme Aging, WP-91-22, International Institute for Applied Systems Analysis, Laxenburg, Austria.

Lutz, W., Prinz, Ch., and Langgassner, J., 1993, World population projections and possible ecological feedbacks, *POPNET*, **23**:1–11.

Macklin, E., 1978, Nonmarital heterosexual cohabitation, *Marriage and Family Review*, **1**:1–12.

Manting, D., 1992, The Break-Up of Unions: The Role of Cohabitation, Paper presented at the EAPS/BIB seminar on Demographic Implications of Marital Status, 27–31 October, Bonn, Germany.

Meyer, S., and Schulze, E., 1983, Nichteheliche Lebensgemeinschaften: Alternativen zur Ehe? (Consensual Unions: Alternatives to Marriage?), *Kölner Zeitschrift für Soziologie und Sozialpsychologie*, **35**:735–754.

Morgan, M., 1980, Marital status, health, illness and service use, *Social Science and Medicine*, **14**A(6):633–643.

Mulder, C., and Wagner, M., 1992, Migration and Marriage: A Study of Synchronized Events in the Life Course, Paper presented at the EAPS/BIB seminar on Demographic Implications of Marital Status, 27–31 October, Bonn, Germany.

Murphy, M., 1992, Marital Status and Mortality: An Epidemiological Viewpoint, Paper presented at the EAPS/BIB seminar on Demographic Implications of Marital Status, 27–31 October, Bonn, Germany.

Nelissen, J.H.M., 1992, Microsimulation of Household and Labor Market Behavior, Paper presented at the workshop on Recent Issues in Household Modeling, 15 July, Wassenaar, The Netherlands.

Nilsson, A., 1992, Family Formation and Dissolution of Consensual Unions and Marriages in Sweden, Paper presented at the EAPS/BIB seminar on Demographic Implications of Marital Status, 27–31 October, Bonn, Germany.

Oppenheim Mason, K., 1992, Summary of the Seminar on Gender and Family Change in Industrialized Countries held in Rome, 26–30 January, *IUSSP Newsletter*, **44**:18–23.

Ostby, L., 1988, Modern family formation, *Scandinavian Population Studies*, **8**:99–120.

Pearl, D., 1980, Cohabitation in English social security legislation, in J. Eekelaar and S. Katz, eds., *Marriage and Cohabitation in Contemporary Societies: Areas of Legal, Social and Ethical Change*, Butterworth, Toronto, Canada.

Pinelli, A., 1992, Women's Condition, Low Fertility and Emerging Union Patterns in Europe, Paper presented at the IUSSP/IRP seminar on Gender and Family Change in Industrialized Countries, 26–30 January, Rome, Italy.

Pollard, J., 1982, Methodological issues, in *Measurement of Inequality of Death in Mortality in South and East Asia: A Review of Changing Trends and Patterns 1950–1975*, WHO/ESCAP, Manila, Philippines.

Popenoe, D., 1987, Beyond the nuclear family: A statistical portrait of the changing family in Sweden, *Journal of Marriage and the Family*, **49**:173–183.

Preston, S., 1987, Estimation of certain measures in family demography based upon generalized stable population relations, in J. Bongaarts, T. Burch, and K. Wachter, eds., *Family Demography: Methods and Their Applications*, Clarendon Press, Oxford, UK.

Prinz, Ch., 1991a, Marital Status and Population Projections, WP-91-12, International Institute for Applied Systems Analysis, Laxenburg, Austria.

Prinz, Ch., 1991b, Marriage and Cohabitation in Sweden, Paper presented at the European Population Conference, 21–25 October, Paris, France.

Prinz, Ch., 1995, Changing family structure and an emancipatory pension policy in Austria, in J.P. Gonnot, N. Keilman, and Ch. Prinz, eds., *Social Security, Household and Family Dynamics in Aging Societies*, Kluwer, Dordrecht, The Netherlands.

Prinz, Ch., Nilsson, A., and Sellerfors, H., 1995, Alternative options for living arrangement models: A sensitivity analysis, in E. van Imhoff, A. Kuijsten, P. Hooimeijer, and L. van Wissen, eds., *Household Demography and Household Modeling*, forthcoming.

Rindfuss, R., and van den Heuvel, A., 1990, Cohabitation: A precursor to marriage or an alternative to being single?, *Population and Development Review*, **4**:703–726.

Rogers, A., 1975, *Introduction to Multiregional Mathematical Demography*, John Wiley and Sons, New York, NY, USA.

Roussel, L., 1989, Types of marriage and frequency of divorce, in E. Grebenik, Ch. Höhn, and R. Mackensen, eds., *Later Phases of the Family Life Cycle: Demographic Aspects*, Clarendon Press, Oxford, UK.

Roussel, L., 1992, La famille en Europe Occidentale: Divergences et convergences (The family in Western Europe: Divergences and convergences), *Population*, **47**(1):133–152.

Roussel, L., and Festy, P., 1978, *L'évolution récente des attitudes et comportements à l'égard de la famille dans les états membres du Conseil de l'Europe* (Recent developments in attitudes and behavior regarding the family in the member states of the Council of Europe), INED, Paris, France.

Sardon, J.-P., 1986, Evolution de la nuptialité et de la divortialité en Europe depuis la fin des années 1960, *Population*, **41**(3):463–482.

Scherbov, S., and Grechucha, V., 1988, DIAL: A System for Modeling Multidimensional Demographic Processes, WP-88-36, International Institute for Applied Systems Analysis, Laxenburg, Austria.

Schoen, R., 1981, The harmonic mean as the basis of a realistic two-sex marriage model, *Demography*, **18**:201–216.

Schoen, R., 1988, *Modeling Multigroup Populations*, Plenum Press, New York, NY, USA.

Shryock, H., Siegel, J., and Stockwell, E., 1976, *The Methods and Materials of Demography*, Academic Press, New York, NY, USA.

Sogner, S., 1986, Changing marriage patterns: A commentary on three papers submitted to the round table session The Family in History, in J. Rogers, ed., *The Nordic Family: II, Perspectives on Family Research*, Uppsala University, Department of History, Uppsala, Sweden.

STG Netherlands, 1988, Lifestyles, Living Conditions and Health in the Netherlands, Background Report, The Netherlands.

Straver, C., van der Heiden, A., and Robert, W., 1980, Lifestyles of cohabiting couples and their impact on juridical questions, in J. Eekelaar and S. Katz, eds., *Marriage and Cohabitation in Contemporary Societies: Areas of Legal, Social and Ethical Change*, Butterworth, Toronto, Canada.

Tapp, P., 1980, The social and legal position of children of unmarried but cohabiting parents, in J. Eekelaar and S. Katz, eds., *Marriage and Cohabitation in Contemporary Societies: Areas of Legal, Social and Ethical Change*, Butterworth, Toronto, Canada.

Thornton, A., 1988, Cohabitation and marriage in the 1980s, *Demography*, **25**(4):497–508.

Trost, J., 1975, Married and unmarried cohabitation: The case of Sweden, with some comparisons, *Journal of Marriage and the Family*, **37**(August):677–682.

Trost, J., 1980, Cohabitation without marriage in Sweden, in J. Eekelaar and S. Katz, eds., *Marriage and Cohabitation in Contemporary Societies: Areas of Legal, Social and Ethical Change*, Butterworth, Toronto, Canada.

Trost, J., 1985, Marital and non-marital cohabitation, in R. Rogers and H. Norman, eds., *The Nordic Family: Perspectives on Family Research*, Uppsala University, Department of History, Uppsala, Sweden.

Trost, J., 1988, Cohabitation and marriage: Transitional pattern, different lifestyle, or just another legal form, in H. Moors and J. Schoorl, eds., *Lifestyles, Contraception and Parenthood*, Vol. 17, NIDI CBGS Publications, Amsterdam, The Netherlands.

United Nations, 1990, *Patterns of First Marriage: Timing and Prevalence*, Department of International Economic and Social Affairs, United Nations, New York, NY, USA.

United Nations, 1992, *Long-Range World Population Projections: Two Centuries of Population Growth 1950–2150*, Department of International Economic and Social Affairs, United Nations, New York, NY, USA.

Vallin, J., and Nizard, A., 1977, La mortalité par état matrimonial (Mortality by marital status), *Population*, **32**:95–125.

van de Kaa, D., 1987, Europe's second demographic transition, *Population Bulletin*, **41**(1).

van de Wiel, A.M., 1980, Cohabitation outside marriage in Dutch law, in J. Eekelaar and S. Katz, eds., *Marriage and Cohabitation in Contemporary Societies: Areas of Legal, Social and Ethical Change*, Butterworth, Toronto, Canada.

van Imhoff, E., 1990, The exponential multidimensional demographic projection model, *Mathematical Population Studies*, **2**(3):171–182.

van Imhoff, E., 1992, A general characterization of consistency algorithms in multidimensional demographic projection models, *Population Studies*, **46**(2).

van Imhoff, E., and Keilman, N., 1991, *LIPRO 2.0: An Application of a Dynamic Demographic Projection Model to Household Structure in the Netherlands*, Swets and Zeitlinger B.V., Lisse, The Netherlands.

Verbrugge, L., 1979, Marital status and health, *Journal of Marriage and the Family*, **41**(May):267–285.

von Krbek, F.S.E., 1980, Cohabitation: A possible German civil law solution, in J. Eekelaar and S. Katz, eds., *Marriage and Cohabitation in Contemporary Societies: Areas of Legal, Social and Ethical Change*, Butterworth, Toronto, Canada.

von Münch, I., 1985, Artikel 6 Grundgesetz, der Wandel familiärer Lebensmuster und das Familien- und Sozialrecht (Article 6 of the Basic Constitutional Law, the Change of Family Life Patterns and the Family and Social Law), *Schriftenreihe des Deutschen Sozialrechtsverbandes*, **27**:69–89.

Weingarten, H., 1985, Marital status and well-being: A national study comparing first-married, currently divorced, and remarried adults, *Journal of Marriage and the Family*, **47**(August):653–662.

Wiersma, G., 1983, *Cohabitation, An Alternative to Marriage? A Cross-national Study*, Martinus Nijhoff Publishers, Boston, MA, USA.

Willekens, F.J., and Drewe, P., 1984, A multiregional model for regional demographic projection, in H. ter Heide and F. Willekens, eds., *Demographic Research and Spatial Policy: The Dutch Experience*, Academic Press, London, UK.

Wingen, M., 1985, Wandlungen im Prozeß der Ehe- und Familienbildung (Changes in the Process of Starting a Marriage or Family), *Schriftenreihe des Deutschen Sozialrechtsverbandes*, **27**:31–68.

Wunsch, G., and Termote, M., 1978, *Introduction to Demographic Analysis: Principles and Methods*, Plenum Press, New York, NY, USA.

Author Index

Country Index

Subject Index